Youth Entrepreneurship

Thea van der Westhuizen

Youth Entrepreneurship

An Ecosystem Theory for Young
Entrepreneurs in South Africa and
Beyond

Thea van der Westhuizen ⓘ
University of KwaZulu-Natal
Westville, South Africa

ISBN 978-3-031-44338-1   ISBN 978-3-031-44339-8   (eBook)
https://doi.org/10.1007/978-3-031-44339-8

This work is based on research supported in part by the National Research Foundation of South Africa (Grant Number: 122002-Shape).

This Palgrave Macmillan imprint is published by the registered company Springer Nature Switzerland AG
The registered company address is: Gewerbestrasse 11, 6330 Cham, Switzerland

Foreword

Delivering a student-focused interaction that blends theory, industry practice and community consciousness, to help an individual find meaning and success in life, is the challenge of teaching entrepreneurship in an experiential mode. The targeted student is nurtured and oriented to be an economic driver through the cultivation of creative and innovative thinking. This is critical in an environment of high unemployment and increased social inequalities, where solutions are not easily generated or are probably not well applied.

Often, we fail to recognise the tremendous amount of innovation that educators bring to solving an array of challenges in today's classrooms. It is the teaching philosophy of; 'learning from and learning by experience' that empowers the entrepreneurship student to construct his/her own knowledge from previous and current experiences, being guided by future expectations. A futuristic orientation embeds in the student, a questioning and envisioning mindset. This principle is anchored in the work by Kolb (1984), who espoused that knowledge is created through the transformation of experience, and that holistic approaches are therefore needed to provide bridges across life situations.

Thea's experiential pedagogy which find expression in this book, provides these bridges. Effective youth entrepreneurship is transformational. This is in line with what scholars on experiential teaching believe, that students learn best when they are engaged in hands-on activities and are involved in a process of enquiry, discovery and interpretation. They interact with practising entrepreneurs, business leaders, government agencies and other business networks, that are an integral part of the learning ecosystem. Thea has always believed and applied this approach from the time she started her own business, initially as a student and later as a full-time entrepreneur to the present time she is sharing these practices in this book.

She has lived and worked in the Middle East where she applied many aspects of the experiential entrepreneurship ecosystem model as a Local Economic Development Strategy in the Al Gharbia region, Abu Dhabi, United Arab Emirates. Through the approach a desert landscape was successfully transformed into a thriving economic hub. She later initiated (in the KwaZulu-Natal province of South Africa) a very successful systemic action learning and action research programme called SHAPE (Shifting Hope, Activating Potential Entrepreneurship), a refinement of an experiential entrepreneurship teaching ecosystem model I had developed earlier. She developed this approach and validated it through practice. The SHAPE became a successful programme financed by the National Research Fund, the EThekwini Municipality and The University of KwaZulu Natal. The programme won the 'Global Innovative Youth Incubator Awards' in Washington D.C., in 2018. It has become a youth development flagship programme at the University of KwaZulu Natal.

She shares experiences accumulated over the years, in different geographical settings and business roles, such as project management, entrepreneurship, academia and youth empowerment; all interwoven into thoroughly researched and clearly articulated topics. These different attributes on the scholarship of teaching and learning, covering action learning, experiential learning and youth development, are found in this book **Youth Entrepreneurship: An Ecosystem Theory for Young Entrepreneurs in South Africa and Beyond**.

Thea and I share the underlying principles on the scholarship of teaching and learning of Entrepreneurship. This book is an invaluable contribution to youth empowerment and development. Youth entrepreneurship is the future of our country and the continent.

Professor of Entrepreneurship

South Africa   Shepherd Dhliwayo

Acknowledgements

This work is based on research supported in part by the National Research Foundation of South Africa (Grant Number: 122002-Shape).

Wade Krieger (M.Com.): for contributions to Chapters 4 and 8–10 as part of the research project work: Krieger, W., 2018. Barriers to youth entrepreneurship: a systemic approach (Masters dissertation). University of KwaZulu-Natal.

Riaan Steenberg (Ph.D.): co-investigator and research member to SHAPE; Director of the Stellenbosch Graduate Institute. Contributions are evident in Chapters 1 and 10.

Janine Upton (Ph.D. Candidate): co-investigator and research member to SHAPE. Contributions evident in Chapters 4 and 7–10.

Technical Contributions

R. Klopper	Graphic design and illustrations
F.B. Green	Initial language editing and manuscript formatting
J. Upton	Empirical primary data quality assurance
D. Griffin	Secondary data quality assurance

R. du Plessis   Manuscript formatting

Peer Review Declaration

The publisher, Springer Nature, endorses the South African 'National Scholarly Book Publishers Forum Best Practice for Peer Review of Scholarly Books'. The manuscript was subjected to a rigorous two-step peer-review process prior to publication, with the identities of the reviewers not revealed to the authors or contributors. The reviewers were independent of the publisher and/or the authors in question. The reviewers commented positively on the scholarly merits of the manuscript and recommended that the manuscript should be published. Where the reviewers recommended revision and/or improvements to the manuscript, the author responded adequately to such recommendations.

Organisation of the Book

The book is divided into two parts and ten chapters.

Part 1 (Chapters 1–3) introduces youth entrepreneurship, provides a background to the SHAPE ecosystem strategy for developing youth entrepreneurship and illustrates the SHAPE YES (youth entrepreneur support) Network for youth entrepreneurs.

Part 2 (Chapters 4–10) looks empirically, from a systemic perspective, at different theoretical models that aim to develop student entrepreneurs. It describes the research methodology and justifies the research design and approach, empirically portraying the findings and results of the quantitative investigation. Each research objective is critically discussed as well as the demographics of the participants. Interpretations of the results or findings are given and discussed in relation to the literature review.

Clarification of Concepts

Barriers to Entrepreneurship

As mentioned in the Introduction, we use the word 'barrier' to describe challenges or obstacles that hinder or prevent youths from making progress in seeking to become entrepreneurs. Personal barriers (concerning systemic intermediaries) experienced by the individual are included because they are perceived as external influences. Identifying these barriers provides useful knowledge to assist youth entrepreneurs.

Various authors have described external barriers to entrepreneurship. Among these are business environmental barriers, such as tax burden, unfair competition and inadequate finance, as well as external environment dynamism, technological opportunities, industry growth and demand for new products.[1]

Ecosystem

An ecosystem is a complex whole whose functioning depends on its parts and the interactions between those parts[2] where systemic elements affect the whole, rather than just parts, and refers to the interrelatedness and integration of systems.[3] An approach can be described as 'the process of going towards something'. The term 'ecosystemic' in the context of this study signifies an emphasis on enablers and barriers of a whole (systemic-connectivity)[4] rather than to disparate entities (systemic-disconnectivity). An ecosystemic approach was adopted in this research to provide information on the seven constructs listed in Chapter 1.

---

[1] Krasniqi 2007
[2] Jackson 2003
[3] Leonard 2010
[4] Jackson 2003

Entrepreneurial Heartset

The entrepreneurial heartset refers to the neurological processes that occur within an individual, shaping and cultivating their entrepreneurial mindset and behavioural actions.

Entrepreneurial Mindset

An entrepreneurial mindset is the end product of thought and a state of mind characterised by a focus on entrepreneurial activities and outcomes. It represents a specific mindset that drives individuals to seek opportunities, foster innovation and create new value. Those with entrepreneurial mindsets possess a natural inclination towards entrepreneurship, demonstrating a propensity for identifying and capitalising on opportunities for growth and success.

Entrepreneurial Handset

Entrepreneurial handset refers to the observable behavioural actions taken by individuals in pursuit of entrepreneurial activities and goals.

Intermediaries to Student Entrepreneurs

The external barriers encountered by student entrepreneurs concerning systemic intermediaries were examined by expert and experienced scholars,[5] using a systematic approach towards the six categories mentioned in the Introduction.

---

[5] Dhliwayo 2008; Van der Westhuizen 2016

Learning a Living

Young people will need to be developed not only to earn a living but to 'learn a living'.[6] Learning a living relies on the quality of relevant skills and competencies of learners. Globally, mobile labour, competition and increasingly sophisticated technology pressurise learners to be well-equipped with skills and self-efficacy to perform successfully in the demands these new trends bring.[7]

SHAPE

SHAPE, an acronym for Shifting Hope, Activating Potential Entrepreneurship, is an academic concept designed to foster entrepreneurship within South African Higher Education Institutions (HEIs) and beyond. The concept recognises the importance of shifting heartsets and mindsets, instilling hope and activating the potential of individuals towards entrepreneurial endeavours. SHAPE emphasises the need to create a multi-disciplinary enabling environment that encourages and supports entrepreneurial feeling, thinking, learning and action. Through targeted interventions, such as curriculum development, experiential learning opportunities, mentorship programmes, action research and access to resources, SHAPE aims to equip students with the necessary confidence, skills and knowledge to embark on entrepreneurial ventures. By incorporating SHAPE into HEIs, South Africa can harness the transformative power of entrepreneurship, driving economic growth, job creation and societal development.

SHAPE YES Network

The SHAPE YES Network is an academic concept that fosters an entrepreneurial ecosystem for young entrepreneurs. It spans various domains, including the youth's internal traits, and interacts with external

---

[6] Hannon, Gillinson & Shanks 2013

[7] Van der Westhuizen 2017

entities. The network includes Higher Education Institutes as project hosts, with government agencies providing support units and mentorship programmes. Private sector agencies offer platforms and guidance, while communities provide crucial encouragement. Collaboration with entrepreneurs and small businesses is also emphasised. Internships and on-the-job learning opportunities are offered by corporations. By integrating the SHAPE YES Network, South Africa can cultivate a thriving environment for young entrepreneurs, promoting entrepreneurship, economic growth and innovation.

Social Technology

Social technology can be defined as a 'process of innovation, conducted collectively and participative by actors interested in building that desirable scenario'. Social technology is a way of using human, intellectual and digital resources to influence social processes.

Student Entrepreneurs

A student entrepreneur is 'an individual who participates in an experiential learning programme about entrepreneurship while having an infrastructure of intermediaries to support the learning process'.[8] The student entrepreneurs, who are the subject of this book, were studying at the University of Kwazulu-Natal, intending to become successful small business owners or managers engaged in entrepreneurship activities. All the student entrepreneurs participated in the SHAPE social technology described previously.

---

[8] Dhliwayo 2008

Systemic Action Learning and Action Research (SALAR)

SALAR is an extension of action learning and action research and can be defined as 'interactive processes' between local stakeholders and the researcher that enable individuals involved to bring diverse knowledge to a dialogical process and to a problem or challenge that allows the researcher to observe and act upon dynamics at the systemic level.[9]

In this study, 'systemic action learning and action research' applies specifically to the 2014–2015 SHAPE project where research and action-based study focused on understanding systems in relation to their complex parts.

Systemic Approach

The term 'systemic intermediaries' applies to the investigation of linked systems and their joint effects on youth entrepreneurship.[10] An 'approach' can be described as the process of going towards something. For this research, a systemic approach implies attention to the whole support structure for youth entrepreneurs as set out by scholars specialising in this doctrine.[11]

Systemic Levels

The four systemic levels that apply to this study are the mundo-, macro-, meso- and micro-levels. The 'mundo-system' refers to global governance, the 'macrosystem' refers to national governance, the 'mesosystem'

---

[9] Schweikert, Meissen & Wolf 2013
[10] Jackson 2003
[11] Dhliwayo 2008; Van der Westhuizen 2016

refers to organisations and culture and the 'microsystem' refers to individuals.[12] Different systemic levels may have an integrative effect on entrepreneurship.[13]

Systems Thinking

In this study, systems thinking is applied in the reviewing of information from a holistic perspective. It attempts to solve problems by encouraging people to view a problem from different perspectives to understand the parts that constitute a whole; it is an approach for solving complex problems in the interests of change, and it becomes a key element in decision-making.[14]

Triple H of Entrepreneurship

The Triple H of Entrepreneurship refers to the interconnectedness of our entrepreneurial Heartset, Mindset and Handset in fostering the psychological development of entrepreneurial behaviour. The term 'entrepreneurial heartset' pertains to the neurological processes that shape our mindset, while 'entrepreneurial mindset' represents the resulting framework of our thoughts. Lastly, 'entrepreneurial handset' signifies the behavioural actions we take towards entrepreneurship. Essentially, it encompasses the dynamic tapestry of intertwining entrepreneurial heart, head and hand (Triple H).

Youth Entrepreneurs

In the South African National Youth Policy for 2015–2020, youths are defined as 'all people between the ages of 14 and 35 years', while the legal age in South Africa for children to enter the labour market is 15.[15] In

---

[12] Scharmer 2009
[13] Scharmer & Kaüfer 2013
[14] Briscoe 2016
[15] Republic of South Africa 2015

this study, 'youths' is accordingly defined as people between the ages of 15 and 35, and 'youth entrepreneurs' are persons in that age group who are attempting to become entrepreneurs.

Youth Entrepreneurship

Youth entrepreneurship refers to the practical elements of personality involved in enterprising activities, such as initiative, innovation, creativity and risk-taking in the working environment (either in self-employment or in employment in small start-up firms) and using skills necessary for success in that environment.[16] For this research, youth entrepreneurship implies entrepreneurial activities being undertaken by youths between the ages of 15 and 35 who are in the process of applying entrepreneurial qualities, including the individual entrepreneurial orientation (IEO) factors of taking a risk and being innovative and proactive.

In addition, entrepreneurship signifies the process of creating and launching a new business.[17] For this study, the term 'youth entrepreneurship' refers to youths seeking to commence a new business.

Youth Entrepreneurship Programmes

Youth entrepreneurship programmes are initiatives to encourage and support youths in being more entrepreneurial. In this study, the term applies to both structured and unstructured events aiming to promote business-mindedness among youths.

References

Briscoe P. 2016. Global systems Thinking in education to end poverty: Systems leaders with a concerted push. International Studies in Educational Administration, 43(3):5–19.

---

[16] Chigunta 2002
[17] Roland 2016

Chigunta F. 2002. Youth entrepreneurship: Meeting the key policy challenges. Oxford: Education Development Centre, Wolfson College.

Dhliwayo S. 2008. Experiential learning in entrepreneurship education: A prospective model for South African tertiary institutions. Education and Training, 50(4):329–340.

Hannon V, Gillinson S & Shanks L. 2013. Learning a living: Radical innovation in education for work. Dohar: Bloomsbury.

Jackson M. 2003. Systems thinking: Creative holism for managers. Chichester, UK: Wiley.

Krasniqi BA. 2007. Barriers to entrepreneurship and SME growth in transition: The case of Kosova. Journal of Developmental Entrepreneurship, 12(1):71–94.

Leonard A. 2010. The story of stuff: How our obsession with stuff is trashing the planet, our communities, and our health – and a vision for change. New York: Simon & Schuster.

Republic of South Africa. 2015. National Youth Policy 2015–2020. Cape Town: The Presidency Republic of South Africa. https://www.gov.za/sites/default/files/gcis_document/201610/nationalyouthpolicy.pdf

Roland P. 2016. Comments by South African business owner. Personal communication to Wade Krieger.

Scharmer CO & Käufer K. 2013. Leading from the emerging future: From ego-system to eco-system economies. Oakland, CA: Berrett-Koehler Publishers.

Scharmer CO. 2009. Theory U: Learning from the future as it emerges. San Francisco: Berrett-Koehler Publishers.

Schweikert S, Meissen JO & Wolf P. 2013. Applying Theory U: The case of the creative living lab. In: O Gunnlaugson, C Baron & M Cayer (eds), Perspectives on Theory U: Insights from the Field. Hershey, PA: IGI Global.

Van der Westhuizen T. 2016. Developing Individual entrepreneurial orientation: A systemic approach through the lens of Theory U. PhD thesis. Durban: UKZN.

Van der Westhuizen T. 2017. Theory U and individual entrepreneurial orientation in developing youth entrepreneurship in South Africa. Journal of Contemporary Management, 14:531–553.

Contents

About the Author

Professor Thea van der Westhuizen, PhD/CPRP Primary investigator and project leader of SHAPE, University of KwaZulu-Natal, School of Management, Information Technology and Governance: Discipline of Management and Entrepreneurship (Academic Leader); Chairperson: Entrepreneurship Development in Higher Education (EDHE) Community of Practice for Learning and Teaching.

Abbreviations and Acronyms

ADB	African Development Bank (also AfDB)
B-BBEE	Broad-Based Black Economic Empowerment
BEP	Breakeven point
BRICS	Brazil, Russia, India, China, South Africa (economic grouping)
CBT	Community-based tourism
CSI	Corporate social investment
DHET	Department of Higher Education and Training
DSBD	Department of Small Business Development
EA	Entrepreneurial Action(s)
EDHE	Entrepreneurship Development in Higher Education
EI	Entrepreneurial intent/intentions
ESE	Entrepreneurial self-efficacy
EU	European Union
GDP	Gross Domestic Product
ICT	Information (and) communication technology
IEO	Individual entrepreneurial orientation
NAFCOC	National African Chamber of Commerce
NGO	Non-Governmental Organisation
SALAR	Systemic action learning and action research

Seda	Small Enterprise Development Agency
SHAPE	Shifting Hope, Activating Potential Entrepreneurship
SME	Small-and-medium-sized enterprise
DTI	Department of Trade and Industry
TIA	Technology Innovation Agency
UKZN	University of KwaZulu-Natal
USD	United States (of America) dollars
VIF	Variance inflation factor
YE	Youth entrepreneur/ship
YES Network	Youth Entrepreneur Support Network

List of Figures

List of Tables

Part I

Connecting Systems

1

Introduction to Youth Entrepreneurship

1.1   Introduction

South Africa is facing its biggest crisis ever in relation to youth unemployment. Under the expanded definition of total national unemployment, which includes discouraged job seekers, the rate rose to a record of 43.2% in the first quarter of 2021 from 42.6% in the previous quarter. Underscoring the gravity of the situation, the youth's jobless rate based on the expanded definition now stands at 74.7%, which means that only one in four school leavers who are 24 or younger have a job in South Africa. This should urgently be addressed as a matter of national priority and is a national crisis Adelakun and Van der Westhuizen (2021), Awotunde and Van der Westhuizen (2021a), Van der Westhuizen (2017a).[1] A link between youth unemployment and low economic development is evident in South Africa, and the low economic growth influences the total labour market. It is important to examine the effects that unemployment has on youth development

---

[1] Stoddard (2021).

because unemployed youths are unable to gain valuable entrepreneurial skills.

Entrepreneurship is often seen as a strategy to improve youth unemployment, but by no means can it be seen as a save-it-all strategy for national social-economic development. Attempting to investigate possible support strategies for youth entrepreneurs, the SHAPE ecosystem for youth entrepreneurs was first theoretically created and then practically applied over time. The key barriers and enablers to youth entrepreneurship were identified as perceived by youths in relation to the ecosystem and results are presented in part two of the book. Youth unemployment and mitigating barriers to youth entrepreneurship are everybody's business, and all systems are held responsible for overcoming this crisis collectively. Failure to do so will result in a national socio-economic collapse. Awotunde and Van der Westhuizen (2021b), Van der Westhuizen (2019), Van der Westhuizen (2022).

1.2   Systems and Ecosystems

The world around us consists of integrated and interrelated systems, and these systems are facing severe challenges in all aspects.[2] The decay in systems in the different environments around us is the cause of collective deconstructive actions of people, and only a transformation of collective consciousness towards sustainable and responsible systemic development practices will bring forward possible solutions to turn around the decay within our systems.[3] The need for not only change but the deep systemic transformation has come to a boiling point where global governing practices such as the United Nations are reviewing sustainability approaches. Systemic transformation needs enablers of transformation which brings forward the desired change.[4] A system can be described as a complex whole whose functioning depends on its parts and the interactions

---

[2] Van der Westhuizen (2016).
[3] Gunnlaugson et al. (2013).
[4] Fitch and O'Fallon (2013).

between those parts,[5] where systemic elements affecting the whole, rather than just parts of it, refers to the interrelatedness and integrativeness of systems.[6]

Systems are distinguished on four different levels: mundo-level, macrolevel, meso-level and micro-level systems.[7] The *mundo-system* refers to global governance, the *macrosystem* refers to national governance or institutionalising, the *mesosystem* refers to organisations and culture and the *microsystem* refers to individuals and their thinking.[8] From a multi-level systemic perspective, the global society in relation to the global economy is described as the mundo-system, society at large as the macrosystem, organisational structure, culture and climate as the mesosystem and the personal characteristics and traits of an individual as the microsystem.[9]

Characteristics of systems and their components and determinants include[10]:

- A system has processes and certain outputs since the system is something.
- When components are added or removed from a system, these actions change the system.
- When any component is added to a system, it is affected by being included in the system.
- When components are added to a system, it is perceived that relating hierarchical structures are formed.
- The survival of a system requires certain forms of control and communication which support system survival.
- Some of the system's properties are emergent and not easy to predict.
- The system has a boundary.
- The external environment to the boundary of the system affects the system.

---

[5] Jackson (2003).
[6] Leonard (2010).
[7] Scharmer (2009).
[8] Townsend and MacBeath (2011).
[9] Mark Edward's as cited in Thompson and Bevan (2013).
[10] Waring (1996).

Systems can further be distinguished between physical or natural structures as hard systems and people, organisations and their culture as soft systems.[11] Hard systems operate in a process that goes from extraction to production, distribution, consumption and ultimately disposal—otherwise referred to as the materials economy.[12] The materials economy system is in crisis because it is confined to a linear sequence of hard systems which minimally incorporate soft-systems approaches.[13] On this topic, twenty-first-century scholars concur that systems at all levels are in a crisis.[14] It is important to highlight the need for collective change within systems because the impact of irresponsible and unsustainable leadership practices results in the decay of all systemic environments, whether it is a political, economic or ecological environment. These systemic challenges are evident in both developed and developing countries.

Soft-systems development scholars propose an anthropomorphic descriptive terminology of the system. They suggest, for example, that integrative systems cannot 'breathe' without one another or that systems are 'living', 'dying' and being 'reborn'.[15] Viewing systems as anthropomorphic ties in with the term 'ecosystem'. An ecosystem, derived from the Greek *oikos* (house or habitation) and *systema* (organised whole) is derived from biology, denoting the complexity of relationship of living things to their environment. An ecosystem describes how various organisms live closely together, their mode of interaction with each other and how they depend on each other for existence and survival. Ecosystems are complex, supporting elements that are both biotic (living) and abiotic (non-living). The biotic are divided based on their type of nutrition: some of them are producers, others are consumers IGI Global (2020).[16]

---

[11] Jackson (2003).

[12] Leonard (2010).

[13] Leonard (2010).

[14] Scharmer (2009) and Goleman and Senge (2014).

[15] Checkland (1999), Jackson (2003), Senge et al. (2008a, 2008b), Scharmer (2009), and Scharmer and Käufer (2013).

[16] Moore (1996).

Similarly, youth entrepreneurs function in an ecosystem and they need a systemic support network to exist—and vice versa—because of the co-dependency of systems.

1.2.1 Systems in Crisis

Globally, social systems are in a crisis and dying. In the same process, something else is being reborn. Death and rebirth of systems, specifically ecosystems, are associated with disruption and change, which can be a painful process for individuals. Hard systems on the planet that are dying include its ecology and the functioning of the materials economy as we know it, and on a soft systemic level traditional leadership and policy approaches are changing beyond recognition. In reflecting on systems and their disconnect, there are three basic feelings shared by many people in the world[17]:

- We live in a world in which we hit the wall with larger systems. Our civilisation is in the process of dying. And that is happening right now, visible among other things in the disruptions around us and between us.
- I want to be part of another story of the future that I want to help create through my life and work; and
- I do not know.

In the rebirth of socio-economic development, the microsystem takes priority, with the values, heartset and mindset of the individual shaping the integrative actions of the system as a whole. The 'spinners' of systemic development going forward are individual values, vision and levels of self-confidence.[18] These aspects are essential for the sustainability of national wealth creation of the flow of goods and services. Wealth creation is

[17] Scharmer (2009).
[18] Senge et al. (2008a, 2008b), Song et al. (2010), Hermans (2012), Hannon et al. (2013), and Hoy (2013).

complex and abstract and not synonymous with the accumulation of vast amounts of money Van der Westhuizen (2017b), Ruba et al. (2021).[19]

1.3   Youth Entrepreneurship

A world without entrepreneurs would be a world without newness and any uncertainty.[20] The youth entrepreneur then evolves as someone searching for profit and initiating new combinations and innovates products, processes, sources of supply, selling markets and organisational forms.

Youth entrepreneurship refers to practical elements of personality in enterprising activity such as taking the initiative, innovation, creativity and risk-taking in the working environment (either in self-employment or employment in small start-up firms) and using skills necessary for success in that environment.[21] Entrepreneurship is a social function whose ultimate objective is value creation through recognition of enabling factors. This involves four processes: innovation and creativity, enabling-creation, creating a market and creating an identity formation.[22] Youth entrepreneurship is not an isolated concept. It takes place within a nondual social-economic environment comprised of people who are entrepreneurs, employees and customers of businesses. For this book, youth entrepreneurship is taken as those entrepreneurial activities being undertaken by youths in the process of applying enterprising qualities, including the individual entrepreneurial orientation (IEO) factors of taking risks and being innovative and proactive. In addition, youth entrepreneurship signifies the process of creating and launching a new business.[23]

The entrepreneurial journey's premise is said to be that of 'new' value creation in which new identities, new ideas, new products and services,

---

[19] Remenyi (2021).

[20] Stefanović and Stošić (2012).

[21] Chigunta (2002).

[22] Goss (2005).

[23] Roland (2016).

new companies and new entrepreneurs are collectively co-created by the entrepreneur and their interaction with society.[24] Youth entrepreneurship education is an initiative to encourage and support youths in becoming more entrepreneurial and facilitate interactions with society. These initiatives can be academic or non-academic with a common denominator to enrich the entrepreneurial experiences of youths with the aim to potentially facilitate entrepreneurial action (EA). The term applies to both structured and unstructured events aimed at promoting business-mindedness among the youth.

The activity of youth entrepreneurship in the informal economy is difficult to determine. However, the *Quarterly Labour Force Survey* released by Statistics South Africa shows that approximately 2.9 million people were actively involved in the informal economy in the first quarter of 2020.[25] With youth unemployment peaking in the formal economic activities, it is essential for policymakers and academics—in particular—to review the current relevance of entrepreneurship strategies to enable sustainable and effective youth entrepreneurship. Equally important for youths is to recognise available national strategies and enabling initiatives that can support them in co-initiating an entrepreneurial ecosystem. Key success factors for an effective youth entrepreneur ecosystem strategy include recognising and bridging systemic disconnect, emphasising microsystemic transformation, innovation strategy formulation for economic development and social growth in an environment of sharply competitive globalisation.[26]

The popularity of youth entrepreneurship has been attributed to its positive influence on wealth and job creation,[27] with particular importance of entrepreneurship as a self-employment option for present-day graduates who can no longer count on the security of wage employment after completing their studies.[28] In a similar vein, youth entrepreneurship can be seen as a tool that minimises unemployment levels and is a source

---

[24] Bruyat and Julien (2000) and Henry et al. (2005).
[25] Statistics South Africa (2020).
[26] Béchard and Toulouse (1998), Matlay and Westhead (2005), and Schaper and Volery (2004).
[27] Gürol and Atsan (2006) and Kantis et al. (2002).
[28] Brown (1996) and Kamau-Maina (2006).

of sustainable economic development.[29] However, there are key barriers within the youth entrepreneur ecosystem that need to be addressed to increase efficiency, success rates and, most importantly, sustainability Van der Westhuizen (2018a), Van der Westhuizen (2018b), Nhleko and van der Westhuizen (2022).

The demographic significance of youth entrepreneurship in South Africa needs to be considered. Highly successful and efficient youth entrepreneurship is related to value creation in a location-specific context. In addition, youth entrepreneurship in South Africa is impaired by factors such as bureaucratic obstacles to accessing finance, a shortage of specialised skills and a general lack of innovation.[30] Young South Africans are nonetheless positively disposed towards entrepreneurship.[31] The driver for young people venturing into business is increasingly considered as being a wish to pursue perceived opportunities rather than merely from basic necessity[32] (Fig. 1.1).

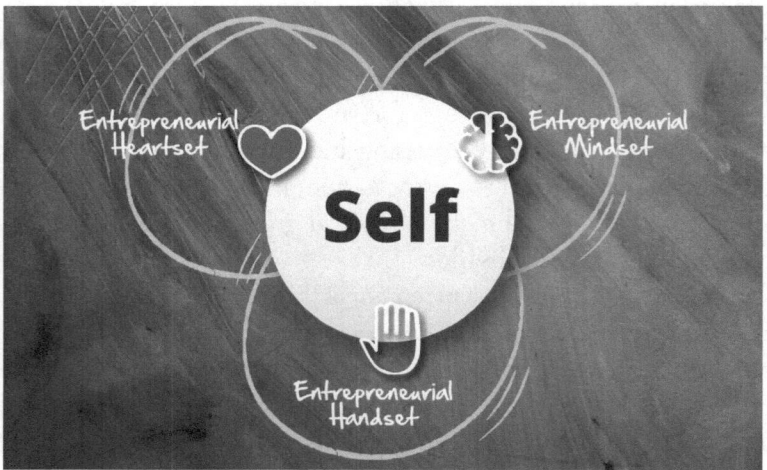

Fig. 1.1 The triple H of entrepreneurship (*Source* Van der Westhuizen, T [2022])

---

[29] Awogbenle and Iwuamadi (2010).

[30] Steenekamp et al. (2011).

[31] Maas and Herrington (2007).

[32] Mpafa (2008).

To acquire entrepreneurial self-efficacy (ESE) in meeting business challenges and succeed in business communication and interpersonal negotiations: youths will need to develop a sense of self-responsibility over their own lives and a resilient desire and capacity to influence the world around them; consciously helping to shape a new world and participate in it; actively making a difference to improve the crisis various systems are in.[33] Another factor consistently identified as important in youth entrepreneurship promotion in South Africa is the level of education and grades achieved at school.[34] Entrepreneurship education is fundamental to youth entrepreneurial development. Figure 1.2 shows the youth entrepreneur development process.

As the diagram shows, youth entrepreneurship is the total of psychological, social, commercial and economic interactions. The entrepreneurial process can be decomposed into three major phases:

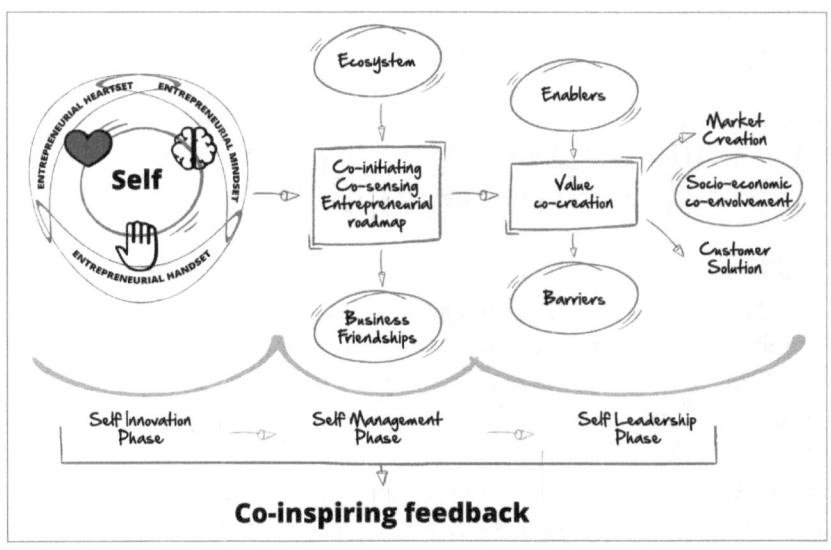

Fig. 1.2 The youth entrepreneur development process (*Source* Van der West-huizen [2022])

---

[33] Hannon et al. (2013) and Scharmer (2009).
[34] Maas and Herrington (2007).

self-innovation, self-management and self-leadership.[35] It is evident that self-development for youth entrepreneurs is embedded in actions of co-inspiring and feedback from their ecosystem: thus, connecting a support system with each other and engaging with feedback through dyadic conversations where discussions and feedback-looping are essential.

The entrepreneurial heartset, mindset and handset of youths is fundamental to their entrepreneurial journey and is described in more detail in Chapter 2. In the self-innovation phase, youths will need to break down their old mental models and start looking at the world with fresh eyes—growing in developmental maturity and transforming the 'Self'. In the self-management phase, youths are taking EA and co-initiating, co-sensing and co-inspiring with role-players in their ecosystem to establish business friendships and explore how value creation can occur through collaborative efforts. In the self-leadership phase, youths take an instrumental role in bringing change to their socio-economic environment, contributing to market creation and inspiring customer solutions for collective socio-economic development.

1.4 Shifting Hope, Activating Potential Youth Entrepreneurship (SHAPE)

SHAPE, an acronym for Shifting Hope, Activating Potential Entrepreneurship, is an academic concept designed to foster entrepreneurship within South African Higher Education Institutions (HEIs) and beyond. The concept recognises the importance of shifting heartsets and mindsets, instilling hope and activating the potential of individuals towards entrepreneurial endeavours. SHAPE emphasises the need to create a multi-disciplinary enabling environment that encourages and supports entrepreneurial feeling, thinking, learning and action. Through targeted interventions, such as curriculum development, experiential learning opportunities, mentorship programmes, action research and access to resources, SHAPE aims to equip students with the necessary confidence, skills and knowledge to embark on entrepreneurial

---

[35] Shambare et al. (2020).

ventures. By incorporating SHAPE into HEIs, South Africa can harness the transformative power of entrepreneurship, driving economic growth, job creation and societal development.

SHAPE was created initially as a theoretical framework and then validated through creating the proposed youth entrepreneurial ecosystem. The practical application of the strategy's sustainability was further validated through a series of assessments. The 'SHAPE' strategy refers to processes on the journey to developing the entrepreneurial heartset, mindset and handset of an individual. This process occurs through moving from reactive response fields to generative response fields, where ideation of entrepreneurial possibilities can be brought into action.

The proposed strategy aims to assist youths in transforming (grow in developmental maturity) personality traits through focusing on ESE, IEO, entrepreneurial intent (EI) and EA. Self-development occurs within a support network, also referred to as the youth entrepreneurial ecosystem. Facilitation of the youth entrepreneurial ecosystem is initially co-initiated by educational institutes, where functions shift as the youth entrepreneurial system develops towards self-sustainability.

As SALAR, the SHAPE strategy consists of three cycles, executed through eleven phases to bring about the desired entrepreneurial change and empirically measure development over time. As a theoretical framework, SHAPE can assist in boosting youth entrepreneurship through starting, inspiring and developing the entrepreneurial heartset, mindset and handset of youth entrepreneurs. SHAPE is designed to connect youths with a support network and leadership (ecosystemic connection) to inspire them to become successful entrepreneurs.[36] These successful youth entrepreneurs are described as individuals who are consistently motivated to achieve financial sustainability and feel confident of overcoming challenges by being proactive. The continuum of high youth unemployment in South Africa forces many youths into finding a way to survive, therefore becoming grassroots entrepreneurs. Youths are limited by their perceptual framework, value system, culture and

---

[36] Van der Westhuizen (2016).

work experiences.[37] Thus, youths' culture, family, role models, education and work experience affect their growth and survival.[38] Youths pursue entrepreneurship because they perceive it to offer flexibility in an improved work-life balance, but they often do not understand what it takes to become a successful entrepreneur. Connecting to a support network in the youth entrepreneur ecosystem might assist the youth entrepreneurs to take EA, more importantly, to sustain their entrepreneurial efforts.

1.5   SHAPE Ecosystem Strategy for Youth Entrepreneurs

The SHAPE ecosystem strategy for youth entrepreneurs identifies internal and external domains for youth entrepreneur support. These domains consist of seven categories that form a support network—ecosystem—needed by youths. The youth entrepreneurial ecosystem may help youths propel their nascent business idea into a reality through a journey *en route* to EA. The young entrepreneur's ecosystem is therefore the same as their youth entrepreneur support network.

The SHAPE YES Network, an acronym for the SHAPE Youth Entrepreneurship Support Network, is an academic concept that represents an entrepreneurial ecosystem tailored for young entrepreneurs. This network holds immense potential for implementation in South African Higher Education Institutes (HEIs) and beyond. It encompasses multiple domains, starting with the youth's internal domain, which encompasses their personality traits and characteristics. This internal domain interacts with several external domains to create a comprehensive support network for youth entrepreneurs.

The external domains of the SHAPE YES Network include the Higher Education Institute (HEI), which serves as the project host and provides leadership, facilitation, administrative support and monitoring for the support network. Government agencies play a crucial role by offering

---

[37] Meyer et al. (2016).
[38] Geldhof et al. (2014).

a business support unit, integrating entrepreneurial strategies at the municipal level, and providing mentorship and support programmes for youth entrepreneurs. Private sector agencies, such as local chambers of commerce and other organisations, contribute by offering platforms and mentorship opportunities to young entrepreneurs.

Communities, including local communities, families and friends, form an essential part of the support network, providing encouragement and support to youth entrepreneurs. Additionally, the SHAPE YES Network incorporates collaboration with entrepreneurs and small to medium-sized businesses, establishing an ecosystem of support and knowledge exchange. Lastly, corporations and large businesses offer internships and on-the-job learning opportunities, creating platforms for practical experience and skill development.

By integrating the SHAPE YES Network into HEIs and beyond, South Africa can cultivate a robust environment for young entrepreneurs. This comprehensive ecosystem enables youth, leverages external support systems and facilitates collaboration across various domains, fostering entrepreneurship, economic growth and innovation. Figure 1.3 illustrates these eight aspects, which are discussed throughout the book.

1.6 Typologies of Youth Entrepreneurs in South Africa

There are at least seven types of definitions of 'youth entrepreneurs' and 'youth entrepreneurship' that have been found in literature[39]:

1. Whom the youth entrepreneur is (focusing on the entrepreneur as a particular type of person or the entrepreneur as the product of a particular type of environment).
2. What the youth entrepreneur does (focusing on the entrepreneur as performing a particular role in society).
3. The youth entrepreneur as a type of business owner.

---

[39] Steenberg (2017).

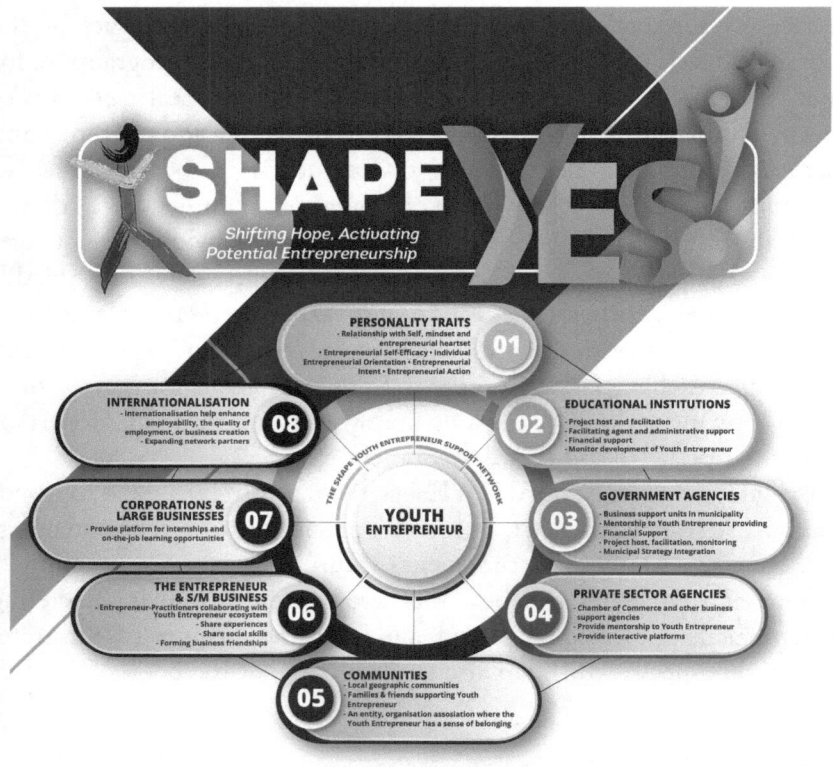

Van der Westhuizen, T. 2023. Effective Youth Entrepreneurship. Sunbonani Scholar. South Africa. 447 pages.

Fig. 1.3 The SHAPE YES Network for youth entrepreneurs (expanded)

4. The process that the youth entrepreneur experiences, entrepreneurial events and entrepreneurial input into the economy.
5. The youth entrepreneur as an innovator, an actor in the creation of future goods and services.[40]
6. Definitions focusing on the fact that youth entrepreneurs own small businesses.
7. Archetypal definitions that classify different types of youth entrepreneurs into broad categories.

---

[40] Sarasvathy and Venkataraman (2011).

It seems that these definitions have all been operationalised for different purposes and thus serve different purposes in the literature.

There are multiple definitions of the term 'youth entrepreneur', and an applicable description within the context of this book is that they are rogues who actualise a market potential. This is consistent with the early nineteenth-century coining of the term 'entrepreneurship' as the process of shifting economic resources from an area of low productivity into situations that have higher yields.[41] Also popular is the definition of radical 1980s scholars, which is that youth entrepreneurs take advantage of opportunities without regard for the resources they currently control.[42]

The traditional nomenclature of youth entrepreneurial activities revolves around two forms of youth entrepreneurship: necessity (survivalist) and opportunity-driven youth entrepreneurship. These are generally distinguished as follows: Youths who are initially unemployed before starting businesses are defined as 'necessity' youth entrepreneurs and youths who are not unemployed (e.g. wage or salary workers, enrolled in school or college or not actively seeking a job) before starting businesses are defined as 'opportunity' youth entrepreneurs.[43]

While the foregoing is taken in the literature as a widely accepted practice, this book adopts a different and more comprehensive approach to classifying entrepreneurial activities. In considering the development of youth entrepreneurs: it is often assumed that entrepreneurship is competence and that when entrepreneurs start out, they are incompetent. Literature has failed to answer why some people are better at starting businesses than others, as the construct for the definition of entrepreneurship has not been focused on a market-based view of entrepreneurial activity.

---

[41] Say (1851).
[42] Gartner et al. (2017).
[43] Fairlie and Fossen (2018).

The definition above describes the entrepreneur as an essential mechanism for translating the demand of customers into supply.[44] It also differentiates the entrepreneur from the business owner, as an entrepreneur develops a sustainable business.

More work needs to be done to create a complete ontology of entrepreneurs.[45] Figure 1.4 combines the work of various authors in an attempt at a description of various types of entrepreneurs as observed in the literature. There are many different descriptions of what we call entrepreneurs today.[46]

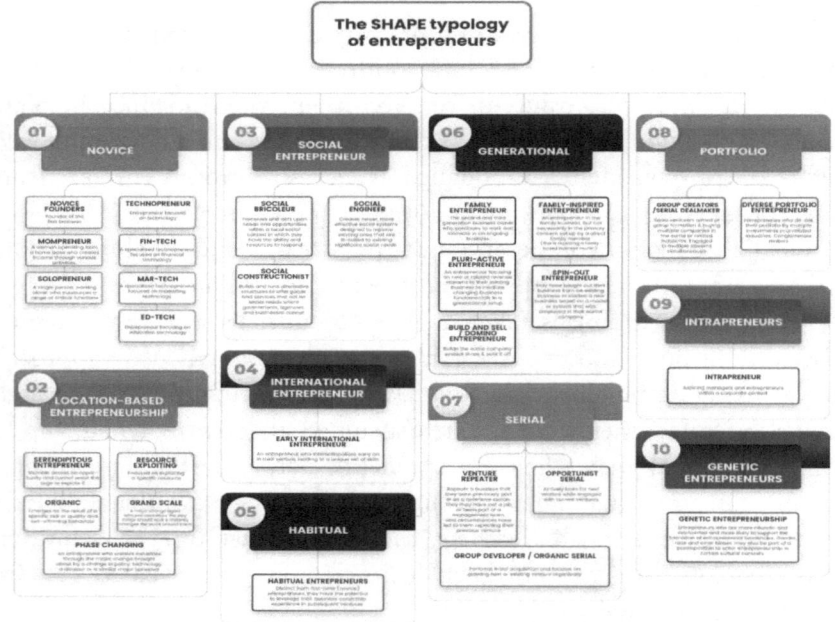

Fig. 1.4 The SHAPE typology of entrepreneurs (*Source* Steenberg [2017])

---

[44] Steenberg (2017).

[45] Ucbasaran et al. (2008).

[46] Rogoff and Lee (1996).

1.7   Entrepreneurship Frameworks and Models

There is a myriad of approaches to entrepreneurship in general. Broadly attempting to understand youth entrepreneurship better, Fig. 1.5 illustrates general entrepreneurship frameworks and key theories.

Entrepreneurship is also broadly classified as process-based, events-based, strengths-based, market-based and functional skills-based models, as shown in Fig. 1.6.

At a broad level, entrepreneurship scholarship is a process undertaken by many authors, and it shows potential in terms of finding a valid approach to entrepreneurship education.[47]

Fig. 1.5 Entrepreneurship frameworks and key theories (*Source* Van der Westhuizen [2022])

---

[47] Steenberg (2017).

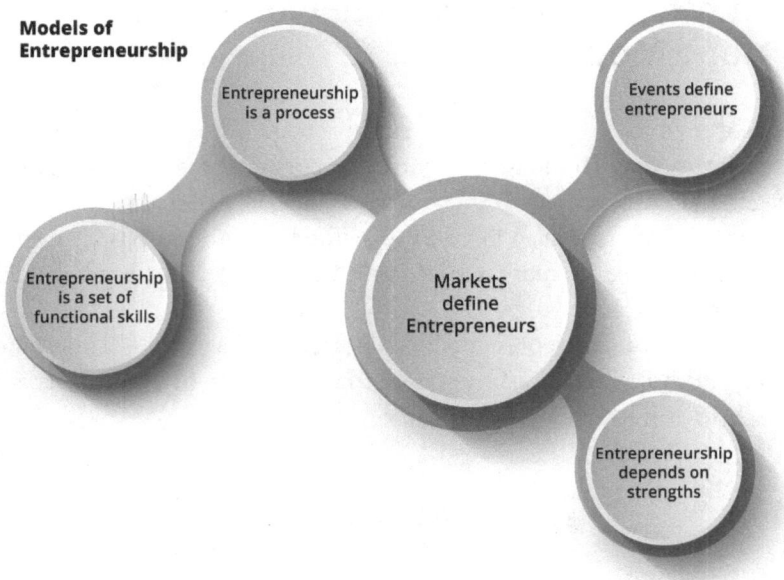

Fig. 1.6 Models of entrepreneurship (*Source* Steenberg [2022])

1.8   Youth Entrepreneurship: Enablers and Barriers

Enablers can be defined as a person, thing or phenomenon that makes, or helps make, something possible. Barriers are obstacles that block the processes of youths' EA. Earlier research on youth entrepreneurship education tends to argue that it is increasingly difficult to become a successful youth entrepreneur. Data from the *2019–2020 Global Entrepreneurship Monitor*[48] show that worldwide youth entrepreneurial activity is low and shows no signs of improvement occurring currently.[49]

---

[48] GERA (2020).
[49] Herrington and Kew (2016).

The low level of youth entrepreneurial activity is exacerbated by inadequate support from government projects and policies, private sector agencies, communities and educational institutions.[50]

As a consequence of these barriers, a multitude of 'daily management challenges' are experienced by youth entrepreneurs. Finding ways to overcome some of the identified barriers could help to alleviate the crisis of youth unemployment.[51] A revised approach to teaching entrepreneurship is required Adelakun and Van der Westhuizen (2021), Awotunde and Van der Westhuizen (2021a, b), IGI Global (2020), Nhleko and van der Westhuizen (2022), Ruba et al. (2021).[52] The revised approach used in SHAPE focuses on action-based learning and encourages youth entrepreneurs to practise experiential learning, problem-solving and creativity. This provides practical experience representative of real-world scenarios. It occurs from a nondual perspective where the youth entrepreneurship ecosystem is created to effectively enable a support network for youth entrepreneurs.[53]

Youth entrepreneurs face both internal and external barriers. Internal barriers affect the entrepreneurial heartset, mindset and handset, which is a specific state of being that orientates human conduct towards entrepreneurial activities and outcomes. Youths with an entrepreneurial mindset are often drawn to opportunities, innovation and new value creation.[54] Elements of the entrepreneurial heartset, mindset and handset specifically noted are ESE, IEO, EI and EA.[55]

Systemic external barriers, which youths who are in the process of becoming youth entrepreneurs encounter in generating momentum for their nascent business ideas, can be identified. These external barriers affect the entrepreneurial mindset and often give rise to further internal barriers within the entrepreneurial mind.[56]

---

[50] Van der Westhuizen (2016).
[51] Meyer et al. (2016).
[52] Dhliwayo (2008).
[53] Van der Westhuizen (2016).
[54] Fayolle (2013).
[55] Cox et al. (2002), Kickul and D'Intino (2005), and Ramkissor (2013).
[56] Kickul and D'Intino (2005).

The study upon which this book is based investigates enablers and barriers that youth entrepreneurs face in South Africa in relation to the theoretical youth entrepreneurial ecosystem, as illustrated in Fig. 1.3.[57]

The youth's perceived enablers and barriers are summarised and illustrated in Fig. 1.7.

The theoretical model of the youth entrepreneur ecosystem, known as the SHAPE YES Network, highlights the significance of a robust support network for young entrepreneurs. This network encompasses educational institutions, government agencies, private sector entities, communities, SMEs and large businesses and corporations. These stakeholders collectively contribute to providing the necessary resources, mentorship and opportunities to empower and enable youth in their entrepreneurial endeavours. By recognising the pivotal role of these interconnected entities, the SHAPE YES Network emphasises the importance of collaboration and integration across various sectors to create a conducive environment that facilitates the growth and success of young entrepreneurs through facilitating an increased enabling environment and overcoming perceived barriers.

1.9   Conclusion

Youth entrepreneur development has been identified as fundamental to any country's long-term socio-economic development, but not a save-it-all solution to the deep socio-economic crisis global systems face. Developing the entrepreneurial heartset, mindset and handset can lead to EA and potential value creation. To create value, youth entrepreneurs need to co-initiate and co-sense an entrepreneurial roadmap within their ecosystem and form crucial business friendships. During these processes, they will encounter barriers and enablers, but an anchored sense of Self can help youth entrepreneurs conquer barriers and optimise enabling factors. Processes of self-innovation, self-management and self-leadership will strengthen positive personality traits to conquer the

---

[57] Van der Westhuizen (2016).

Fig. 1.7 Top 10 barriers and enablers in the youth entrepreneurial ecosystem (*Source* Van der Westhuizen [2022])

barriers encountered, especially if these barriers relate to psychological health aspects.

This chapter introduced SHAPE social technology, which was used as a strategy for the empirical research described in this book. The SHAPE support network, which illustrates a youth entrepreneur ecosystem, is used as the key model for the empirical premise of the book.

References

Adelakun, Y., & Van der Westhuizen, T. (2021). Delineating government policies and individual entrepreneurial orientation. *Journal of Sociology and Social Anthropology, 12*(3–4), 106–117. https://doi.org/10.31901/245 66764.2021/12.3-4.371

Awogbenle, A. C., & Iwuamadi, K. C. (2010). Youth unemployment: Entrepreneurship development programme as an intervention mechanism. *African Journal of Business Management, 4*(6), 831–835.

Awotunde, O. M., & Van der Westhuizen, T. (2021a). Entrepreneurial self-efficacy development: An effective intervention for sustainable student entrepreneurial intentions. *International Journal of Innovation and Sustainable Development, 15*(4), 475–495.

Awotunde, O. M., & Van der Westhuizen, T. (2021b). *Entrepreneurial self-efficacy and the SHAPE ideation model for university students.* ECIE 2021 16th European Conference on Innovation and Entrepreneurship, Vol. 1, p. 37.

Béchard, J. P., & Toulouse, J. M. (1998). Validation of a didactic model for the analysis of training objectives in entrepreneurship. *Journal of Business Venturing, 13*(4), 317–332.

Brown, S. P. (1996). A meta-analysis and review of organizational research on job involvement. *Psychological Bulletin, 120*(2), 235–255 (Retrieved 29 May 2020).

Bruyat, C., & Julien, P. A. (2000). Defining the field of research in entrepreneurship. *Journal of Business Venturing, 16*(2), 165–180.

Checkland, P. (1999). *Systems thinking, systems practice: Includes a 30-year retrospective.* Wiley.

Chigunta, F. (2002). *Youth entrepreneurship: Meeting the key policy challenges.* Education Development Centre, Wolfson College.

Cox, L. W., Mueller, S. L., & Moss, S. E. (2002). The impact of entrepreneurship education on entrepreneurial self-efficacy. *International Journal of Entrepreneurship Education, 1*(2), 229–245.

Dhliwayo, S. (2008). Experiential learning in entrepreneurship education: A prospective model for South African tertiary institutions. *Education and Training, 50*(4), 329–340.

Fairlie, R. W., & Fossen, F. M. (2018). *Opportunity versus necessity entrepreneurship: Two components of business creation* (IZA Discussion Paper No. 11258). Forschungsinstitut zur Zukunft der Arbeit [Research Institute on the Future of Work], University of Bonn.

Fayolle, A. (2013). Personal views on the future of entrepreneurship education. *Entrepreneurship and Regional Development, 25*(7–8), 692–701.

Fitch, G., & O'Fallon, T. (2013). Theory U applied in transformation development. In O. Gunnlaugson, C. Baron, & M. Cayer (Eds.), *Perspectives on Theory U: Insights from the field*. IGI Global.

Gartner, W. B., Teague, B. T., Baker, T., & Wadhwani, R. D. (2017). A brief history of the idea of opportunity. In C. Leger-Jarniou & S. Tegtmeier (Eds.), *Research handbook on entrepreneurial opportunities* (pp. 47–65). Edward Elgar.

Geldhof, G. J., Porter, T., Weiner, M. B., Malin, H., Bronk, K. C., Agans, J. P., Mueller, M., Damon, W., & Lerner, R. M. (2014). Fostering youth entrepreneurship: Preliminary findings from the Young Entrepreneurs Study. *Journal of Research on Adolescence, 24*(3), 431–446.

GERA (Global Entrepreneurship Research Association). (2020). *Global Entrepreneurship Monitor: 2019/20 Global report*. GERA, London Business School.

Goleman, D., & Senge, P. (2014). Seeking the big picture: Systems thinking for schools. *Education Week, 34*(2), 22–23.

Goss, D. (2005). Schumpeter's legacy? Interactions and emotions in the society of entrepreneurship. *Entrepreneurship Theory and Practice, 29*(2), 205–218.

Gunnlaugson, O., Baron, C., & Cayer, M. (Eds.). (2013). *Perspectives on Theory U: Insights from the field*. IGI Global.

Gürol, Y., & Atsan, N. (2006). Entrepreneurial characteristics amongst university students. *Education and Training, 48*(1), 25–38.

Hannon, V., Gillinson, S., & Shanks, L. (2013). *Learning a living: Radical innovation in education for work*. Bloomsbury.

Henry, C., Hill, F., & Leitch, C. (2005). Entrepreneurship education and training: Can entrepreneurship be taught? Part 1. *Education and Training, 47*(2), 98–111.

Hermans, C. A. M. (2012). Towards a 'U-turn' by the churches: How (not) to possibilise the future. *Religion & Theology, 19*(3/4), 237–264.

Herrington, M., & Kew, P. (2016). *Is SA heading for an economic meltdown?* (Global Entrepreneur Monitor: South African Report 2015/16). www.gem consortium.org/report/49537 (Retrieved 15 January 2018).

Hoy, F. (2013). Handbook of research on innovation and entrepreneurship edited by David B. Audretsch, Oliver Falck, Stephan Heblich and Adam Lederer. *Science & Public Policy (SPP), 40*(2), 274–275.

IGI Global. (2020). *What is social technology?* www.igi-global.com/dictionary/social-technology/37941 (Retrieved 12 May 2020).

Jackson, M. (2003). *Systems thinking: Creative holism for managers*. Wiley.

Kamau-Maina, R. (2006, June 2). *Structured qualitative methods, stimulating youth entrepreneurship in Kenya* (EDMP 638. Concept Paper, pp. 1–38). Weatherhead School of Management.

Kantis, H., Ishida, M., & Komori, M. (2002). *Entrepreneurship in emerging economies: The creation and development of new firms in Latin America and East Asia*. Inter-American Development Bank.

Kickul, J., & D'Intino, R. S. (2005). Measure for measure: Modeling entrepreneurial self-efficacy onto instrumental tasks within the new venture creation process. *New England Journal of Entrepreneurship, 8*(2), 6.

Leonard, A. (2010). *The story of stuff: How our obsession with stuff is trashing the planet, our communities, and our health—And a vision for change*. Simon & Schuster.

Maas, G., & Herrington, M. (2007). *Global Entrepreneurship Monitor: South African report 2007*. Graduate School of Business, University of Cape Town.

Matlay, H., & Westhead, P. (2005). Virtual teams and the rise of e-entrepreneurship in Europe. *International Small Business Journal: Researching Entrepreneurship, 23*(3), 279–302 (Retrieved 10 May 2020).

Meyer, N., Meyer, D. F., & Molefe, K. N. (2016). Bariery rozwoju malych nieformalnych przedsiebiorstw i przedsiebiorczosci: Przypadek regionu emfuleni [Barriers to the development of small informal enterprises and entrepreneurship: The case of the Emfuleni region]. *Polish Journal of Management Studies, 13*(1), 121–133.

Moore, J. F. (1996). *The death of competition: Leadership & strategy in the age of business ecosystems.* HarperBusiness. ISBN 0-88730-850-3.

Mpafa, D. (2008). *Youth positive about being entrepreneurs.* http://www.gem. consortium.org/document.aspx?id=778 (Retrieved 15 February 2012).

Nhleko, Y., & van der Westhuizen, T. (2022). The role of higher education institutions in introducing entrepreneurship education to meet the demands of industry 4. 0. *Academy of Entrepreneurship Journal, 28*(1), 1–23.

Ramkissor, M. S. (2013). *The entrepreneurial orientation and intention of UKZN MBA students* (MCom thesis). University of KwaZulu-Natal (UKZN), Durban.

Remenyi, D. (2021). *7th e-Learning Excellence Awards 2021: An anthology of case histories.* University of Applied Sciences.

Rogoff, E. G., & Lee, M.-S. (1996). Does firm origin matter? An empirical examination of types of small business owners and entrepreneurs. *Academy of Entrepreneurship Journal, 1*(2), 1–17.

Roland, P. (2016). *Comments by South African business owner.* Personal communication to Wade Krieger.

Ruba, R. M., Van der Westhuizen, T., & Chiloane-Tsoka, G. E. (2021). Influence of entrepreneurial orientation on organisational performance: Evidence from Congolese Higher Education Institutions. *Journal of Contemporary Management, 18*(1), 243–269.

Sarasvathy, S. D., & Venkataraman, S. (2011). Entrepreneurship as method: Open questions for an entrepreneurial future. *Entrepreneurship Theory and Practice, 35*(1), 113–135.

Say, J.-B. (1851). *A treatise on political economy; or the production, distribution, and consumption of wealth.* Translated from the 4th Edition of the French. Clement, C. B. (Ed.) & Prinsep, C. B. (Trans.). Lippincott, Grambo & Co.

Schaper, M., & Volery, T. (2004). *Entrepreneurship and small business: A Pacific Rim perspective.* Wiley.

Scharmer, C. O., & Käufer, K. (2013). *Leading from the emerging future: From ego-system to eco-system economies.* Berrett-Koehler Publishers.

Scharmer, C. O. (2009). *Theory U: Learning from the future as it emerges.* Berrett-Koehler Publishers.

Senge, P., Scharmer, C. O., Jaworski, J., & Flowers, B. S. (2008a). *Presence: Human purpose and the field of the future.* Doubleday.

Senge, P., Smith, B., Kruschwitz, N., Laur, J., & Schley, S. (2008b). Anatomy of inspiration. *T & D, 62*(8), 52–55.

Shambare, R., Chakuzira, W., & Shambare, J. (2020). Revisiting entrepreneurship marketing research: Towards and framework for SMEs in developing countries. In S. Nwankwo & A. Gbadamosi (Eds.), *Entrepreneurship marketing: Principles and practice of SME marketing.* Routledge.

Song, L. Z., Song, M., & Parry, M. E. (2010). Perspective: Economic conditions, entrepreneurship, first-product development, and new venture success. *Journal of Product Innovation Management, 27*(1), 130–135.

Statistics South Africa. (2020). *Quarterly Labour Force Survey: Q1 2020.* https://www.statssa.gov.za/publications/P0211/P02111stQuarter2020.pdf (Retrieved 12 May 2020).

Steenberg, R. (2017). *The entrepreneurial spirit—Towards an education model for entrepreneurial success in South African entrepreneurs* (PhD thesis). Texila American University in association with the University of Central Nicaragua, Georgetown, Guyana.

Steenberg, (2022). *The Entrepreneurial Spirit.* In Van der Westhuizen, T. (Ed.), Effective youth entrepreneurship. Sunbonani. https://omp.sunbonani.co.za/index.php/sunbonani/catalog/book/6

Steenekamp, A. G., Van der Merwe, S. P., & Athayde, R. (2011). An investigation into youth entrepreneurship in selected South African secondary schools: An exploratory study. *South African Business Review, 15*(3), 46–75.

Stefanović, S., & Stošić, D. (2012). Specifics and challenges of female entrepreneurship. *Economic Themes, 50*(3), 327–343.

Stoddard, E. (2021, June 1). *First-quarter unemployment rate hits record high of 43.2%, youth jobless rate 74.7%.* Business Maverick. https://www.dailymaverick.co.za/article/2021-06-01-first-quarter-unemployment-rate-hits-record-high-of-43-2-youth-jobless-rate-74-7/

Thompson, M. J. B. D., & Bevan, D. (2013). *Wise management and organisational culture.* Palgrave Macmillan.

Townsend, D., & MacBeath, J. (2011). *International handbook of leadership for learning.* Springer.

Ucbasaran, D., Alsos, G. A., Westhead, P., & Wright, M. (2008). *Habitual entrepreneurs.* Now Publishers.

Van der Westhuizen, T. (2016). *Developing Individual entrepreneurial orientation: A systemic approach through the lens of Theory U* (PhD thesis). UKZN, Durban.

Van der Westhuizen, T. (2017a). The use of Theory U and Individual Entrepreneurial Orientation to increase Low Youth Entrepreneurship in South Africa. *Journal of Contemporary Management, 14*, 531–553.

Van der Westhuizen, T. (2017b). A systemic approach towards responsible and sustainable economic development: Entrepreneurship, systems theory and socio-economic momentum. In Z. Fields (Ed.), *Collective creativity for responsible and sustainable business practice*. IGI Global.

Van der Westhuizen, T. (2018a). The SHAPE project: Shifting hope, activating potential entrepreneurship In D. Remenyi & D. A. Grant (Eds.), *Incubators for young entrepreneurs—20 case histories*. ACPIL.

Van der Westhuizen, T. (2018b). *Open heart, open mind and open will in transformative individual entrepreneurial orientation pedagogies*. Academic Conferences and Publishing International Limited, Redding, UK, pp. 443–448.

Van der Westhuizen, T. (2019). *Action! Methods to develop entrepreneurship*. 18th European Conference on Research Methodology for Business and Management Studies, pp. 331–337.

Van der Westhuizen, T. (2021). Applying Theory U through SHAPE to develop student's individual entrepreneurial orientation in a university eco-system. In O. Gunnlaugson & W. Brendel (Eds.), *Advances in pre-sensing Volume III: Collective approaches, in Theory U* (pp. 395–435). Trifoss Business Press.

Van der Westhuizen, T. (2022). *Effective youth entrepreneurship*. Sunbonani. https://omp.sunbonani.co.za/index.php/sunbonani/catalog/book/6

Waring, A. (1996). *Practical systems thinking*. International Thomson Business Press.

2

Internal Domains Entrepreneurial Heartset, Mindset and Handset

2.1 Introduction

On the assumption that raising levels of self-confidence and value expectations for individuals, as definers of the microsystem, constitutes a fundamental starting point for extended development at higher systemic levels; value-centred development of individuals will, in turn, require from them deeper levels of knowledge both about themselves and about the larger system, with the ability to relate on a multi-dimensional level with everything around them. Therefore, a change in an individual's attitude towards transforming different systemic levels might lead to bridging the decay within systemic development. No matter if these individuals are from developed or developing countries, collective transformation is needed Adelakun and Van der Westhuizen (2021), Awotunde and Van der Westhuizen (2021a, b).[1]

The SHAPE ecosystem strategy for youth entrepreneurs introduces youths' internal domains as the cornerstone and starting point of creating

---

[1] Weinberg (2014).

© University of Kwazulu-Natal 2023
T. van der Westhuizen, *Youth Entrepreneurship*,
https://doi.org/10.1007/978-3-031-44339-8_2

an entrepreneurial ecosystem, referred to as the SHAPE YES Network (youth entrepreneur support network). It starts by maturing a relationship with oneself through fostering an entrepreneurial heartset, mindset and handset. In other words, the entrepreneurial heart, head and hand—the Triple H of Entrepreneurship.

A youth entrepreneur's personality traits are both enablers and personal barriers for themselves. It can also enable or obstruct crucial relationships with other role-players in the ecosystem. Core personality traits needed by youth entrepreneurs to execute entrepreneurial tasks effectively can be listed as vision, resilience, teamwork, innovation, passion, leadership, integrity, customer focus and flexibility. These personality traits can also be seen as being a nonconformist at the same time as being a team player; being motivated, driven, focused and persistent; being 'an architect of one's personal view'; being able to build an ecosystem or community of people able to achieve an outcome; being able to find opportunities and niches in the market, and living following one's belief system, therefore aligning values.[2] An internal locus of control is positively linked with youth entrepreneurship through a desire to solve problems and a willingness to seek out niches in the market. It also assists youth entrepreneurs because of the social benefits derived through networking within the ecosystem[3] (Fig. 2.1).

The way forward to transform (change) global systems and steer collective creativity for responsible and sustainable business practice starts with individual human beings. Unless people change their attitudes or perspectives towards collective transformation, the desired change will not kick in. A change in people's levels of self-confidence (self-efficacy), as well as their individual entrepreneurial orientation (IEO), might lead to a transformation in their attitudes and perspective towards systemic change, therefore, increasing entrepreneurial intent (EI) and action (EA).

---

[2] Ernst & Young (2017).
[3] Hsiao et al. (2016).

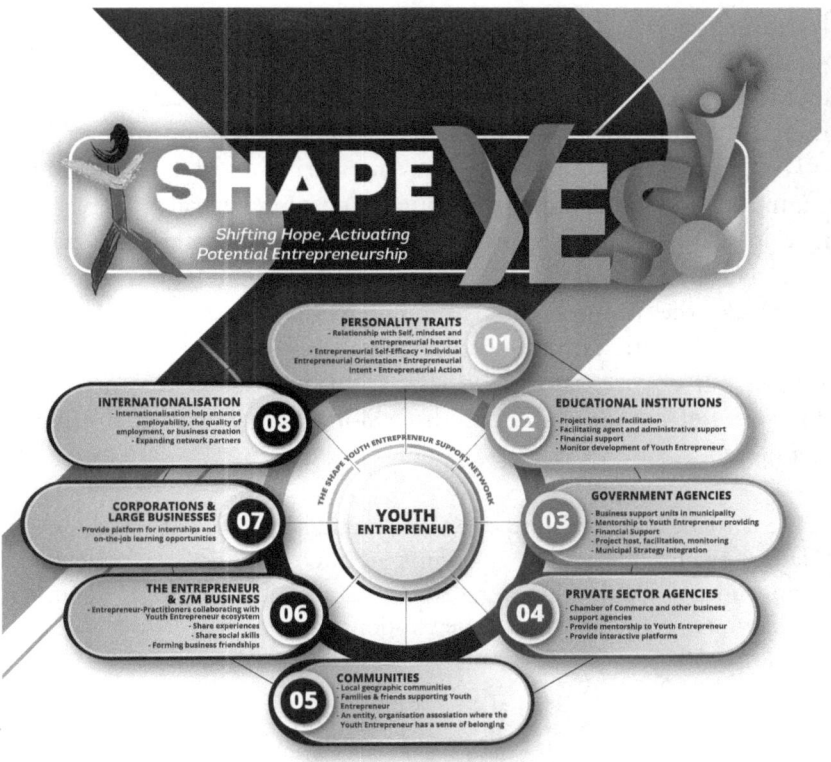

Van der Westhuizen, T. 2023. Effective Youth Entrepreneurship. Sunbonani Scholar. South Africa. 447 pages.

Fig. 2.1 Internal domains of youth entrepreneurs (*Source* Van der Westhuizen [2022])

2.2 The Entrepreneurial Heartset and Mindset

The mind is the biggest part of a human being and includes thinking, feeling and choosing. The mind is not the brain; it is produced by the brain. The mind and brain are separate. Brain activity rather reflects mind activity. The mind uses the brain when thinking, feeling and choosing in response to life experiences. This pushes energy through the brain, and the brain responds to the energy electromagnetically, chemically and genetically and builds the mind-energy into physical protein thought-trees within the brain. Thoughts are the end-product of the mind which is thinking, feeling and choosing. Thoughts also propel us into action. Therefore, looking at behaviours, one can deduce one's thoughts, and by looking into thoughts, one can deduce mindset.[4]

This study uses the terms 'entrepreneurial mindset' as a concept relating to the end-product of thought, 'entrepreneurial heartset' as the neurological process of creating a mindset and 'entrepreneurial handset' as behavioural action. In other words, the entrepreneurial heart, head and hand—the *Triple H* of Entrepreneurship (Fig. 2.2).

Various definitions have been proposed for 'entrepreneurial mindset' and what it encompasses, especially from a psychological perspective. However, for the purpose of this discussion, the following definition will be adopted:

> The entrepreneurial mindset refers to a specific state of mind which orientates human conduct towards entrepreneurial activities and outcomes. Individuals with entrepreneurial mindsets are often drawn to opportunities, innovation, and new value creation.[5]

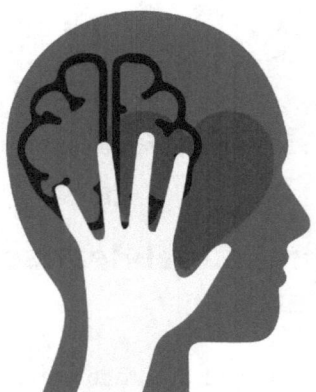

Fig. 2.2 The triple H of entrepreneurship: heart, head and hand (*Source* Van der Westhuizen [2022])

---

[4] Leaf (2013).
[5] Fayolle (2015).

The SHAPE ecosystem strategy focuses on developing youths' personality traits through concepts empirically associated with an entrepreneurial heartset, mindset and handset. These concepts comprise entrepreneurial self-efficacy (ESE), IEO, EI and entrepreneurial actions (EA)[6] Van der Westhuizen (2017a, b, 2018a, b 2021) (Fig. 2.3).

The entrepreneurial heartset, mindset and handset and their relationship to the entire ecosystem need to be interpreted as nondual. The notion of nonduality is a philosophical perspective of non-separation, which implies that impulses of the entrepreneurial heartset, mindset and handset, as noted above, emerge from the overall being of the individual as a whole, rather than as linear or fragmented sequential processes. Nonduality can be defined as 'not two' or 'non-separation'.[7] It is the sense that all things are interconnected and not separate, while at the same time, all things retain their individuality. An awareness

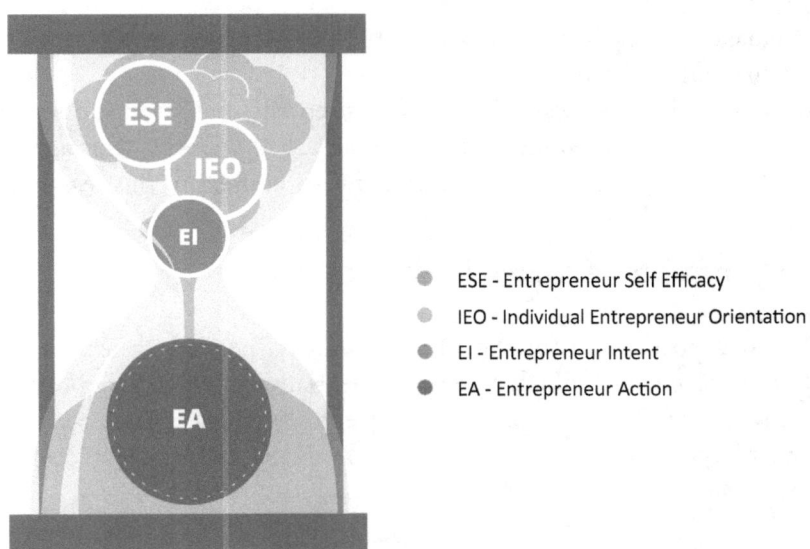

ESE - Entrepreneur Self Efficacy

IEO - Individual Entrepreneur Orientation EI

EI - Entrepreneur Intent

EA - Entrepreneur Action

Fig. 2.3 Elements of entrepreneurial heartset and mindset that lead to entrepreneurial action (handset) (*Source* Van der Westhuizen [2022])

---

[6] Cox et al. (2002) and Kickul and D'Intino (2005).
[7] Pillay (2014).

of nonduality gives individuals a bigger perspective on life, a greater sense of freedom, and brings them more stable happiness.[8] Building on the philosophy of nondualism, the environment external to the individual cannot be divorced from the internal state of an individual.[9] How the entrepreneurial heartset, mindset and handset develop, thus is a combination of an internal orientation in relation to the external whole, forming an individual's perceived reality.

> [The] world is not just a system of interconnected objects and processes – a concept that has been pioneered by systems thinking for more than six decades – but that there is no separate, solid, physical world existing independently of consciousness.[10]

Therefore, the entrepreneurial heartset, mindset and handset (heart, head and hand) apply to both individuals and collectives: thinking and acting entrepreneurially (having an entrepreneurial mindset) is as significant for managers or employees in an established company as it is for the individual entrepreneur.[11]

Illustrating how processes within the entrepreneurial internal domains should be seen from a nondual perspective, Fig. 2.4 sets out the interrelationship between these various aspects in the context of this research.

2.2.1 Entrepreneurial Self-Efficacy (ESE)

ESE is described as a construct that measures a person's belief in their ability to successfully launch an entrepreneurial venture. Belief in oneself is necessary for the development of entrepreneurship. Individuals with a higher degree of self-confidence are more likely to become successful entrepreneurs and sustain EA.

---

[8] Katz (1997).
[9] Pillay (2014).
[10] Pillay (2015).
[11] Covin and Slevin (2002).

Fig. 2.4 Elements of the entrepreneurial heartset, mindset and handset (*Source* Van der Westhuizen [2022])

ESE includes levels of self-confidence for achieving success and meeting difficult objectives in business start-up and can be broken down into four task-specific types:

- Self-efficacy in identifying opportunities and developing new market offerings
- Relationship self-efficacy: being able to build investor relationships
- Managerial self-efficacy: perception of economics and financial management capabilities; and
- Tolerance self-efficacy: perception of the ability to cope with stress and change.

These self-efficacy dimensions reinforce the importance of personality traits and the ability to interact with the forces at play within the environment.

Existing validated empirical research on ESE proposes a comprehensive theoretical framework of ESE factors determining the success of an entrepreneur, which extends to ten task-specific entrepreneurial skills in four venture creation phases, as illustrated in Fig. 2.5.

ESE and its associates' skills sets, in relation to the venture creation process, was tested and validated to have a significant and positive relationship to IEO, EI and EA. ESE is an important factor in shaping youths' reactions to the environment, and low ESE will reduce youths'

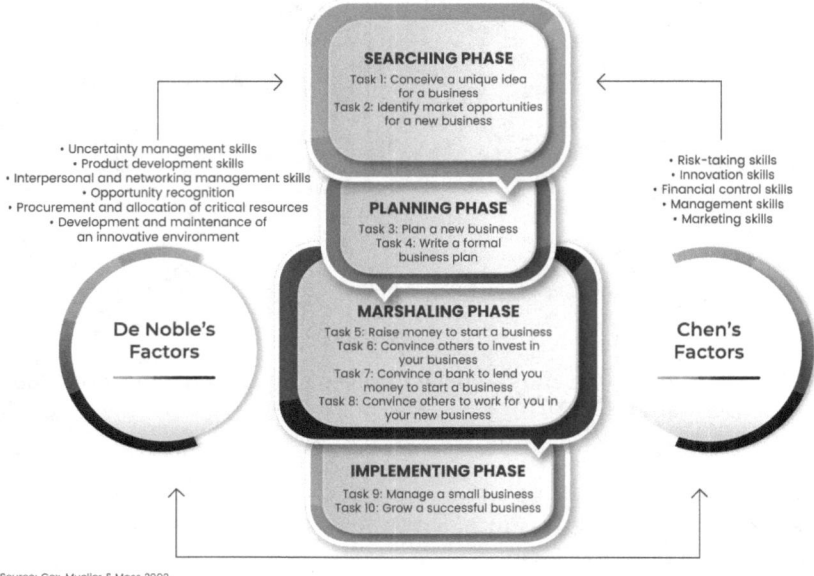

Source: Cox, Mueller & Moss 2002.

Fig. 2.5 Relationship of self-efficacy to tasks and roles in the entrepreneurial life cycle (*Source* Cox et al. [2002])

intention to start a business and youths' confidence in embracing opportunities. ESE is therefore positively correlated with youths' intention to start a business in the belief that it can be achieved. Youths' level of ESE in relation to a given task can affect their willingness to undertake the task.

A possible way to raise ESE towards skills sets is to enhance the individual in question through training or coaching. The SHAPE ecosystem strategy proposes that an ecosystem is necessary to support youth entrepreneurs' ESE development and strengthen crucial relationships with networks. Therefore, the development of ESE levels can take place as intrapersonal development processes where the individual enhances his or her own ESE through exposure to a variety of external processes and support networks.

A possible technique that pivots ESE development, either as an interpersonal or intrapersonal process, is called co-inspiring. In the psychological and neurological literature on the entrepreneurial heartset, mindset and handset, the term 'co-inspiring' is proposed as a technique to enable innovative thought to occur as an internal pre-cognitive process within the individual. This technique was proved to transform (grow developmental maturity) an individual's ability to innovate by moving from reacting to cognitions to generative new innovative cognitions. Co-inspiring signifies the birth of a creative and novel idea that can lead to innovation or an 'aha moment'. The part of the brain identified as reflecting the 'aha moment' is the anterior portion of the superior temporal gyrus of the non-dominant hemisphere and is associated with a short burst of Gamma EEG activity of 40 Hz. The profoundness of the innovation might relate to an individual's psychoneuro-endocrinological (PNE) engagement with their source of inspiration and will. PNE is terminology from neurological sciences, which implies that mind, body and soul are an interactive whole with no separation between these functions. Therefore, the integrativeness and interrelations of the entrepreneurial heartset, mindset and handset. PNE relates directly to the paradigm of nondualism which was introduced at the beginning of this chapter. As a result, low or high levels of ESE directly influence low or high levels of IEO when co-initiating and taking risks in the entrepreneurship process.

ESE development towards the new venture creation process and perceptions of own skills cannot be measured in a quantitative manner because this approach leaves no scope for incorporating individuals' PNE levels, feelings and emotions. Therefore, a qualitative or mixed-method approach is a better fit to measure ESE and its relation to entrepreneurial skills.

Entrepreneurship education often and commonly focus on entrepreneurial management and planning skills but often without addressing the deep fundamental underpinnings of ESE. More specifically, youth entrepreneurship development courses in entrepreneurship tend to teach technical skills with little or no focus in their planning of cognitive or belief systems on the part of the youths, which might underpin entrepreneurial attitudes and perceptions. Another way for youths to develop ESE, IEO and EI might be to observe youth entrepreneurs and actual settings where entrepreneurship takes place. Therefore, creating the SHAPE ecosystem for youth entrepreneurship development has value to enable shared learning experiences within a wide-reaching support network—learning from each other's experiences and co-inspiring one another.

2.3   Individual Entrepreneurial Orientation (IEO)

IEO signifies the processes, practices and decision-making activities of an individual that lead to entrepreneurship. The entrepreneurial decision-making process is influenced by external and internal domains. Internal domains include factors of risk-taking, proactivity and innovation, and external domains include aspects of the economy, society, technology, competition and politics. IEO is considered to have a direct impact on the entrepreneurial performance and EA of youths.

A country's socio-economic development relates directly to individuals who make up the microsystemic attitudes, activities and aspirations. For socio-economic development to occur through acts of entrepreneurialism (and intrapreneurialism), it is necessary to develop individuals' ability to take risks, proactivity and degree of innovativeness. These propensities of development will require individuals to connect with a much deeper level of knowledge Nhleko and van der Westhuizen (2022), Ruba et al. (2021).

Deep action learning, especially to spark innovative thought in the field of entrepreneurship and intrapreneurship, might be necessary for successful socio-economic development. A possible strategy is SHAPE, of which the theoretical model and its application are introduced in this book.

2.3.1   Individual Risk-Taking

The risk-taking propensity is described as the perceived probability of receiving the rewards associated with the success of a proposed situation, which is required by an individual before subjecting to the consequences associated with failure. The alternative situation provides less reward as well as less severe consequences than the proposed situation. Important predictors in risk-taking are how the risk problem is framed, results of past risk-taking and ability to perform under risky conditions.

Risk-taking propensity is a behavioural dimension of IEO that helps to trigger the pursuit of an opportunity. It involves major decisions individuals need to take, which might bring high rewards. The process includes an element of uncertainty and self-management of ESE task-related skills necessary to enable individual risk-taking qualities and reduce the fear associated with possible future barriers. This can also be regarded as a cognitive orientation directed towards EA since, in an IEO perspective, the youth entrepreneur acts in an individual capacity. Youth entrepreneurs, therefore, bear the personal risk intrinsic to the occupational choice being made.

Two different aspects of entrepreneurial risk are distinguished: the general risk-taking propensity of a potential entrepreneur and the perceived probability of failure. General risk-taking propensity is described as accessibility to research across role-players within the entrepreneurial ecosystem due to differences in individual venture probabilities for success and failure. By choosing to take EA, the youth entrepreneur becomes a risk-bearer and liable for personal choices associated with taking business risks.

Youth entrepreneurs operate within their entrepreneurial ecosystem. Therefore, economic failure and barriers do not solely fall on the youth entrepreneur; it is the responsibility of the ecosystemic role-players to help bear risk factors and mitigate barriers in the process of enabling socio-economic development from a bigger-picture systems perspective.

2.3.2 Individual Innovation

Innovation, as in the creation and development of new products and processes, lies at the heart of youth entrepreneurship and entrepreneurship in general. The generation of new business ideas and innovation is positively linked to the success of effective youth entrepreneur business development. Entrepreneurial innovation is described as the willingness to support creativity and experimentation in introducing new products/

services, novelty, technological leadership and research and development in developing new processes. As an IEO propensity, innovation is an important means of pursuing opportunities.

Individual innovation is exemplified as the youth entrepreneur who most strictly confines him or herself to the characteristic entrepreneurial function: carrying out new combinations. It is also interpreted as the purest type of entrepreneur genus. Individual innovation is a process of creative destruction by which wealth is created when existing market structures are disrupted by the introduction of new goods or services. Innovation by youth entrepreneurs is linked to learned behaviours reflected in the pursuit of entrepreneurial opportunities.

In society, emphasis is placed by SMEs and large corporations on research and development that might lead to the innovation of new products and services. This occurs on a business, enterprise or organisational level. On the contrary, there is a disconnect and gap in the entrepreneurial ecosystem to provide all-round support to youth entrepreneurs, including the provision of transformative entrepreneurial education (growth in developmental maturity to produce generative thought). The importance for youth entrepreneurs and their ecosystem to apply co-inspiring strategies to reach individual innovation is crucial for effective youth entrepreneurship development and sustainability.

For national socio-economic development, especially in developing countries, more is needed than just improving entrepreneurial ability and reducing the pressure for necessity entrepreneurship. It also implies that governments must focus on a deeper and more people-centred level to enhance individual youth entrepreneurs' innovative abilities and their levels of education and skills. Given the important role that entrepreneurial attitude, aspirations and actions play in socio-economic development, it is recommended that governments should have an innovation policy in place for the promotion of youth entrepreneurship, youth entrepreneurs in developing countries such as South Africa have a considerable propensity for innovation and these personality traits are not given sufficient recognition in literature or by policymakers.

In South Africa, as a developing country, stimulation of innovation has not on the whole been a key focus area for youth entrepreneurial ecosystem role-players such as development agencies, private sector development programmes or national programmes in support of entrepreneurship. In governmental youth entrepreneurship support programmes, the main concern needs to be people-centred approaches to advance innovation which could engender the kind of dynamic efficiency that would drive job creation, transformation (growth in developmental maturity) and entrepreneurial ecosystemic growth.

Where innovation policy is apparent in government programmes, it often has a dualistic character, combining structuralist approaches with laissez-faire, non-interventionist approaches derived from the neo-liberal school of thought. A possible reason why structuralist approaches are used might be that the leaders who facilitate these types of government programmes see policymaking for innovation from the stereotypical perspective of the national economy as a set of separate structures and processes rather than as an integrative whole—a nondual paradigm. Both approaches see innovation policy as an infrastructural development factor in government strategies for hard- and soft-system development. However, innovation policy alone most certainly cannot inspire youths' EA towards innovation. Therefore, the emphasis in moving towards individual innovation by youth entrepreneurs is placed on connecting the entrepreneurial ecosystem. Within the youth entrepreneurship ecosystem, enabling mechanising is created in a process to co-initiate, co-sense, co-inspire, co-create and co-evolve. The process of 'co' is proven to facilitate entrepreneurial heartset, mindset and handset to lever from reactive to generative responses, therefore, birthing individual innovation.

Adopting a national government approach towards including policies to enable individual innovation and facilitate innovative entrepreneurial ecosystems are fairly new on all systemic levels. Measuring instruments for government innovation policy to enable individual innovation for entrepreneurial ecosystems is difficult to create because of the fast and continuous pace of youth entrepreneurship development initiatives.

Successful innovative socio-economic development requires governments to increase the development impact of entrepreneurship by readjusting their policy frameworks and focus. The key for governments in addressing the developmental impact of socio-economic challenges might be to focus on creating deeper-level youth entrepreneurial ecosystems where the emphasis is on entrepreneurial heartset, mindset and handset. Without a deep transformation and innovation of individual introspective processes of total ecosystems, a broader level of national socio-economic development will remain in a crisis as youth unemployment and sustainability issues continue to soar.

In summary, individual innovation's 'aha moment' is linked to increased levels of ESE and IEO. Individual Innovation is further liked to transformation (growth in development maturity). Youth entrepreneurs, especially in developing countries, reaches an 'aha moment' with great difficulty because they are entrapped within barriers of disconnected entrepreneurial ecosystems. It might be helpful if there are innovation policies from the national government. However, commitment from all role-players is needed for efficient implementation and sustainability, which is vastly and all-round complex.

2.3.3 Individual Proactiveness

Individual proactiveness is related to initiative and first-mover advantages through the pursuit of new opportunities and acting in anticipation of future problems. The importance of proactiveness is its 'forward-looking perspective' for entrepreneurial activity and innovation. Proactiveness is a behavioural trait where youth entrepreneurs and role-players in the entrepreneurial ecosystem are constantly seeking opportunities and having a forward-looking perspective. Young entrepreneurs or individuals entering the market for the first time need to be proactive in looking for new opportunities since they do not have a high profile in the market. These opportunities might include access to finance, partnerships or skills development. Proactivity also links to the ESE skill set of management (Fig. 2.3) since proactive individuals adopt an active management style.

Although youths displaying proactive propensities are more likely to display leadership traits, being proactive and having leadership qualities does not guarantee that they will have a competitive pioneer advantage or be able to sustain EA; likewise, increased earnings might not necessarily be predictably associated with higher levels of proactiveness. This would depend on the specific context and dimension of IEO.

Proactiveness stands at one end of a continuum with passiveness as its opposite end. Proactiveness can therefore be seen as a form of reactiveness or a reactive response. The IEO proactivity propensity is closely associated with the ESE skill set of opportunity identification. High levels of IEO support opportunity recognition and opportunity creation. While individuals may change their goals and aspirations to match the requirements of changing environments around them because they see new opportunities to raise their level of performance, these proactive steps may not necessarily be efficient or bring increased earnings unless the individual reconfigures his or her own resources and adapts to the changing environment in a renewed manner.

Proactiveness may thus lead youths to perform differently, but not necessarily more effectively, should the efficiency of the individual not be improved. Proactiveness will not contribute to increased performance or successful attainment of personal goals and aspirations. Not all contexts will necessarily offer the opportunity for the individual to increase efficiency through proactive behaviour.

If proactiveness is associated with seizing the initiative and acting opportunistically in order to shape the environment and increase demand, then the intent of proactiveness is growing willingness. Willingness can be described as a measure of the degree to which the intention to increase demand exists, and growth willingness is therefore taken to represent a measure of proactiveness. In addition, education is likely to have a strong influence on growth willingness, both in encouraging an entrepreneur to aim higher and in boosting overall ESE.

2.3.4 The Illusion of External Opportunity Identification as an Act of Individual Proactivity

In cognitive sciences, the concepts of individual proactivity and opportunity identification are often seen as synonymous. Within this context, the entrepreneurial opportunity is central to the scholarship of entrepreneurship since entrepreneurs are individuals who pursue entrepreneurial opportunities, therefore, acting proactively. Conceptually speaking, without entrepreneurial opportunities, there could be no entrepreneurship. It could, however, be argued that the idea of 'entrepreneurial opportunity' is a misconception. Could it then be described that those entrepreneurial opportunities are external factors existing in the entrepreneurship ecosystem or nexus, independent from an individual's personality traits and the core of our being (an individual's entrepreneurial heartset and mindset)?

Entrepreneurial opportunities can be regarded as situations where products and services can be sold at a price greater than the cost of production. From this, it can be argued that to make a profit, action needs to be taken by the youth entrepreneur pursuing an entrepreneurial opportunity. Business situations—situations that are profit-driven—do exist, and there are many businesses making money and exploiting niche markets or gaps in the market.

However, a dichotomy lies within the concept of entrepreneurial opportunity. It is a future-orientated action: How does one know that a profitable opportunity did exist before the youth entrepreneur tried it out? The dichotomy is this: Before youth entrepreneurs pilot the opportunity and try to sell the products or services, they do not have a confirmation or a certainty that selling these products or services will be profitable. If the youth entrepreneurs make money, then an entrepreneurial opportunity must have existed because the EA resulted in a profit. But if a loss was made or the venture failed in some other way, was it because not enough market research was put into ideating or prototyping the product or service, or was the opportunity not even there in the first place?

If people are not able to establish beforehand whether an entrepreneurial opportunity exists, then the concept of risk-taking towards an entrepreneurial opportunity advises youth entrepreneurs to act in post-facto risk calculation.

A future opportunity can be said to exist as an abstract phenomenon; it becomes tangible only when combined with the personality traits and actions of the entrepreneur. It can, therefore, be said that the entrepreneurial heartset + the entrepreneurial mindset + EA = pursuit of entrepreneurial opportunity. This can further be deconstructed into 'opportunities for someone' and 'opportunities for me'. A potential business opportunity in the entrepreneurial ecosystem may be a real opportunity for 'me' only if 'I' possess the right qualities to make a profit in pursuing it. A further dichotomy is created within this argument because, without involving clinical experts, it is difficult to determine what qualities are needed to pursue a specific entrepreneurial opportunity and whether the youth entrepreneur does have such traits. Even if the youth entrepreneur knows that he or she has the right qualities in relation to a specific opportunity, they will still need to act to determine—after the event—the success, or otherwise, of the action they have taken.

Another lens on the concept of opportunity identification is to shift focus from 'opportunity discovery' to 'opportunity creation'. This philosophy is aligned with several schools of thought supporting youth entrepreneurs moving from reactive thought to generative thought, which will bring forth innovation in thought and potential prototypes of business models, products and services. Youth entrepreneurs can discover niches in markets and opportunities that already exist. However, this viewpoint of opportunity creation leads to a tautology inherent in the concept of 'entrepreneurial opportunity': What if the youth entrepreneur tries to create an opportunity and fails? Were they not entrepreneurial because an opportunity was created, and because they failed? Using a practical example: Before Instagram, there was PhotoMe; Instagram founders are billionaires; PhotoMe founders are not. The 'opportunity creation' school suffers from the same tautology as the 'opportunity discovery' school because of its focus on the opportunity: all it does (from an entrepreneurship-scholarly lens) is to spark entrepreneurial momentum for youth entrepreneurs to take calculated risks.

Therefore, if the concept of an entrepreneurial opportunity is dichotomic and its schools of thought are tautological, how should youth entrepreneurs move forward to gain entrepreneurial momentum? Is taking a calculated risk, after performing various paper-based activities such as writing a business plan, budgeting and market research, only a projection of something which could potentially result in an opportunity? The results of a written business plan are often very different from those envisaged (and often discarded) once the youth entrepreneur's venture meets the realities and barriers in the ecosystem or nexus.

In summary, the IEO concept with its associated propensities relates to stimuli within an individual as well as external domains. The internal and external domains interact with one another in a nondual manner. Only through diminishing systemic disconnect, socio-economic will gain momentum.

2.4   Entrepreneurial Intention (EI)

EI is linked to ESE, IEO and its effects on entrepreneurial personality traits, perception and actions. EI is related to the likelihood or desirability of becoming an entrepreneur. Further, EI is a determinant for youth entrepreneurs to engage with EA and the sustainability of the actions. Figure 2.2 gives a schematic representation of the way aspects of ESE and IEO contribute to levels of EI. Without relationships to ESE and IEO, EI cannot exist as a single entity.

The outflow of EI leads to taking EA, where the action does not necessarily equate to a start-up. EI involves process building up to a possible business start-up. When youth entrepreneurs are developing EI, the entrepreneurial heartset and mindset actively combine to further develop the entrepreneurial handset (EA). Therefore, an action-orientated and enabling process occurs.

Participation of individuals in a facilitated entrepreneurial ecosystemic intervention might potentially enhance youths' EI, as well as the role-players in their direct support network. Personal entrepreneurial exposure and support expected for a variety of intermediaries and entrepreneurial disposition all influence the levels of EI that individuals might form through participating in a facilitated intervention or strategy, for example, the SHAPE ecosystem strategy for youth entrepreneurs (Fig. 2.6).

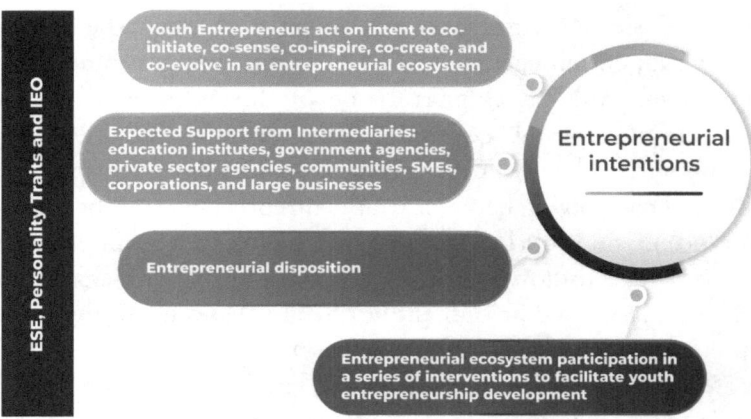

Fig. 2.6 Youth entrepreneurial intentions (EI) (*Source* Van der Westhuizen [2022])

2.5 Entrepreneurial Action (EA)

Following the schematic indication set out in Fig. 2.2 of EA as a process that results from ESE, IEO and EI. Therefore, EA is conceived as emanating from an inner place of an individual's being.[12] This inner place from which an individual's intentions and actions arise are associated with an individual's being, described as an individual's values, aspirations and dreams—the purpose behind entrepreneurial passion.[13] These elements of heartset and mindset are propelled by various processes that result in an individual's actions. The combination of the inner sources from which individuals act and the processes that follow eventuate in the results of individual behaviour, which might include EA, not necessarily in the form of a new venture, but with the possibility that youths' actions become entrepreneurial.

For some youth entrepreneurs, without guidance and developmental support, EA might result in a continuum process of being *en route* to 'X' because of not being purpose-orientated and purpose-driven. It is impossible to apply linear planning to a nondual youth entrepreneurial

---

[12] Scharmer and Käufer (2013).

[13] Hayes in Gunnlaugson et al. (2013).

ecosystem. Instead of trying to pin down what might be merely an illusion, youth entrepreneurs should be experimenting: prototyping and piloting taking EA. The emphasis is on producing generative response fields—innovation—and executing entrepreneurial activities through fresh, innovative lenses. Co-initiating, co-sensing, co-inspiring, co-creating and co-evolving between youth entrepreneurs and the ecosystem starts to occur and propel as new ideas are created as a result of collective interactions. If a prototype does not work, then pivot—change direction. The initial deep development of ESE, IEO and EI will boost youth entrepreneurs who engage with EA to sustain self-confidence and vision when an initial prototype does not work. The combination of enhanced internal and external domains helps youth entrepreneurs to start with an idea and continue to ideate and not give up entrepreneurial hopes and dreams.

Further emphasis is on the continuum of cyclical processes for youth entrepreneurs to take action and then collaborate with the ecosystem and potential customers to co-create and co-evolve a value-based outcome for all concerned. Therefore, creating entrepreneurial momentum towards socio-economic development.

Youth entrepreneurs should put less emphasis on long-term and potentially outdated business planning and (within reasonable limits) put more emphasis on action. Youth entrepreneurs need to focus on their entrepreneurial heartset and mindset because, ultimately, these will determine the success of their EA (handset). Their internal qualities are thus not barriers anymore, but rather the vehicle sparking entrepreneurial momentum. Instead of chasing 'opportunities' in an abstract 'market', it is essential for the youth entrepreneur (as a microsystem) to integrate with other systemic role-players, therefore, taking responsibility for co-creating and co-evolving a potential sustainable support structure. Ideally, those with whom the youth entrepreneurs choose to collaborate are individuals with like-minded, like-hearted and like-willed qualities.

One can argue that 'entrepreneurial barriers' can only be experienced by youth entrepreneurs once they have taken 'entrepreneurial action'. Therefore, acting on a possible opportunity and proactively taking a potential risk without having a guarantee that the opportunity will result in wealth creation. The premise of youth entrepreneurs' ability to experience barriers in the external environment in relation to their EA implies that they demonstrated initial signs of positive qualities associated with being entrepreneurs. Therefore, they demonstrate qualities of ESE, IEO and EI.

As life continuously moves on for youth entrepreneurs, the future scenario becomes the current one. The current problem-solving situations that EA youth entrepreneurs face are necessary to fulfil their entrepreneurial aspirations. Therefore, they grow to think and act upon new experiences in the process of developing their entrepreneurial heartset, mindset and handset en route to potential EA. Therefore, their journey through transforming (growing in developmental maturity) might have moved youth entrepreneurs to crystallise their ideas (envisioning the new), prototype them (enacting the new) and perform them (the new in praxis).[14] This implies that they are developing new knowledge—generative thought[15]—through embodying new experiences.

Might this imply that the lived-through experiences of youth entrepreneurs might self-teach them to overcome barriers and exposure to entrepreneurial realities within the ecosystem is necessary to sustain EA?

2.6 Conclusion

In the SHAPE ecosystem strategy for youth entrepreneurs, enabling the development of youths' personality traits, ESE, IEO, EI and EA occur through educational institutes playing the facilitating role to co-initiate. Entrepreneurship education, inter and cross-curricula, in both formal academic programmes and informal youth development initiatives is an essential starting point. From a nondual perspective, youth entrepreneurs and role-players in the entrepreneurial ecosystem need to share the vision and purpose for EA. This can be facilitated through education institutes,

---

[14] Cox (2013).
[15] Scharmer (2009).

especially in higher education universities. The role of entrepreneurial-orientated universities to facilitate the creation of an entrepreneurial ecosystem for youths and sustain crucial relationships might help bridge the systemic disconnect and unite people through an inspiring vision for wealth creation through socio-economic development.

In summary, transformative academic entrepreneurship education can facilitate ESE, EIO, EI and EA through learning, teaching and research. It was actioned by youths, education institutes, government agencies, private sector agencies, communities, SMEs and corporations/ large businesses. Within the SHAPE youth entrepreneurial ecosystem strategy, an educational institute such as a university can be the facilitating agent to co-initiate the ecosystem creation for youths. However, the SHAPE strategy is flexible to allow movement, generalisation and adaptation of role-players, and location-specific aspects will influence the unique co-creating of a youth entrepreneurial ecosystem to add value in a location-specific context and a broader sense. This is further investigated in the next chapter.

References

Adelakun, Y., & Van der Westhuizen, T. (2021). Delineating government policies and individual entrepreneurial orientation. *Journal of Sociology and Social Anthropology, 12*(3–4), 106–117. https://doi.org/10.31901/245 66764.2021/12.3-4.371

Awotunde, O. M., & Van der Westhuizen, T. (2021a). Entrepreneurial self-efficacy development: An effective intervention for sustainable student entrepreneurial intentions. *International Journal of Innovation and Sustainable Development, 15*(4), 475–495.

Awotunde, O. M., & Van der Westhuizen, T. (2021b). *Entrepreneurial self-efficacy and the SHAPE ideation model for university students. ECIE 2021 16th European Conference on Innovation and Entrepreneurship*, Vol. 1, p. 37.

Covin, J. G., & Slevin, D. P. (2002). The entrepreneurial imperatives of strategic leadership. In M. Hitt, R. D. Ireland, S. M. Camp, & D. Sexton (Eds.), *Strategic entrepreneurship: Creating a new mindset*. Blackwell.

Cox, L. D. (2013). Presencing our absencing: A collective reflective practice using Scharmer's 'U' model. In O. Gunnlaugson, C. Baron, & M. Cayer (Eds.), *Perspectives on Theory U: Insights from the field*. IGI Global.

Cox, L. W., Mueller, S. L., & Moss, S. E. (2002). The impact of entrepreneurship education on entrepreneurial self-efficacy. *International Journal of Entrepreneurship Education, 1*(2), 229–245.

Ernst & Young. (2017). *Entrepreneurs share core traits: Decoding the DNA of the entrepreneur*. www.ey.com/gl/en/services/strategic-growth-markets/ey-nature-or-nurture-5-entrepreneurs-share-core-traits (Retrieved 15 September 2017).

Fayolle, A. (2015). Entrepreneurial mindset. *Financial Times* Lexicon. http://lexicon.ft.com/Term?term=entrepreneurial-mindset (Retrieved 21 August 2015).

Gunnlaugson, O., Baron, C., & Cayer, M. (Eds.). (2013). *Perspectives on Theory U: Insights from the field*. IGI Global.

Hsiao, C., Lee, Y.-H., & Chen, H.-H. (2016). The effects of internal locus of control on entrepreneurship: The mediating mechanisms of social capital and human capital. *The International Journal of Human Resource Management, 27*(11), 1158–1172.

Katz, J. (1997). *Nonduality.com—An introduction*. http://www.nonduality.com/lrn.htm (Retrieved 15 September 2015).

Kickul, J., & D'Intino, R. S. (2005). Measure for measure: Modeling entrepreneurial self-efficacy onto instrumental tasks within the new venture creation process. *New England Journal of Entrepreneurship, 8*(2), 6.

Leaf, C. (2013). *Switch on your brain: The key to peak happiness, thinking, and health*. Baker Books.

Nhleko, Y., & van der Westhuizen, T. (2022). The role of higher education institutions in introducing entrepreneurship education to meet the demands of industry 4.0. *Academy of Entrepreneurship Journal, 28*(1), 1–23.

Pillay, K. (2014). Learning, the whole and Theory U: Reflections on creating a space for deep learning. *Problems and Perspectives in Management, 12*(4), 340–346.

Pillay, K. (2015, July 6). *Learning and the illusion of solid and separate things: Troublesome knowledge and the curriculum.* Edge Hill University Centre for Learning and Teaching University Learning and Teaching Day Conference.

Ruba, R. M., Van der Westhuizen, T., & Chiloane-Tsoka, G. E. (2021). Influence of entrepreneurial orientation on organisational performance: Evidence from Congolese Higher Education Institutions. *Journal of Contemporary Management, 18*(1), 243–269.

Scharmer, C. O., & Käufer, K. (2013). *Leading from the emerging future: From ego-system to eco-system economies.* Berrett-Koehler Publishers.

Scharmer, C. O. (2009). *Theory U: Learning from the future as it emerges.* Berrett-Koehler Publishers.

Van der Westhuizen, T. (2017a). The use of Theory U and Individual Entrepreneurial Orientation to increase Low Youth Entrepreneurship in South Africa. *Journal of Contemporary Management, 14*, 531–553.

Van der Westhuizen, T. (2017b). A systemic approach towards responsible and sustainable economic development: Entrepreneurship, systems theory and socio-economic momentum. In Z. Fields (Ed.), *Collective creativity for responsible and sustainable business practice.* IGI Global.

Van der Westhuizen, T. (2018a). The SHAPE project: Shifting hope, activating potential entrepreneurship In D. Remenyi & D. A. Grant (Eds.), *Incubators for young entrepreneurs—20 case histories.* ACPIL.

Van der Westhuizen, T. (2018b). *Open heart, open mind and open will in transformative individual entrepreneurial orientation pedagogies.* Academic Conferences and Publishing International Limited, Redding, UK, pp. 443–448.

Van der Westhuizen, T. (2019). *Action! Methods to develop entrepreneurship.* 18th European Conference on Research Methodology for Business and Management Studies, pp. 331–337.

Van der Westhuizen, T. (2021). Applying Theory U through SHAPE to develop student's individual entrepreneurial orientation in a university eco-system. In O. Gunnlaugson & W. Brendel (Eds.), *Advances in pre-sensing Volume III: Collective approaches, in Theory U* (pp. 395–435). Trifoss Business Press.

Van der Westhuizen, T. (2022). *Effective youth entrepreneurship.* Sunbonani. https://omp.sunbonani.co.za/index.php/sunbonani/catalog/book/6

Weinberg, I. (2014). *The complete triangles model: Exploring the foundations of neuromodulation.* http://www.pninet.com/articles/Memory.pdf (Retrieved 1 September 2017).

3

Youth Entrepreneur Ecosystem

3.1 Introduction

The previous chapter established that the mind uses various brain processes when thinking, feeling and choosing responses to life experiences. Youth entrepreneurs gain said life experiences through being and interacting within ecosystems. This chapter, therefore, proposes the establishment of an ecosystem to promote youth entrepreneurship. This proposed theoretical ecosystem model has been practically created and applied to youth entrepreneurs as a means to test their entrepreneurial mindset and discover the enablers and barriers that youth entrepreneurs come into contact with in relation to their own ecosystems. The application and findings related to this model are discussed further in Part II of this book.

3.1.1 Context

The SHAPE ecosystem, which has been created to promote youth entrepreneurship strategies, fundamentally starts with education, training, skills development and mentorship within the microsystem.

© University of Kwazulu-Natal 2023
T. van der Westhuizen, *Youth Entrepreneurship*,
https://doi.org/10.1007/978-3-031-44339-8_3

Since youths are central to this ecosystem, they form both the recipients of stimuli and, in return, offer shared experiences and insights to the various role-players operating within their ecosystem. The process of this model is, thus, dynamic, interactive and reflective, with the facilitating agent of this ecosystem being the education institute that drives the system's creation and evolution Van der Westhuizen (2017a, b, 2018a, b, 2019, 2021).

In order for higher education institutions in South Africa to effectively provide the necessary skills and learning for entrepreneurial development in our emerging economy, a radical change in intellectual and educational priorities is needed.[1] Higher-order thinking or a deeper dimension to and towards entrepreneurship learning is especially necessary to address the current socio-economic crisis and rising youth unemployment rates.[2] Similar to other living-theory approaches (e.g. Theory U, systemic action learning and action research (SALAR)), SHAPE-activated learning experiences are proposed to have the potential to enable a paradigm shift among youth entrepreneurs and their intermediaries that can help to advance socio-economic development in pursuit of macro- and mundo-system visions.[3]

With pedagogy in the field of entrepreneurship shifting the emphasis from classroom teaching to action learning, 'static' or 'content-orientated' teaching, which has been common practice for more than two decades, is now frequently criticised as it is no longer appropriate in or for South Africa's complex and change-driven society.[4] Such traditional educational methods, focusing on theory and information, are now regarded as inappropriate for content and pedagogy.[5] Rather, entrepreneurship curriculum pedagogies based on discovery and creation theories now provide a basis for shifting from static classroom approaches to an action learning methodology.

---

[1] Chia (2014).
[2] Scharmer and Käufer (2013).
[3] Chia (1996, 2014), Harrison et al. (2007), Nonaka, Chia et al. (2014), and Paton et al. (2014).
[4] Sahay and Nirjar (2012).
[5] Garavan and O'Cinneide (1994) and Oyugi (2014).

Most current undergraduate curricula in South African higher education have adopted principles from discovery theory, where the emphasis is on creativity, scanning, shaping ideas and developing business plans.[6] Developing and presenting an entrepreneurship programme needs a suitable programme process to help aspirant entrepreneurs assimilate entrepreneurial practice. This process should be action-orientated and include appealing themes that promote student-centredness and encourage reflective thinking.[7]

While the discovery approach is prominent in the complex and continually evolving South African context, there are also cases for adopting pedagogic approaches that draw on principles from creation theory. In such an approach, the emphasis is on overall programme processes and how ideas transform over time. Programme participants, in this instance, have the opportunity to practice entrepreneurship skills by adapting initial ideas in response to new knowledge and information.

One key benefit of the creative entrepreneurship programme approach is how it can help students to problem-solve through the creation of a challenging environment where students have to face relevant challenges and learn to overcome these through taking action (learning by doing). This approach is, thus, also referred to as experiential learning or action learning. By promoting action, such a programme helps to promote self-direction and adaptability in its participants, which, in turn, makes it easier to assess the overall impact of an entrepreneurship endeavour. By comparison, more traditional programme participants would merely be allocated a 'pass' or 'fail' with little to no consideration of the broader implications. The cyclical approach of the experiential or action learning process thus shapes students into lifelong learners.[8]

Despite this move towards less traditional teaching and learning approaches, entrepreneurship programmes in South Africa currently still face a number of challenges, including:

---

[6] Sahay and Nirjar (2006) and Rahimi et al. (2015).

[7] Chia (2014), McIntyre-Mills et al. (2014), and Yeo and Marquardt (2015).

[8] Rahimi et al. (2015).

- Making students aware of (the need for) socio-economic change. Otto Scharmer and Peter Senge believe that society has a 'blind spot' in respect to deeper dimensions of systemic change. This blind spot can be related to the systems thinking paradigm, where systems are seen only as interconnected and interrelated and, as such, might imply fragmentation of systems.[9] Our current era, however, calls for new levels of cognition processes that adopt a nondual perspective.[10] This more holistic and unified understanding could potentially allow youths to create a future filled with greater opportunities.[11]
- Enhancing levels of self-efficacy, individual entrepreneurial orientation (IEO) and entrepreneurial intent (EI) among programme participants. Young people often lack commitment, work ethic and motivation, and South Africa has the third-lowest level of youth entrepreneurship globally.[12]
- Developing problem-solving thought processes and generating new ideas to solve existing problems. Strategy-making processes in both public and private sector organisations can provide a basis for entrepreneurial initiatives and create opportunities for young people to be involved in decisions and actions.[13]
- Developing a support network for youth entrepreneurs. In South Africa, it is difficult for youth entrepreneurs to engage with an entrepreneurial ecosystem, as not enough private sector organisations or small- and medium-sized enterprise (SME) owners are willing to form 'business friendships' with youth entrepreneurs to harness their entrepreneurial drive and help them develop sustainable entrepreneurial skills.[14]

These common challenges facing entrepreneurship programmes call for the reframing of their focus on enhancing programme participants'

---

[9] Pillay (2015b).

[10] This is where systems are perceived as a whole and stemming from a single source; Pillay (2015a) and Scharmer (2009).

[11] Scharmer (2009).

[12] Xavier et al. (2013).

[13] Bolton and Lane (2012).

[14] DTI (2017).

levels of self-confidence and motivation Nhleko and Van der West-huizen (2022), Ruba et al. (2021). Thus, entrepreneurship programmes presented at higher education institutes should embrace active learning that includes practices aimed at teaching both *for* entrepreneurship (e.g. by offering case studies, guest speakers, group projects, business plans, student oral presentations, survey-participation) and *about* entrepreneurship (e.g. lecturers, set tests, individual assignments and written exams).[15] These programmes should also aim to develop students' entrepreneurial self-efficacy (ESE) and individual entrepreneurial orientation (IEO) so that they make the pursuit of entrepreneurship a primary goal.

A further consideration is that youths require comprehensive facilitation and mentorship in order to develop a deeper cognitive perception of the challenges and issues faced both by young entrepreneurs and the broader socio-economic context. Such understanding could help students to develop their own internal domains.

The challenge is to develop an innovative action model—a kind of 'living theory'—that truly inspires youths on a much deeper level and brings about the needed attitude change at an ontological level.

Shepherd Dhliwayo, who wrote this book's preface, previously indicated that 'to ensure effective sustainability of youth entrepreneurial endeavours', it is necessary to link youth entrepreneurs' gained life experiences to an interrelated ecosystem (a support structure). Several support structures[16] aimed at developing and aiding youth entrepreneurs already exist. However, youth entrepreneurs frequently experience barriers caused by these very intermediaries who, at times, may obstruct rather than promote entrepreneurial growth.

---

[15] Oyugi (2014).
[16] Also referred to as 'intermediaries' or 'nexus'.

3.2   The SHAPE Ecosystem Strategy for Youth Entrepreneurship

The concept of youth entrepreneur ecosystems is relatively new to the body of knowledge on youth entrepreneurship but has begun gaining in popularity over the past few years. Entrepreneurial systems, on the other hand, have been discussed in the literature for more than 30 years.[17] In terms of the newer youth entrepreneur ecosystem literature, special attention is currently paid to policy circles, as the government seeks ways to address the crisis of high national youth unemployment in South Africa. There are still several empirical shortcomings within the literature surrounding youth entrepreneur ecosystems:

1. There remains a need for a clear analytical framework to explicitly demonstrate what causes and effects such ecosystems currently lack. Due to the varied locations and culture-specific nature of youth entrepreneurial ecosystems, it might not be possible to create a 'one-solution-fits-all' framework; multiple frameworks are necessary to effectively address the complex adaptive nature of these systems.
2. Although it is a systemic concept, the (youth) entrepreneur ecosystem still needs to incorporate insights from network theory to further exploit the co-initiation of the ecosystem. The interconnectivity and integrativeness of relationships between various internal and external domains are not currently clear.
3. Institutions or agents' impact and special scale on the structure and performance of youth entrepreneur ecosystems remains unclear.
4. Studies have often focused on the (youth) entrepreneur ecosystem in a single region or cluster. Thus, the literature lacks a comparative and collective perspective.
5. The literature on (youth) entrepreneur ecosystems tends to provide a static framework that does not consider these systems' evolution over time.[18]

---

[17] Alvedalen and Boschma (2017, 887–903).
[18] Ibid.

As a longitudinal intervention, the SHAPE ecosystem model has been created to support youth entrepreneurs' thinking, feelings and decisions surrounding entrepreneurial behaviours and actions. The model aims to facilitate entrepreneurial 'heartset' by promoting an entrepreneurial mindset and 'handset'. The facilitating agents of this model have built on Shepherd Dhliwayo's model for experiential learning in entrepreneurship education, which proposes a prospective model for South African tertiary institutions. SHAPE is also grounded within Theory U's premise that a process of shifting from reactive to generative thought is necessary for deep transformative socio-economic development. In Theory U, the pinnacle of an 'aha moment' is referred to as 'presencing' (synonymous with 'co-inspiring' or 'innovative thought'). The presencing process occurs through youth entrepreneurs and role-players who, as Theory U states, co-initiate, co-sense, co-inspire, co-create and co-evolve.

The occurrence of Shifting Hope, Activating Potential Entrepreneurship is seen as essential to addressing the deep-rooted socio-economic crisis faced by various systems in this country (Chapter 1). Therefore, the SHAPE YES (Youth Entrepreneur Support) Network (Fig. 3.1) was put into practice, and the related ecosystem was created, applied and facilitated for the purposes of this research. The SHAPE ecosystem model was also validated through a series of assessments over seven years.

In a biological ecosystem (see Chapter 1), the heterogeneous concept of 'home' interrelates and interacts in an interdependent and complex relationship (non-dually). The youth entrepreneur ecosystem is similarly positioned within systemic levels, as described in Chapter 1 (micro-, meso-, macro- and mundo-systems). Therefore, from a non-dualistic perspective, the youth entrepreneur ecosystem and its systemic levels cannot be separated due to the interrelatedness common to the source of origin (see Chapter 5).[19] Powerful centripetal forces, thus, bring youth entrepreneurs' internal and external domains together into a single ecosystem.[20]

One starting point in creating the youth entrepreneur ecosystem may be to look into the entomological origin of the word 'home'; how

---

[19] Ibid.
[20] Brown and Mason (2017, 11–30).

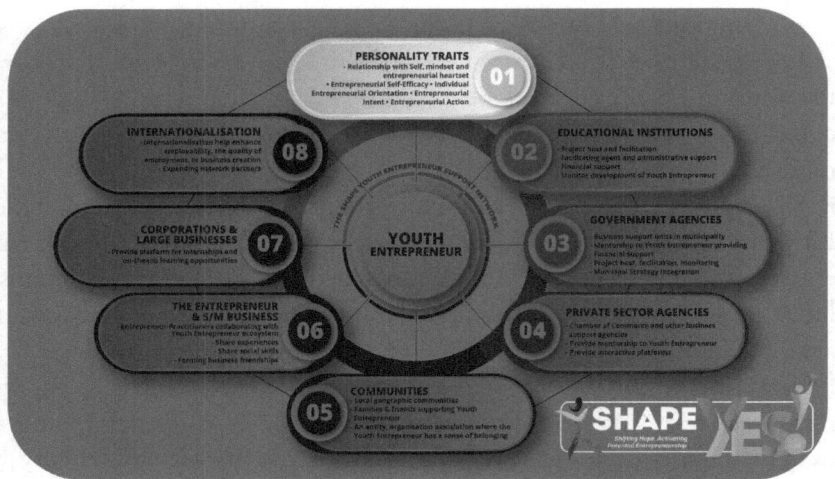

Fig. 3.1 The SHAPE YES Network for youth entrepreneurs—personality traits[21] (*Source* Van der Westhuizen, 2022)

it relates to connecting components forming the youth entrepreneur environment. The facilitating agent from a given education institute, who is responsible for co-initiating the architecture of the proposed model, could start by bringing together a support network from within the same geographical location. These parties would, and should, be mutually dependent on one another for their own existence, as these location-specific characteristics make up a youth entrepreneur ecosystem (a 'home').

Since this support network and the youth entrepreneurs in the area share a common location, it is assumed that they can easily reach out to one another and draw support from one another. Of further note is that while technology could further broaden the scope and reach of the network role-players, a deeper understanding is still needed in respect to the physical location of 'home'. There is a need to better understand the location-specific problems and opportunities that youth entrepreneurs encounter in order to find the best niche market for value creation. There

---

[21] *The Shape Youth Entrepreneur Support (YES) Network. First submitted for publication consideration to the International Journal of Entrepreneurial Behavior and Research.

is also the understanding that, due to the location-specific nature of the microsystem, the architecture of bringing together different role-players will be different for each location.

Besides location-specific aspects, the youth entrepreneur ecosystem can also be industry-specific, depending on the youths' needs and available value creation opportunities. The youth entrepreneurial ecosystem can, therefore, be a highly variegated, multi-actor and multi-scalar phenomenon that requires bespoke policy interventions.[22] The SHAPE strategy could allow for better adaptation and movement across different geographical locations as well as within the understanding of the nature of 'home'.

One common denominator within the youth entrepreneurial ecosystem is the commitment to sustainable socio-economic development. This means that the contribution(s) from each actor must add value to systemic development. All parties must also share a vision to address multiple systemic crises (see Chapter 1).

The centripetal forces in the youth entrepreneurial ecosystem's complex environment demand competitive advantage and innovation for existence, survival, and growth. The competition around resources within this ecosystem is, however, extremely high, as the same actors within the same ecosystem require access to the same resources. Despite this competitive nature, there still exists co-creation and co-evolvement among actors, which enables a conducive environment. According to Theory U, it is necessary for like-minded, like-hearted and like-willed individuals to engage in the process of social emergence ('economies of creation'), as, without cooperation, a continuation of systemic disconnect and social pathology ('economies of destruction') will occur.[23]

Since the nature and scope of the youth entrepreneur ecosystem, along with its centripetal forces linked to location and industry, differ, Fig. 3.2 provides only a basic taxonomy of youth entrepreneurial ecosystems.

Theory U implies that for socio-economic development to occur—as in the development of (youth) entrepreneurship—on different systemic

---

[22] Ibid.
[23] Scharmer (2011).

Fig. 3.2 Basic taxonomy of a youth entrepreneurial ecosystem (*Source* Brown & Mason, 2017[24])

---

[24] Brown and Mason (2017, 11–30).

levels, the co-growth of all role-players is necessary. Five stages are proposed in this regard[25]:

3.2.1 Co-initiating

Co-initiating entails working with others from the outset, as there exists a strong connection between people who share common ground. In the case of entrepreneurs, having similar connections helps to build long-lasting relationships with like-minded individuals. When there is a shared vision for a country, there is also greater synergy because people have similar goals. The SHAPE social technology focuses on building common intent through macrosystemic initiatives similar to those set out in South Africa's *National Development Plan (NDP) 2030*.

3.2.2 Co-sensing

Co-sensing, in the South African context, connects entrepreneurs and key stakeholders through an in-depth understanding of all relevant interconnected systems. Understanding the dynamics can provide entrepreneurs and key stakeholders greater clarity and increase the likelihood of achieving mutual benefits. This is not necessarily a simple matter, and all parties need to understand clearly the challenges involved.

3.2.3 Co-inspiring

Co-inspiring (also referred to as 'presencing') is the ability to focus on new thought processes while removing inhibiting ideologies and pre-existing theories. This practice relates to developing the ability to react appropriately in new, unexperienced situations. Developing this ability gives entrepreneurs a competitive edge in unpredictable and difficult scenarios, as well as greater confidence in tackling difficult problems and making difficult decisions.

---

[25] Scharmer and Käufer (2013) and Van der Westhuizen (2016).

3.2.4 Co-creating

Co-creating relates to 'exploring the future by doing' and focusing on the needs of entrepreneurs' projected businesses in order to remove obstacles that prevent them from achieving their objectives.

3.2.5 Co-evolving

Finally, co-evolving occurs after the formulation of a prototype solution. In this stage, the focus is on the impact of the given solution on the entire system. Co-evolving can also pertain to creating initiatives based on the interacting meso- and macro-fields involved.

3.3   Educational Institutions

An educational institute is, in essence, a business. The SHAPE youth entrepreneurial ecosystem strategy positions higher education institutes (universities) as key centripetal forces and facilitators for co-initiating, co-sensing, co-inspiring, co-creating and co-evolving the support network for, and of, youth entrepreneurs. Indeed, entrepreneurial-orientated institutions can provide would-be entrepreneurs with the necessary foundation to start a business through providing necessary formal and/or informal training and skills development that increase entrepreneurial self-confidence (Fig. 3.3).

In *The University of the Future*, edited by Dan Remenyi, Kenneth A. Grant and Shawren Singh, there is an emphasis on how educational institutes, especially universities, are under considerable pressure to change towards producing work-ready graduates. Specifically, the work argues:

> Universities reflect society and thus they are always a work-in-progress, continually in need of reinventing themselves.[26]

---

[26] Remenyi et al. (2019).

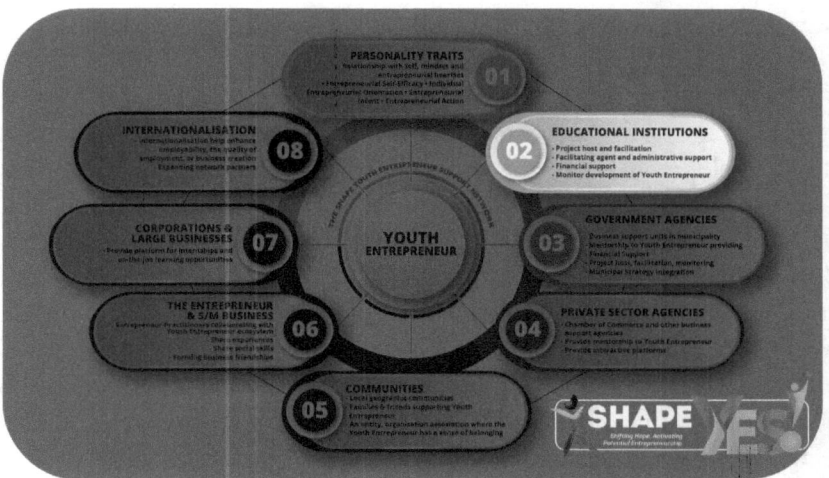

Fig. 3.3 The SHAPE YES Network for youth entrepreneurs—educational institutions

They have been criticised for their intense focus on research which has sometimes been said to have been at the cost [of] their mandate to educate.[27]

There are also ongoing debates between scholars as to whether universities should expand their focus towards becoming entrepreneurial in nature and, thereby, facilitate the entrepreneurship of students. Scholars from developing countries, which are generally faced with high graduate unemployment rates, tend to be more eager to support the new direction of universities becoming entrepreneurial, as this could provide greater scope for developing individuals' internal entrepreneurial domains. Developing these inner domains towards entrepreneurial inclinations should occur both inter-disciplinarily and cross-disciplinarily, where all programmes and modules incorporate elements of entrepreneurship. Developing the initial entrepreneurial heart and mindset before tackling the entrepreneurial skillset could also take place both in formal academic

---

[27] Ibid.

programmes as well as through support or supplementary programmes and initiatives.[28]

The South African Department of Higher Education and Training's (DHET) university education branch established the Entrepreneurship Development in Higher Education programme (EDHE) in 2016. The vision was for universities to enable (a) every student and graduate to be fully equipped to participate in the economy, aside from through traditional employment; and (b) teaching, research, innovation, entrepreneurship and commercialisation pipelines that are supported within universities.[29] The EDHE focus on developing entrepreneurial universities, entrepreneurship in academia and student entrepreneurship. The role of the EDHE is discussed in more detail in the next section.

It should be noted at this point, however, that the creation of the EDHE aligns with global trends towards increasingly recognising entrepreneurship as a vital part of a university's role.[30] Development of entrepreneurship should, thus, be executed by academics in the form of academic entrepreneurship, by students in the form of student or graduate entrepreneurship, and by leadership in the form of creating entrepreneurial universities.[31]

3.3.1 The Entrepreneurial University

The concept of an entrepreneurial education institute gained popularity towards the end of the twentieth century due to the socio-economic need for universities, and educational institutes in general, to relook at their business model and sources of income. The entrepreneurial university creates, facilitates and maintains an ecosystem for the youth, which impacts systemic development on micro-, meso-, macro- and mundo-systemic levels.

Both education and research, as an industry, hold scope for entrepreneurial behaviour and approaches like providing services and

---

[28] Preedy et al. (2020).
[29] EDHE (2021).
[30] Davey et al. (2016).
[31] Ibid.

products to clients. The concept of an entrepreneurial university, thus, adopts both a linear and a reverse linear model, thereby enabling entrepreneurship *in* universities. The linear model relates to teaching and research, knowledge, skills and technology transfer. The reverse linear model occurs as these aspects are adapted from the place of research into active use. This transfer is aided by interface capabilities, such as activation and transfer officers. The university's incubator or accelerator facilitators and mentors to youths, whose responsibilities would be to manage and market knowledge as a product and as protected intellectual property, can also aid in this process.

Based on this joint model, it is understood that the entrepreneurial university's primary characteristics include:

1. the university itself, which, as an organisation, becomes entrepreneurial;
2. the members of the university who turn themselves into entrepreneurs; and
3. the interaction of the university with the environment.[32]

Key factors influencing the effective practice of an entrepreneurial university relate to entrepreneurial-orientated inner domains-based leadership, which can enable an entrepreneurial and value-adding environment. The entrepreneurial-orientated staff, as well as learning and teaching, exist in this environment. The entrepreneurial university's success is, furthermore, associated with the presence of leadership with a vision towards addressing various systemic crises and inspiring both staff and youths to generate problem-solving ideas and possible inventions that support spin-off creation.[33]

At many education institutes, working towards such a vision might not be possible through the academic programme alone. In this sense, institutions may require support programmes, initiatives, or units to

---

[32] Röpke (1998).
[33] Dominici and Gagnidze (2021, 13–30).

collate these universities' total entrepreneurial actions (EA). Such collation may take the form of an economic activation unit, which functions as a central institutional point.

Currently, many universities do have incubation, acceleration and technology transfer offices in place that hold the potential to co-initiate the broader sense of the youth entrepreneurial ecosystem. Since students eventually graduate from these education institutes, hopefully with an entrepreneurial concept in place to enable initial career steps, it is the responsibility of the entrepreneurial university to educate and train role-players in students' external support networks to provide effective mentorship and support after graduation. Through support from government agencies, private sector agencies, communities, corporates and large businesses, and SME owners in their direct environment, graduates may be better able to further develop themselves as youth entrepreneurs. These alumni, in return, become part of the future youth entrepreneurial ecosystem through continuous cycles of providing support and mentorship, passing on knowledge and skills, and introducing new role-players to the network. Through this cycle, students graduating from entrepreneurial universities begin to contribute to future interconnected local systems where co-beneficial support structures occur and co-develop.

3.3.2 Academic Entrepreneurship

Value creation is widely recognised as the common core of both academic entrepreneurship and how different stakeholders in society create value for each other. It can, therefore, be reasoned that value co-creation is essential for an effective youth entrepreneur ecosystem. The development of entrepreneurship, as part of a university's role, should, thus, be executed by academics in the form of 'academic' entrepreneurship. University academics, generally through research conducted at universities, are a significant source of entrepreneurial activity, and their role in stimulating economic activity has become more pronounced over the past 30 years.

Initially, academic entrepreneurship was described as involving academics who attempt to generate funds from external agencies as a means of pursuing research at a university. This developing entrepreneurial activity has since manifested in increasing numbers of patents, licencing income, numbers of academic spinouts and start-ups, and applied research conducted with partners and consultancy engagements.[34] Through such developments, more extended research-led community engagements now take place, and the entrepreneurial ecosystem of the university has become a natural outflow of co-engagement, co-creation and co-evolvement processes with the larger external community of the university.

The South African national agenda, through the EDHE goal on academic entrepreneurship, is to

> [...] support (university) academics in instilling an entrepreneurial mindset within all students and graduates through the offering of relevant knowledge, transferral of practical skills and the application of business principles, not only to a specific discipline, but across disciplines.[35]

The idea of infusing elements of entrepreneurship into education has gained great traction in many educational institutes around the world as a response to addressing socio-economic problems and facilitating graduate employment. However, putting this idea into practice poses significant challenges. The initial co-initiating, co-sensing, co-inspiring, co-creating and (eventually) co-evolving of the youth entrepreneur ecosystem are complex and time-consuming for individuals at these education institutes who facilitate the process. Despite these challenges, the positive long-term effects (systemic transformation and value creation) make it necessary to expand this ecosystem as much as possible in a responsible and sustainable manner.

The main problem that educational institutes might initially encounter when establishing a youth entrepreneurship environment is related to the capacity and ability to change. This issue includes, but is

---

[34] Davey et al. (2016).
[35] EDHE (2021).

not limited to, a lack of time and various resources; academic staff's trep-
idation towards commercialism; educational structures that are currently
not able to promote entrepreneurialism; and a lack of clarity,[36] as locations, institutional architecture, programme offerings and staff abilities
differ both within and across institutions.[37]

A further issue is that *what* is meant with 'entrepreneurship *in* education' (or entrepreneurship education) differs significantly across existing
literature reviews. Some perspectives view the concept as a process
involving various academic and non-academic programmes to encourage
students to start up their own enterprises. Other perspectives include
that this concept is, instead, about making students more creative,
opportunities-orientated, proactive and/or innovative towards problem-
solving. Furthermore, regarding promoting entrepreneurship education
in developing countries with high unemployment: the emphasis and
common denominator tend to fall on value creation (training students
to create value for other people). Indeed, value creation is at the
core of systemic development and a key factor in and for addressing
different socio-economic crises on and across various systemic levels (see
Chapter 1). As such, value creation is a key competency required by all
staff and students, no matter what career is being pursued or whether
activities take place internally or externally from an educational institute. Creating new and innovative enterprises could, thus, be viewed as
one of many different means for creating value.[38]

In addition, while *why* entrepreneurship education is relevant is
mostly viewed from a socio-economic development perspective, it can
by no means be seen as a 'save-all' solution for high youth unemployment. This is because as much as entrepreneurship education can work
as a formal academic programme, with elective courses or components
of entrepreneurship being incorporated into general modules or course
learning outcomes within higher education, it can still be problematic
when infused into the primary or secondary levels of education. At
these lower levels, it can, however, still be impactful to trigger students'

---

[36] No 'ten-step plan' of 'how to' infuse entrepreneurship into education.

[37] Lackéus (2015).

[38] Ibid.

entrepreneurial heartsets and mindsets, which could result in deeper learning over time.[39]

Effective youth entrepreneurship is, furthermore, linked to students' resilience within their inner domains. Through resilience, students can become motivated to engage in creating value in their environment based on the knowledge they acquire through entrepreneurial education. Thus, both academic and non-academic entrepreneurship education programmes have certain implications for planning, executing, assessing and co-initiating the youth entrepreneur ecosystem within their respective programme or module offerings.

In comparison with *what* and *why*, *when* to infuse entrepreneurship into education tends to be clearer in its theory (Fig. 3.4). Yet, its practical application is often difficult and will vary between educational institutes, locations and students. The theory ambitiously proposes that entrepreneurship education should be embedded into curricula that are relevant to all students, preferably as early as pre-primary and primary school. Some countries (e.g. in the Middle East) have managed to do so. These countries' success in this endeavour may be related to how their education systems are relatively new and specifically created in response to the need to add value to extreme national problems (e.g. to address the over-extraction of oil and gas and its related potential to reduce income gained from this resource).

At a later stage in the educational system, both academic and non-academic programmes can be complemented by offering youths voluntary enabling opportunities for entrepreneurship practice. Currently, on both the secondary and tertiary levels, most initiatives, besides curricula offerings, focus on business start-ups. This focus is problematic, as it often lacks embeddedness in other teaching subjects. A possible way to better infuse theory and practice could be through the adoption of SALAR. However, effective implementation thereof requires academic staff, support staff and mentors from institutes' external environments to collaborate. Furthermore, an action takes time to co-initiate and sustain, as maintaining relationships is complex, and coordinating the various role-players can be time-consuming for facilitators. In vocational

---

[39] Ibid.

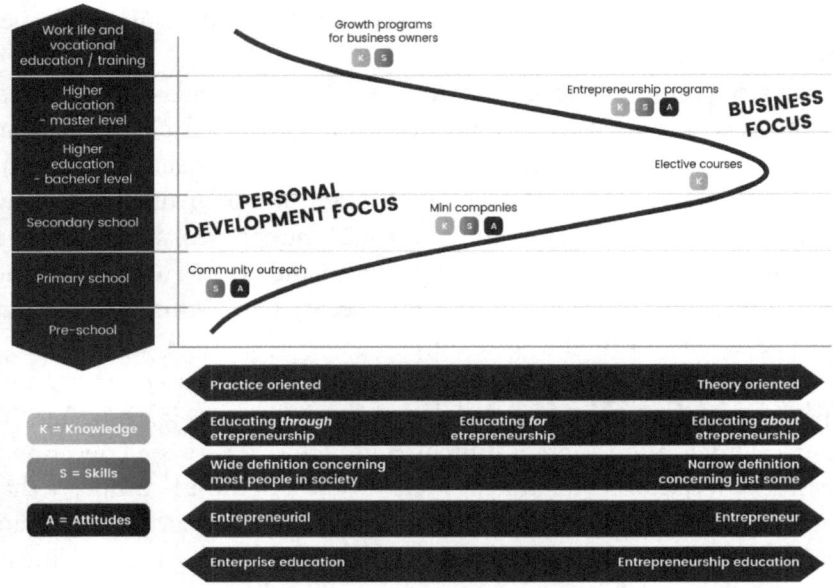

Fig. 3.4 Overview of entrepreneurial education (*Source* Lackeus, 2015)

education and training, youths' EA is also generally associated with the actualisation of learning outcomes and value creation; however, gaps still exist in connecting youths to tools, methods and processes for sustaining actions and the value creation process.

It is necessary, therefore, to determine *how* to develop staff and students with enhanced entrepreneurial heartsets and mindsets in order to address complex situations. While determining this 'how' may be a difficult endeavour, it is still vital, as successfully answering this question could translate into significant reductions in the currently high levels of graduate and youth unemployment.

One popular approach to developing youth entrepreneurial abilities is 'learning-by-doing'. Indeed, there is increasing consensus in the body of knowledge that students working in interdisciplinary teams and inter-acting with people outside the educational institute can be a particularly powerful way to develop entrepreneurial competencies. However, in order to effectively adopt this approach, the *what* (what needs to be learnt by doing?) needs to be properly answered.

If experiential and action learning, similar to learning-by-doing, is based on EA as an outcome, then it could be argued that value creation should occur within the extended youth entrepreneurial ecosystem. By employing such an approach, it may be that role-players outside of educational institutes could significantly benefit from the youths' value creation, both indirectly and directly. While this value creation might not be immediately visible or tangible, there is a vision that the ecosystem could coherently move towards a common 'big picture' vision. For this to occur, however, the facilitating agent within the educational institute needs to draw from other institutional resources to support the scope of activities serving as a node by bringing together total youth EA. Traditionally, acting as a node was not associated with the role, function and/ or mandate of education institute staff.[40]

The Organisation for Economic Co-operation and Development (OECD) created a model to provide an overview of different concepts within entrepreneurship education (Fig. 3.4). The model illustrates youth entrepreneurial progression in the education system and could be a starting point for facilitators when planning to co-initiate the youth entrepreneurial ecosystem.[41] It details the development of the entrepreneurial heartset and mindset from pre-youth years through to higher education conclusion.

According to the model, four approaches[42] can be considered:

1. teaching about entrepreneurship, which pays attention to theoretical concepts[43];
2. education related to entrepreneurial competencies, behaviours, and hard and soft skills;
3. education for entrepreneurship, which creates a platform for training or practice sessions and may demand a form of informal course structure; and

---

[40] Ibid.
[41] Ibid.
[42] Maas (2015).
[43] Davey et al. (2016) and Parsons (1951).

4. education in entrepreneurship for youths or staff who have existing enterprise concepts and demonstrate existing EA.

Entrepreneurship education can offer a way for societies to progress based on problem-solving competencies, innovation, and innovative and creative thinking Adelakun and Van der Westhuizen (2021), Awotunde and Van der Westhuizen (2021a, b).

3.3.3 Studentpreneurship

Studentpreneurship is a term used to describe youths with an open heart, open will, and open mind to connect to their entrepreneurial ecosystem en route to EA. The term refers to youths who are learning to be entrepreneurial or who have, in some cases, initiated a start-up. Student-preneurs develop their heartset, handset and mindsets with support from an educational institute or participate in development or mentorship initiatives from other agents. These studentpreneurs have a responsibility to co-initiate, co-sense, co-inspire, co-create and co-evolve with other people in their youth entrepreneurial ecosystem and to maintain positive interpersonal relationships so as to hopefully gain sustained EA and create value.

Some educational institutes, especially in higher education, enable an environment of entrepreneurial support and allow studentpreneurs to engage in business activities on and off-campus, with or without the support of the educational institute. These institutions do so by offering their students incubation, acceleration, shop-space, patenting and licencing opportunities. Such activities often take place extra-curricularly and are not linked to academic assessment. Oftentimes, educational institutes provide formal studentpreneur policies or agreements that stipulate rules for doing business with, or to the external environment of, the educational institute with support of the educational institute itself.

The EDHE programme of DHET envisions South African universities mobilising national student and graduate resources to create successful enterprises that will eventually lead to both wealth and job creation. Graduates, under this vision, would continue to add value to the ecosystem and, in return, offer support to the new generation of youth entrepreneurs moving into the education system cycle. In this context, wealth refers more to national value creation than the accumulation of money.

3.4 Government Agencies

The SHAPE strategy for developing an effective youth entrepreneurial ecosystem underlines the need for robust links between governmental agencies, educational institutes and the full range of entrepreneurial factors in the ecosystem. In terms of (youth) entrepreneurial development, government plays two important roles. The first is regulatory, which is related to creating and providing conducive policies and responsibly and ethically ensuring justice. The second is developmental, which aligns to initiating various programmes and offering financial and other forms of assistance (e.g. policy creation that enables entrepreneurial ventures and safeguards its interest, including conflict resolution mechanisms, patent policies, taxation laws and other business-related regulations)[44] (Fig. 3.5).

In South Africa, Sector Education Training Authorities (SETAs) are responsible for initiating and sponsoring internships or learnership programmes. In 2005, 22 different economic sector-related organisations were re-established by the South African Minister of Labour. They had since been allocated responsibility for educating and training individuals to develop skills in relation to each specific economic sector (e.g. one for the banking sector, one for information technology, etc.) as a means to implement the global National Skills Development Strategy.[45] A sector is made up of economic activities that are linked and related to macrosystemic socio-economic development. These SETAs provide experiential learning to individuals, with 60% of the training taking place outside the classroom (in a workplace-related milieu). There are currently, however,

---

[44] Mujahid et al. (2019).
[45] Seta's South Africa (2021).

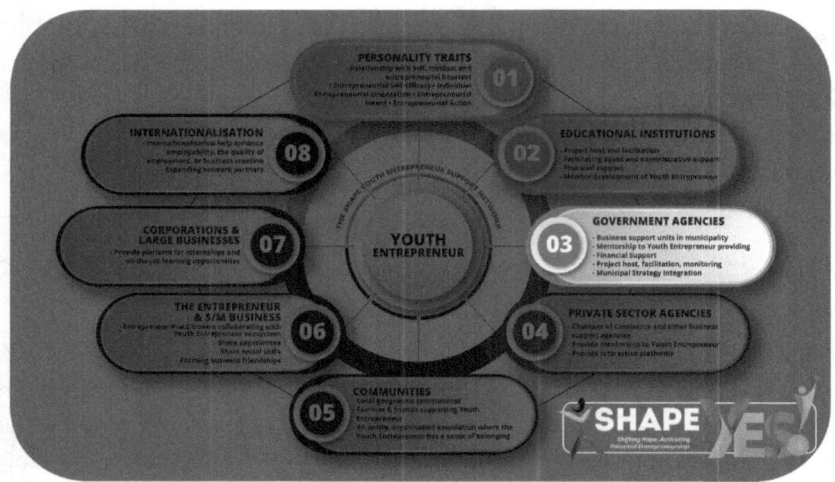

Fig. 3.5 The SHAPE YES Network for youth entrepreneurs—Government agencies

no SETAs specifically allocated to youth entrepreneurship, nor is there any track record of sustainable job creation for youths who undergo SETA-based programmes.[46]

Government bodies, such as local municipalities, also provide business support to youth entrepreneurs and have programmes to boost entrepreneurship. One example of a local municipality in South Africa that has implemented such initiatives is the eThekwini Municipality (in which central Durban is located). In this municipality, 15 types of business support offerings and programmes exist to support individuals and enhance entrepreneurship (Fig. 3.6).[47]

One problem with these kinds of municipality-based business support programmes is a lack of reliable data on their successes or sustainability in the long term. The focus of these programmes also tends to be on the most basic level, with no core focus on innovation, creativity, or sustainable mentorship post-completion of such a programme.

---

[46] Records are available on pass and failure rates.
[47] eThekwini Municipality (2017).

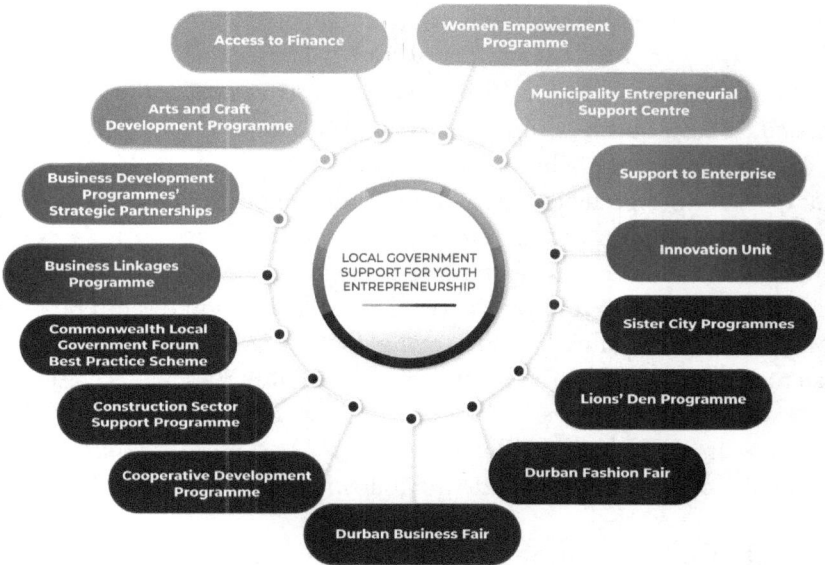

Fig. 3.6 Example of local government support for youth entrepreneurship

3.4.1 Entrepreneurship Development in Higher Education

The EDHE, as a government agency, offers a platform primarily aimed at addressing the issues of graduate unemployment and the need for universities to become more entrepreneurial. It was created in 2016 within the South African DHET and is part of the University Capacity Development Programme (UCDP). The EDHE intends to co-initiate, co-sense, co-inspire, co-create and co-evolve with South African public universities to create a national impact. This intended impact is to (a) equip every student for economic participation through economic activity, with an emphasis on student women; (b) support academics and professionals to develop entrepreneurship through learning, teaching and research across all disciplines; and (c) support universities as entrepreneurial and innovative ecosystems, which include relevant policy development.

This government agency further describes its approach as propelling the economic participation of students and graduates by leveraging strong and existing networks in and through its community of practice (CoPs—detailed a bit later in this section). The EDHE also champions relationships by utilising existing university structures and resources to capacitate each South African university in a lean, scalable way.

It should be noted, however, that the mandate of this agency does not include entrepreneurship in basic education or general entrepreneurship in the community but rather has a specific focus on universities. The vision, thus, needs to mobilise resources across the nation and different universities to promote the desired facilitation of entrepreneurship programmes aimed at improving the systemic crises faced at the macrosystems level. A primary strategy to mobilise these noted resources is to create different CoPs by bringing together university staff and students from various public universities into a central node. Such national CoPs currently include the following:

- EDHE CoP for Student Entrepreneurship (CoP for SE);
- EDHE CoP for Entrepreneurship Learning and Teaching (CoP for ELT);
- EDHE CoP for Entrepreneurship Research (CoP for ER);
- EDHE CoP for Entrepreneurial Universities (CoP for EU);
- EDHE Studentpreneurs (CoP for SPs); and
- Upcoming in 2022, EDHE CoP for Entrepreneurial Alumni (CoP for EA).

The national entrepreneurship/entrepreneurial CoP structure enables the youth entrepreneurial ecosystem to develop between educational institutes, governmental agencies and private sectors (Fig. 3.7).

The EDHE further envisions replicating the national CoP structure of general government agencies within South African universities. This, in turn, could boost the concept of entrepreneurial universities where universities actively collaborate with governmental agencies through establishing an economic activation office as a central internal node (e.g. an existing incubator or accelerator), which would be responsible for facilitating the internal co-creation of the CoP structure. This node would also lever on existing university support structures (Fig. 3.8).

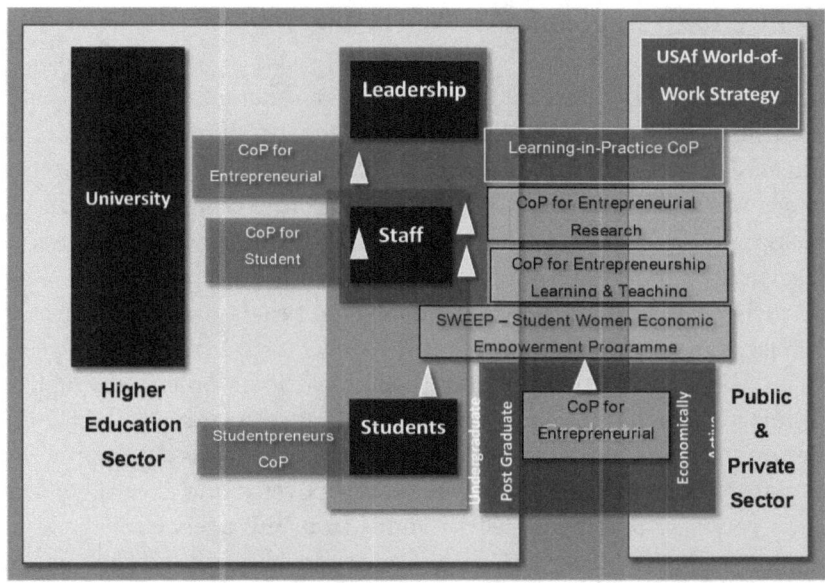

Fig. 3.7 The EDHE CoP landscape (2021–2023) (*Source* EDHE, 2021)

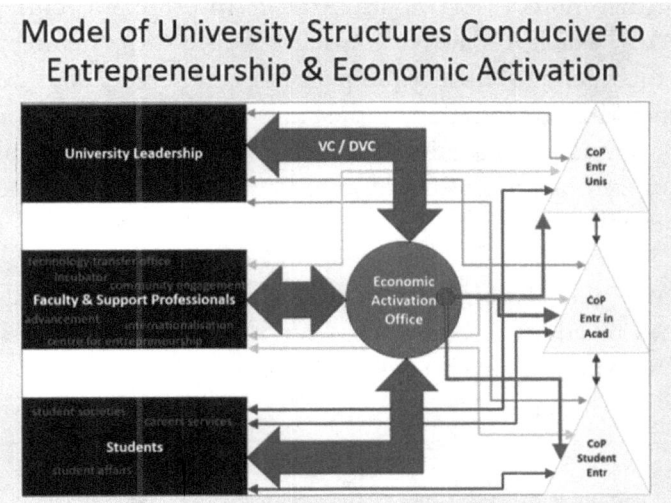

Fig. 3.8 Model of university structures conducive to entrepreneurship and economic activation (*Source* EDHE, 2021)

3.4.2 Other Government Agencies

Aside from the EDHE, there are a number of other government agencies responsible for promoting (youth) entrepreneurship. For example, the Industrial Development Corporation (IDC) is a national development finance institute mandated to promote economic growth and industrial development and improve domestic industrial capacity.[48] This agency is capacitated to develop opportunities for youth entrepreneurs in alignment with development policies and develop programmes and functions in collaboration with educational institutes.

The IDC also promotes entrepreneurial development through its subsidiary, namely the Small Enterprise Finance Agency (SEFA). SEFA is responsible for supporting the establishment and developing and growing SMEs with the aim of reducing poverty and creating jobs.[49] When youth entrepreneurs receive funds from this agency for the establishment of their businesses, such ventures can employ other youths. SEFA also partners with financial intermediaries to foster the support of entrepreneurs and creates an avenue for monitoring allocated funds.

Of further note is the South African Institute for Entrepreneurship (SAIE), which is aimed at impacting South Africa's entrepreneurial culture to foster job creation and promote entrepreneurial behaviour, which should result in reducing the currently high levels of unemployment, poverty and inequality.[50] With a focus primarily on agriculture, education, information technology and enterprise development sectors, SAIE is enabled to develop relevant initiative programmes and methodologies.

Similarly, the National Youth Development Agency (NYDA) was established by an act of parliament (Act 54 of 2008) to address matters relating to youth development at the national, provincial and local

---

[48] SEFA (2021).

[49] SA Institute for Entrepreneurship (2021).

[50] NYDA (2021).

government levels.[51] NYDA ensures that stakeholders, such as Government, the private sector and civil society, give attention to the development of youths by offering programmes to solve challenges and improve their lives. At the micro-level, NYDA provides training, mentorship, and entrepreneurial support to youths, while at the macro-level, it facilitates the contribution of the youth to policy development, partnership and research.

The Chemical Industries Education and Training Authority (CHIETA) was established by the Skills Development Act in 1998[52] and is responsible for the identification of skills needed to be developed to promote growth in the chemical industries sector. Such growth is achieved through training and development initiatives.

Furthermore, the Umsobomvu Youth Fund[53] has been equipped to attract investment partnerships to fund youth entrepreneurs. This Fund helps youth entrepreneurs to grow their ventures by teaching them the required skills and offering programmes, such as franchises, fund-a-loan and the voucher financing system. The Fund also supports entrepreneurship education and training, co-operative training, graduate development training and business consulting service vouchers.

As a macrosystem role-player, governmental agencies set out to support youth entrepreneurship through various programmes and initiatives. These initiatives can be presented on a national, provincial, or local municipal level. The support provided by these agencies can also be through various avenues, including mentorship, resource exchange, leverage and/or possible financial support.

3.5   Private Sector Agencies

Private sector agencies are community, regional, national, or international-based agents operating for the collective promotion of private sector organisations. These agencies have the potential to support

---

[51] CHIETA (2021).
[52] SACCI (2021).
[53] Danns and Danns (2019).

youth entrepreneurs by enabling networking opportunities with other entrepreneurs and business friends. The agencies also assist with forming further business friendships, possible collaboration opportunities in the value chain, possible financing schemes and other support platforms to enable youth entrepreneurs over time (Fig. 3.9).

Networks within private sector agencies are necessary because youth entrepreneurs access intangible resources (e.g. access to new markets, information, trust and knowledge) and tangible resources (e.g. facilities and finances) through these avenues. In the SHAPE ecosystem, specifically, the collaboration between educational institutes and private sector agencies is necessary to facilitate[54] the sharing of resources, such as capital, knowledge, expertise and technologies. Private sector agencies can also serve as incubators by providing business support and physical spaces for youth entrepreneurs through or within their physical proximity or online platforms. Furthermore, many private sector agencies operate on a membership system, where members benefit from various

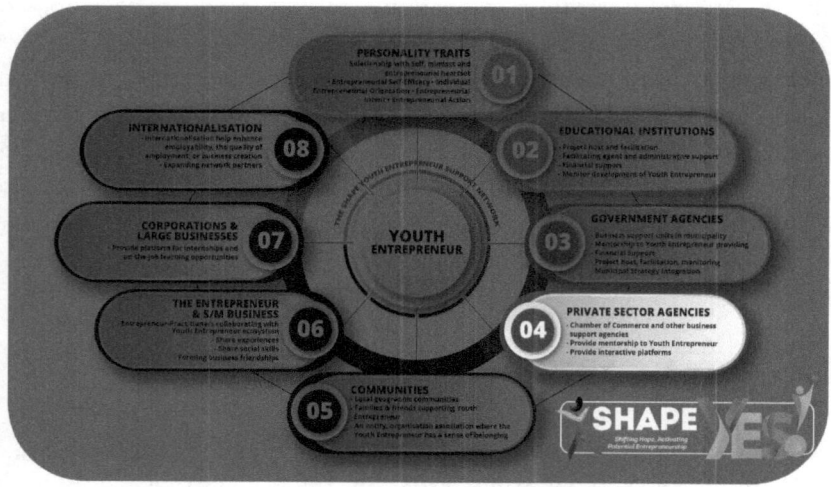

Fig. 3.9 The SHAPE YES Network for youth entrepreneurs—Private sector agencies

---

[54] Hernández-Chea et al. (2021).

organised services offered by respective private sector agencies.[55] The following paragraphs offer more details regarding these kinds of agencies.

The South Africa Chamber of Commerce and Industry (SACCI)[56] represents the interest of businesses by engaging with the government and regulators on matters that pertain to ensuring a conducive business environment for business owners, thereby protecting the interest of the business sector. SACCI's responsibility to entrepreneurs is to promote and lobby potential investors (e.g. the government and other businesses) for conditions that enable the development of start-ups for youth entrepreneurs.[57]

The National African Federated Chamber of Commerce and Industry (NAFCOC),[58] [59]in turn, is aimed at developing and promoting inclusive economic growth among existing and new businesses with memberships of about 5 million SMEs. NAFCOC has existing partnerships with various institutions, including governmental and educational institutions, and builds business relations with international business chambers.

The African Development Bank (AfDB),[60] in conjunction with the European Investment Bank,[61] has instituted an initiative referred to as Boost Africa Empowering Young Entrepreneurs. This initiative assesses possible funding for youth entrepreneurs at the earliest stages of their EA.

3.6   Communities

The concept of 'communities' refers to the context in which youth entrepreneurs are embedded.[62] Communities can be both enabling and barrier factors within and for the youth entrepreneurial ecosystem. The

---

[55] Griffin-El (2015) and Isenberg (2010).

[56] https://sacci.org.za/.

[57] NAFCOC (2021).

[58] Vuk'uzenzele (2021).

[59] https://nafcoc.org.za/.

[60] Crampton (2019) and https://www.afdb.org/en.

[61] https://www.eib.org/en/index.htm.

[62] Shirokova et al. (2013).

notion of 'embeddedness' indicated earlier relates to both contextual and community influences that critically contribute to the formation of youth entrepreneurs' mental models (thinking and feeling). In other words, the spirit and culture of the embedded community can impact youths' shared values and norms, receptivity to education and mentorship, leadership and governance, and infrastructure. All these factors, in turn, impact the youths' EI (Fig. 3.10).

The embeddedness of community is also important for youth entrepreneurs in terms of how communities can provide an 'anchoring' that supports the healthy development of young people's inner domains. Indeed, an enabling community is most likely to contribute to shaping the youths' EA and encourage trust between role-players when co-initiating entrepreneurial ideas. The growth-effectiveness of youth entrepreneurship depends on a shared heart, mind and will; hence, the need for positive community embeddedness.

While such embeddedness can be structural, cultural, political and/ or cognitive, cultural embeddedness most commonly impacts youth entrepreneurs. Cultural embeddedness consists of the beliefs, values,

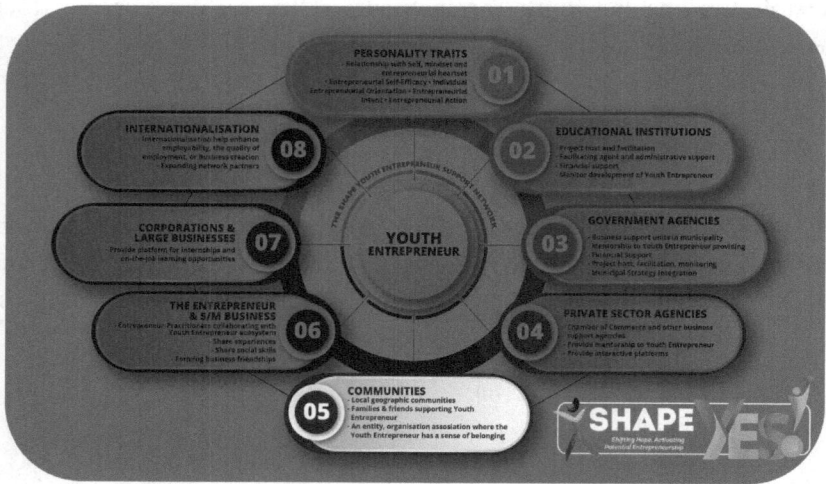

Fig. 3.10 The SHAPE YES Network for youth entrepreneurs—communities

ideologies and norms that exist and develop within a given community (wherein a youth entrepreneur exists) and most often begins within the immediate family. General culture also influences the choice of a young person to become an entrepreneur and his or her response to information.[63]

With this understanding, it can be asserted that current embeddedness and culture run counter to the traditional South African notion of *ubuntu* (an African philosophy that values moral practice and the intention to act in a manner that is respectful and honest). In South Africa, *ubuntu* culture seeks to benefit society rather than just the individual. However, the practice of *ubuntu* is not widespread, and more effort is required for communities to benefit from this concept. South Africa, thus, needs to develop a pervading culture of *ubuntu* to provide collective benefits to and for all entrepreneurs, as such assistance could be crucial in bridging the current disconnect between existing individualistic and collectivist points of view.[64]

As the community spirit often starts with the immediate family, roleplayers can consist of parents, guardians, or siblings who form the primary support system and become the greatest influencers of youth entrepreneurs. Mentors in the broader community (adult allies) or peers are also great social influencers for youth entrepreneurs and can either create an enabling or a disabling environment. That is, youths often perceive especially their peers as trustworthy and relatable, which can create emotional support for youth entrepreneurs, particularly when those peers encourage their pursuits. Other community enabling aspects can include community organisations (e.g. social, sport, or cultural clubs), religious institutions, infrastructure, or facilities, and other public or private organisations located in direct geographical access to the community wherein a youth entrepreneur exists.[65] Conversely, many barriers to youth entrepreneurship occur as a result of a lack of (positive) community support. Without community support, many youths

---

[63] Shirokova et al. (2013).

[64] Nel (2017).

[65] Shirokova et al. (2013).

are left feeling hopeless and helpless in creating an entrepreneurial future for themselves.

When a facilitator in an educational institute co-initiates SHAPE, engagements will naturally occur with youths in the local community wherein they are pursuing their entrepreneurial education. Often, local communities consist of both community-based organisations and NGOs with whom local youth entrepreneurs interact. Local communities are also the principal consumers of the products and services rendered by youth entrepreneurs and form their infrastructure 'business friends'. In this way, local communities both receive value from and create value for youth entrepreneurs. Since these communities also tend to be the same as from where the youth entrepreneur hails, they also add pertinence to the link between 'community' and 'entrepreneurial development'. This link is particularly true in respect to how most South African youths are well-acquainted with the social ills (e.g. crime, corruption, violence and the mismanagement of unemployment) that exist within their own communities[66] and, therefore, aim to address these ills practically through entrepreneurship.

Youth entrepreneurial ability should, thus, begin at home and then proceed to higher education and training.[67] At the tertiary level, partnerships with local communities and SMEs can also better provide opportunities for youth entrepreneurs to form business friendships, thereby widening the scope for beneficial consultation and creating the potential for youth entrepreneurs and their business friends to move forward together in entrepreneurial activity.

The local communities who act as support networks between youth entrepreneurs and the broader entrepreneurial process, thus, become an important supportive pillar in the SHAPE youth entrepreneurial ecosystem.

---

[66] Van der Westhuizen (2016).
[67] Dhliwayo (2008, 329–340).

3.7 Small- and Medium-Sized Enterprises (SMEs)

The terms 'entrepreneur' and 'SME owner' can be used synonymously in relation to their potential for serving as business friends to youth entrepreneurs, as most often, an SME owner is also an entrepreneur.[68] In the SHAPE strategy for youth entrepreneurial ecosystems, the emphasis is on youth entrepreneurs having an initial opportunity to try out social skills with existing entrepreneurs or business owner-managers through the processes of co-initiating, co-sensing and co-inspiring. Further EA might result from these interactions by co-creating and co-evolving business ideas that occur together or individually (Fig. 3.11).

Normative, cognitive and regulatory pillars are associated with the co-initiation phase between youth entrepreneurs and possible business friends, as facilitated through the education institute.[69] The normative pillar underpins social values, norms and beliefs that govern individual

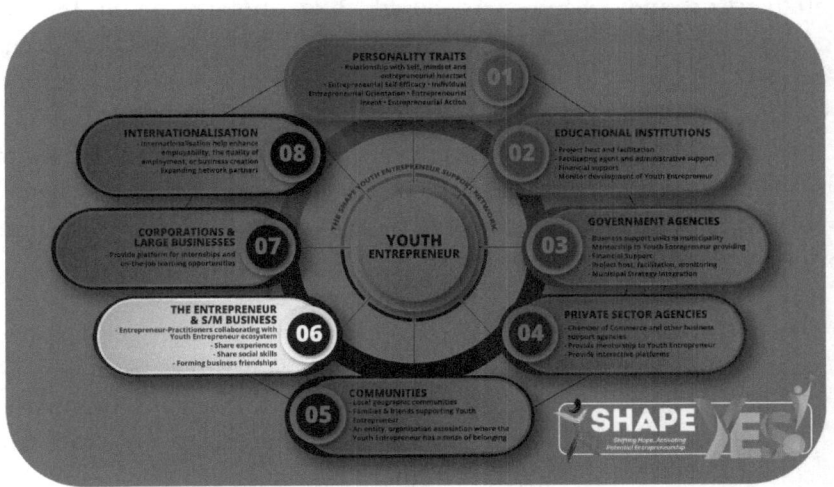

Fig. 3.11 The SHAPE YES Network for youth entrepreneurs—the entrepreneur and S/M business

---

[68] Bagheri and Pihie (2011).
[69] Audretsch et al. (2021).

and organisational behaviour. The cognitive pillar constitutes the 'shared logics of action' among youths and their ecosystem(s). These, in turn, can be used to interpret available information and formulate youths' expectations about the outcome of their entrepreneurial interactions. The regulatory pillar comprises regulations, laws and other aspects that define the 'rules of co-value creation' and legal boundaries.[70]

Building on these three pillars, interactions of skills transfer, mentorship and industry training from SME owners or existing entrepreneurs to youth entrepreneurs who are just beginning their EA are necessary to build an effective ecosystem and add value to socio-economic development. Possibly some of the most productive learning environments for youth entrepreneurs and their business friends occur when actions closely match the day-to-day realities of small-business leadership and networking.[71] Hands-on experience of actual business and industry environments for youths who would otherwise have little sense of the competitive pressures that face new entrants in a business field is also a crucial enabler aspect. The emphasis in these interactions between youth entrepreneurs and SME owners should, thus, primarily be on 'learning the business' by 'experiencing the business'. This process best occurs through the active performance of business operations in the course of an entrepreneurship initiative undertaken at an educational institute.

As part of the 'co' strategy, the possible collaboration between business friendship structures, youth entrepreneurs and SME owner-managers is encouraged by facilitators of an educational institute. Possible emerging business friendships that can result from such collaboration include:

- Youth entrepreneurs who wish to co-create and co-evolve on their own and with their own business ideas become their own business friends.
- Business professionals (non-youth) who wish to draw on their participation in the youth entrepreneurial ecosystem to co-create and co-evolve on their own and with their own business ideas.

---

[70] Ibid.

[71] Dhliwayo (2008).

- Youth entrepreneurs who wish to co-create and co-evolve together with other youth entrepreneurs and with their own and/or joint business ideas.
- Youth entrepreneurs who wish to co-create and co-evolve together with other youth entrepreneurs *and* business professionals with their own or joint business ideas.
- Business professionals who wish to co-create and co-evolve together with other business professionals; these professionals remain part of value creation within the youth entrepreneurial ecosystem.

Youth entrepreneurs who engage with initial EA benefit from their inner and external domain development through business friendships with SMEs that provide possible spin-off new ventures and creation opportunities. Business friendships also strengthen both the individual and the enterprise, especially in challenging business times.[72] Networks that youth entrepreneurs can access through business friendships include

1. information networks, through which opportunities are identified, and resources are acquired (e.g. embracing information communication technology (ICT));
2. networks for value-adding exchange (embracing competition and strengthening value chains); and
3. networks of social influence or status.

This last network type is especially important because youth entrepreneurs can boost their ESE to confidently overcome emotions associated with feeling helpless and/or hopeless about the future when they have social support. The ability of youth entrepreneurs to use existing networks within the ecosystem allows them leverage over their competitors, both within the ecosystem and across other communities.

A possible way for a facilitator at an educational institute to bring youth entrepreneurs together with various potential business friends is to allocate industry mentors to youths. These mentors can provide guidance to their mentees, and the youth entrepreneurs can learn from

---

[72] Mason and Brown (2014).

these mentors' experiences and success stories. Industry mentorship between business friends and youth entrepreneurs can also enhance the collective learning capacity necessary to propel youths' creativity and innovativeness.[73]

3.8   Corporations and Large Businesses

Corporations and large businesses perform important functions in the development of the youth entrepreneurial ecosystem. These organisations generally specialise in attracting a pool of highly skilled individuals, many of whom are graduates with higher education qualifications from various disciplines.[74] In terms of contributing and adding value to the youth entrepreneurial ecosystem, educational institutes and corporations or large businesses can collaborate through both formal and informal agreements to support youth entrepreneurial development. A vibrant, value-adding youth entrepreneurial ecosystem essentially includes major businesses that help to cultivate said ecosystem (purposefully or otherwise).[75] Large businesses rooted locally instead of internationally are also likely to be the most successful in strengthening this ecosystem, as angel investors tend to be indigenous. Top management roles within local-based, larger organisations also tend to be more plentiful, ensuring that the company is generally well connected within the community (Fig. 3.12).

Fewer and fewer jobs are available in the industrial sector due to technological advancements, which calls for new models of social innovation to facilitate youth entrepreneurship, along with new skills development for the new economy and opportunities for transforming resources and skills into value creating endeavours.[76] Current wicked

---

[73] Brown and Mason (2017).
[74] Feldman et al. (2005).
[75] Isenberg (2011).
[76] Gupta et al. (2017).

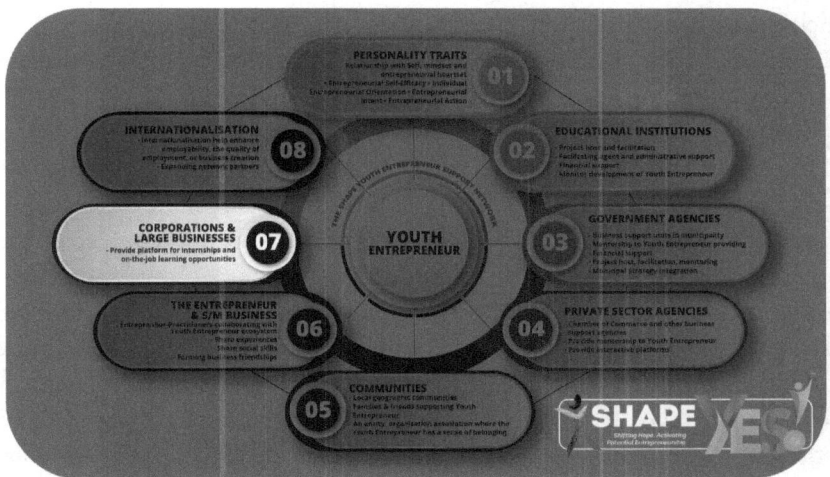

Fig. 3.12 The SHAPE YES Network for youth entrepreneurs—Corporations & large businesses

problems (also referred to as long-term unaddressed systemic problems that cause systemic crises), however, indicate that existing institutional arrangements are insufficient for adding value to socio-economic problem-solving, making new innovations imperative.[77] An open innovation approach towards purposefully blending grassroots ideas, youth entrepreneurial innovations and frugal innovations is still far from being actioned by most large businesses and corporations in South Africa. It is, therefore, essential for a systemic disconnect to be overcome in order to effectively address wicked problems.

The youth entrepreneurial ecosystem could be a significant avenue for overcoming this disconnect, particularly if it is supported to create value through social, open innovations that connect corporations, communities and educational institutes. Social innovation is a creative and connected solution that can be used to address unmet social needs, as it

---

[77] Ibid.

includes adding value and innovation *by* grassroots and youths *for* grass-roots and youths. Through this approach, it becomes easier to co-create a healthy youth entrepreneurial ecosystem.[78]

Corporations and large businesses can further benefit youth entrepreneurs through mechanisms rooted in regulatory obligation. Corporate social investment (CSI), for instance, can provide skills development and mentorship to youth entrepreneurs. It is also crucial that corporations undertake talent recruitment programmes aimed at university graduates that assist with development. These larger businesses can also provide exhibitions to foster youth entrepreneurship and attract graduates. Similarly, skills development and training initiatives (e.g. the South African Skills Development Levy) can be promoted. Since most large businesses and corporations pay a tax towards the SETA to which they are registered, such funding can enable youth entrepreneurs to undergo industrial training and promote academic-industry collaboration with existing large businesses. In this way, youth entrepreneurs can be provided with valuable industry-specific skills.

Such vocational initiatives currently include 40% classroom training and 60% on-the-job training (also referred to as 'learnerships') when linked to obtaining a full accredited qualification. The regulatory pillar of learnership training and skills development similarly includes tri-party agreements between the youth, educational institute, and large business or corporation. In these kinds of agreements, the corporation pays a skills development levy as tax to the industry-affiliated SETA.

CSI refers to business practices involving programmes that benefit the community, including youth development.[79] At both the mundo- (United Nations) and macrosystem levels (national government), CSI (also referred to as corporate social *responsibility*) can help with youth development and the training of youths in entrepreneurial activities. A business's CSI can encompass a wide variety of operations (e.g. assisting the broader socio-economic environment and/or helping people in the community grow through development programmes).

---

[78] Ibid.
[79] Caramela (2016).

As part of CSI, a business should assess its compliance with ethical and international norms and ensure that all its policies are in alignment. Sometimes, companies communicate these policies to better ensure that local communities benefit from these operations. It should be noted, however, that although these initiatives are usually perceived to be effective, they often lack necessary support and strategic management. The criteria for measuring their success also tend to be unclear and subjective, and one possible reason for companies to claim that they implement CSI programmes is to gain credibility and loyalty in the community, without much further substantiation to such a claim being required.

In case-study research, two South African retail banks were investigated to identify whether employees involved in CSI initiatives were supported by the programmes. These studies showed that the banks in question did not, in fact, support employees through CSI programmes and the programmes were, therefore, not effective. There, thus, needs to be better management of CSI programmes to improve their effectiveness and optimise their value for recipients.[80]

Similarly, work-integrated learning provides youths with the opportunity to learn within an industry. This approach can greatly increase EA within the youth by improving their skills and enabling them to gain experience. Inflexible and restrictive regulatory pillars for youths moving into work-integrated learning can, however, cause barriers. Therefore, there is a need to leave scope for flexibility. For example, the eligibility criteria imposed by educational institutions when selecting youths for their programmes often do not include corporate representatives in reviewing the selection process. Corporations and large businesses must be more involved in work-integrated learning if they are to make a significant contribution to the entrepreneurial development of youths, address skills shortages and promote graduate employability.[81]

The importance and effectiveness of educational institutes collaborating with industry to improve work-integrated learning are worth considering, as the investment of resources in this endeavour can learn to provide youths with skills and experiences that make them

---

[80] Penn and Thomas (2017).
[81] Dunn et al. (2016).

more entrepreneurial. Shared resources (e.g. facilities, equipment and specialist expertise) enable all-round strength. Indeed, various case studies from developed countries show evidence that if major universities are supported by 10,000 companies, there are strong contributions from both universities and businesses. Studies from developing countries, conversely, show weak business contributions to work-integrated learning, which is problematic as youths are not provided with valuable work experience.

Despite the current lack of business contribution to work-integrated learning, there are some positive signs found within, particularly, the engineering sector of South Africa. Specifically, commitment and engagement appear to be higher for the work-integrated learning process when industries are financially invested in the process. South Africa could, thus, greatly improve work-integrated learning progress by partnering with both the community and industry to increase commitment from industry.[82]

Apprenticeships (also referred to as the internship method) are another way to link youths, large businesses and educational institutes in a formal manner. To activate effective apprenticeships, designated representatives from large businesses and corporations should match interns with mentors who can manage their development and be accountable for internship outcomes. The interns' educational institutes, in turn, should assess these internship programmes to evaluate their effectiveness and ascertain whether tax incentives are providing a worthwhile return to the economy. Such monitoring could also ensure that when companies abuse these programmes, penalties can be enforced to ensure compliance.[83]

A wide-ranging study conducted in South Africa examined more than 20 South African tertiary education institutes and gathered data on whether the current education programmes include internships. This study found that there were positive outcomes for internships for ESE, IEO and EI.[84]

---

[82] Reinhard et al. (2016).
[83] Naidoo and Hoque (2017).
[84] Botha and Bignotti (2016).

One further example of the importance of a strong partnership between government, industry and educational institutes is illustrated in a one-year internship programme created by the Department of Science and Technology. Two hundred students from across five provinces studying mechanical, electrical, industrial and civil engineering were provided with an opportunity to gain work experience in the industry. Along with the benefit to the youths who took part in this programme, the companies also benefitted by gaining an opportunity to boost their competitiveness by the acquisition of new talent, through the youth who completed the one-year internship and then went on to become permanent employees.[85]

Although many educational institutes in South Africa have educational programmes connected to industry, these programmes often lack resources and financial input from industry. Indeed, while institutions that provide work experience opportunities usually also offer to fund students in these programmes, the South African industry must show more commitment when financially investing in a work experience programme. Since these programmes give students practical experience, youths who complete them tend to be more employable than youths who have not had work exposure.[86] Another possibility would be, therefore, to enable youths is to gain trade accreditation and incubation, facilitated by their educational institute and offered by relevant large businesses or corporations. Such accreditation could provide youths with the necessary knowledge to pursue entrepreneurial activities.[87]

The co-initiation between youth entrepreneurs, educational institutes, and corporations or large businesses is generally viewed through the lenses of two relevant tensions that underscore a systemic paradox, namely the development tension (the inconsistent relationship between the youth entrepreneurial ecosystem and economic performance) and the policy tension (the unclear role of youth entrepreneurial ecosystem policies in respect to improving and adding value to socio-economic

---

[85] Zondi (2016).
[86] Reinhard et al. (2016).
[87] Melass (2015).

outcomes).[88] Radical social innovation is, therefore, necessary to bridge the current systemic disconnect and enable a future of possibilities for youth entrepreneurs.

3.9   Internationalisation

Internationalisation in Higher Education as a concept and strategic agenda in developing youth entrepreneurs is a relatively new, broad and varied phenomenon driven by a dynamic combination of political, economic, sociocultural and academic rationales and stakeholders. Its impact on regions, countries and institutions varies according to their particular contexts[89] (Fig. 3.13).

One of the key reasons for the significance of internationalisation in Higher Education to support a YES Network is its role in promoting cultural exchange and global understanding. South African universities

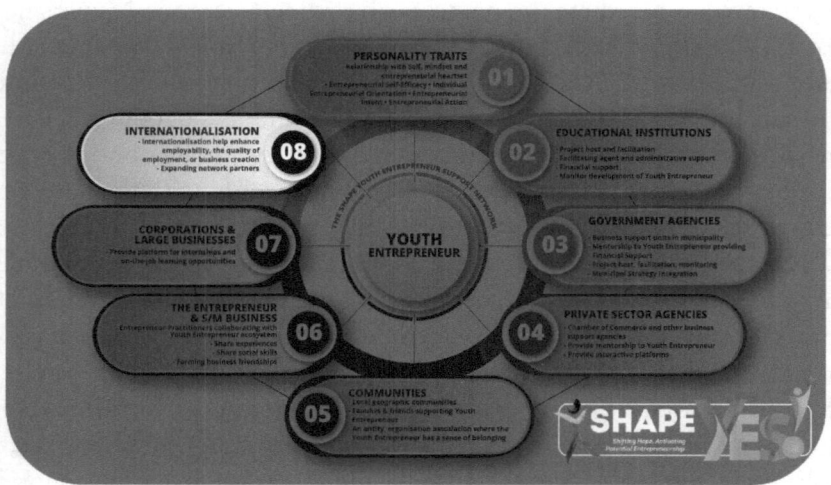

Fig. 3.13 The SHAPE YES Network for youth entrepreneurs—internationalisation

---

[88] Lafuente et al. (2018).
[89] De Wit and Altbach (2021).

that embrace internationalisation create an environment that encourages interaction between local and international youth entrepreneurs. This enables the sharing of diverse cultural experiences, languages and perspectives, enhancing intercultural competence and global awareness among these youth entrepreneurs. Such exposure nurtures open-mindedness, tolerance and respect for different cultures, preparing youth to thrive in an interconnected and diverse world.[90]

Developing countries like South Africa need to rethink and reimagine its socio-economic development orientated problem-solving strategy when responding to developing an enabling environment to maximise the benefits of internationalisation in the context of the 'Knowledge Society' while serving its direct ecosystemic Youth Entrepreneur Support Network, while being part of the global community.[91] The Knowledge Society serves to facilitate the process where information translates into resources to enable youth entrepreneurs taking effective actions (it differs from the information society that only creates and disseminates raw data). The Knowledge Society serves to facilitate the process where information translates into resources to enable youth entrepreneurs taking effective actions (it differs from the information society that only creates and disseminates raw data), therefore, translating output into outcomes.[92]

Internationalisation plays a central role in the Future World-of-Work strategy of higher education institutions in South Africa. It aims to "Africanize" the purposes, functions and curricula of universities, thereby creating a unique YES Network specifically tailored to the local ecosystem. However, young entrepreneurs require stronger support to establish these essential international relationships, which can contribute to their entrepreneurial journey and potentially facilitate the scaling-up of their initiatives. Traditionally, mobility was a key barrier to youth within the African context in internationalisation, where access to funds to enable mobility played a pivotal role. However, the digital transformation of the 'Knowledge Society' enables youth to access global networks,

---

[90] Hénard et al. (2012).
[91] Kishun (2007).
[92] Zhao et al. (2021).

international funding opportunities and cutting-edge technologies to support their entrepreneurial actions.[93]

In summary, internationalisation plays a multifaceted role in South African universities and beyond. It facilitates cultural exchange, broadens mental models of youth entrepreneurs, drives innovation and economic development, and elevates the global competitiveness. Embracing internationalisation is vital for youth South African universities to provide youth entrepreneurs with an opportunity to remain competitive, foster global citizenship and contribute to the socio-economic growth of the nation.

3.10 Synthesis

The key constructs outlined in this chapter translate into the different sections of the empirical investigation discussed in the following chapters. Furthermore, the identified key aspects were translated into factors for empirical investigation in each section of the investigation tool. Figure 3.14 presents a summary of the youth entrepreneurship nexus.

3.11 Conclusion

This chapter also proposed the theoretical conceptualisation of the SHAPE ecosystem model for effective youth entrepreneurship. In this model, youth entrepreneurs feature as central agents, with their internal and external domain factors either enabling or hindering EA. A systematic literature review identified educational institutes as facilitating agents in the youth entrepreneurial ecosystem, with emphasis on higher education institutes and especially universities. Findings from the literature also emphasised that there is a current systemic disconnect and lack of frugal social innovation to address wicked grassroots problems, which has created key barriers to the value chain and value creation aimed towards socio-economic development.

---

[93] Altbach and de Wit (2021).

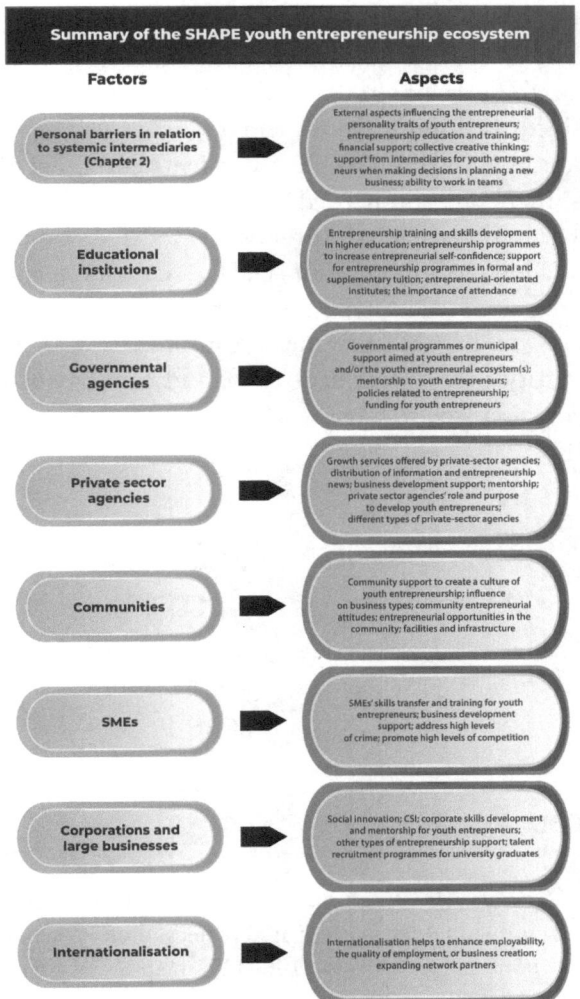

Fig. 3.14 Summary of the SHAPE youth entrepreneurship ecosystem

Since the microsystem is key for improving systems holistically and runs parallel with heartset, handset and mindset development, involvement by youths and other role-players in their ecosystem is essential. The systematic literature review presented in this chapter also provided new insights into the role of educational institutes as facilitating agents responsible for co-initiating, co-sensing, co-creating and co-evolving the youth entrepreneurial ecosystem. A limitation of the review was, however, that there is not much information available regarding the practical co-incorporation of youth entrepreneurs who are not affiliated with an educational institute in the ecosystem. Further research on this inclusivity is, therefore, still needed.

Of further note is that the proposed model is generic and flexible, thereby allowing for location-specific adaptation and movement in creating the architecture of the youth entrepreneurial ecosystem. The theoretical model was implemented in practice at a selected South African university over a period of time, and findings of the practical application are discussed in Chapters 4–8.

References

Adelakun, Y., & Van der Westhuizen, T. (2021). Delineating government policies and individual entrepreneurial orientation. *Journal of Sociology and Social Anthropology, 12*(3–4), 106–117. https://doi.org/10.31901/245 66764.2021/12.3-4.371

Altbach, P.G., & de Wit, H. (2021). The Boston College Center for international education and the emergence of a field of analysis, 1995–2020. In *Higher education in the next decade* (pp. 326–344). Brill.

Alvedalen, J., & Boschma, R. (2017). A critical review of entrepreneurial ecosystems research: Towards a future research agenda. *European Planning Studies, 25*(6), 887–903.

Audretsch, D. B., Belitski, M., & Cherkas, N. (2021). Entrepreneurial ecosystems in cities: The role of institutions. *PLoS ONE, 16*(3), e0247609.

Awotunde, O. M., & Van der Westhuizen, T. (2021a). Entrepreneurial self-efficacy development: An effective intervention for sustainable student entrepreneurial intentions. *International Journal of Innovation and Sustainable Development, 15*(4), 475–495.

Awotunde, O. M., & Van der Westhuizen, T. (2021b, September). Entrepreneurial self-efficacy and the SHAPE ideation model for university students. In *ECIE 2021 16th European conference on innovation and entrepreneurship Vol. 1* (p. 37).

Bagheri, A., & Pihie, Z. A. L. (2011). Entrepreneurial leadership: Towards a model for learning and development. *Human Resource Development International, 14*(4), 447–463.

Bolton, D. L., & Lane, M. D. (2012). Individual entrepreneurial orientation: Further investigation of a measurement instrument. *Academy of Entrepreneurship Journal, 18*(1), 91–98.

Botha, M., & Bignotti, A. (2016). Internships enhancing entrepreneurial intent and self-efficacy: Investigating tertiary-level entrepreneurship education programmes. *Southern African Journal of Entrepreneurship and Small Business Management, 8*(1), 1–15.

Brown, R., & Mason, C. (2017). Looking inside the spiky bits: A critical review and conceptualisation of entrepreneurial ecosystems. *Small Business Economics, 49*(1), 11–30.

Caramela, S., 2016. Understanding what corporate social responsibility (CSR) is, and why it matters, imagine tomorrow.

Chia, R. (1996). Teaching paradigm shifting in management education: University business schools and the entrepreneurial imagination. *Journal of Management Studies, 33*(4), 409–428.

Chia, R. (2014). From relevance to relevate: How university-based business schools can remain seats of "higher" learning and still contribute effectively to business. *Journal of Management Development, 33*(5), 443–455.

CHIETA (Chemical Industries Education & Training Authority). (2021). *Who are we.* https://www.chieta.org.za/

Crampton, N. (2019). 26 of the richest people in South Africa. *Entrepreneur South Africa.* https://www.entrepreneur.com/article/327556

Danns, D. E., & Danns, G. K. (2019). Financing youth entrepreneurship in a developing country. *Quarterly Review of Business Disciplines, 6*(3), 193–217.

Davey, T., Hannon, P., & Penaluna, A. (2016). Entrepreneurship education and the role of universities in entrepreneurship: Introduction to the special issue. *Industry and Higher Education, 30*(3), 171–182.

De Wit, H., & Altbach, P. G. (2021). Chapter 15: Internationalization in higher education. In *Higher education in the next decade*. Brill. Available from: Brill https://doi.org/10.1163/9789004462717_016. Accessed 13 July 2023.

Dhliwayo, S. (2008). Experiential learning in entrepreneurship education: A prospective model for South African tertiary institutions. *Education and Training, 50*(4), 329–340.

Dominici, G., & Gagnidze, I. (2021). Effectiveness of entrepreneurial universities: Experiences and challenges in digital era (a systemic approach). *Interdisciplinary Description of Complex Systems, 19*(1), 13–30.

DTI. (2017). *Department of small business development: Republic of South Africa.* Retrieved 15 September 2017, from www.dsbd.gov.za

Dunn, L. A., Schier, M. A., Hiller, J. E., & Harding, I. H. (2016). Eligibility requirements for work-integrated learning programs: Exploring the implications of using grade point averages for student participation. *Asia-Pacific Journal of Cooperative Education, 17*(3), 295–308.

EDHE (Entrepreneurship Development in Higher Education). (2021). *Background on the EDHE Programme.* https://edhe.co.za/about/

eThekwini Municipality. (2017). *Welcome to the official website of the eThekwini Municipality.* Retrieved 7 December 2017, from www.durban.gov.za/

Feldman, M. A., Francis, J., & Bercovitz, J. (2005). Creating a cluster while building a firm: Entrepreneurs and the formation of industrial clusters. *Regional Studies, 39*, 129–141.

Garavan, T. N., & O'Cinneide, B. (1994). Entrepreneurship education and training programmes: A review and evaluation—Part 1: Literature review of problems associated with entrepreneurship education and training programmes. *Journal of European Industrial Training, 18*(8), 3–12.

Griffin-El, E. W. (2015). Network-based resources for the innovation process of South African micro-entrepreneurs: A conceptual framework. *South African Journal of Business Management, 46*(3), 79–89.

Gupta, A., Dey, A., & Singh, G. (2017). Connecting corporations and communities: Towards a theory of social inclusive open innovation. *Journal of Open Innovation: Technology, Market, and Complexity, 3*(3), 17.

Harrison, R. T., Leitch, C. M., & Chia, R. (2007). Developing paradigmatic awareness in university business schools: The challenge for executive education. *Academy of Management Learning & Education, 6*(3), 332–343.

Hénard, F., Diamond, L., & Roseveare, D. (2012). Approaches to internationalisation and their implications for strategic management and institutional practice. *IMHE Institutional Management in Higher Education, 11*(12), 2013.

Hernández-Chea, R., Mahdad, M., Minh, T. T., & Hjortsø, C. N. (2021). Moving beyond intermediation: How intermediary organizations shape collaboration dynamics in entrepreneurial ecosystems. *Technovation, 108*, 102332.

Isenberg D. (2011). *The entrepreneurship ecosystem strategy as a new paradigm for economy policy: Principles for cultivating entrepreneurship.* Babson Entrepreneurship Ecosystem Project, Babson College.

Isenberg, D. J. (2010). How to start an entrepreneurial revolution. *Harvard Business Review, 88*(6), 40–50.

Kishun, R. (2007). The internationalisation of higher education in South Africa: Progress and challenges. *Journal of Studies in International Education, 11*(3–4), 455–469.

Lackéus M. (2015). *Entrepreneurship in education: What, why, when, how.* Background Paper. Paris: Organisation for Economic Co-operation and Development. https://www.oecd.org/cfe/leed/bgp_entrepreneurship-in-education.pdf

Lafuente, E., Szerb, L., & Ács, Z. J. (2018, November 29). The entrepreneurship paradox: More entrepreneurs are not always good for the economy—The role of the entrepreneurial ecosystem on economic performance in Africa. *Social Science Research Network.* https://papers.ssrn.com/sol3/papers.cfm?abstract_id=3307617

Maas, G. (2015). *Systemic entrepreneurship: Contemporary issues and case studies.* Springer.

Mason, C., & Brown, R. (2014). *Entrepreneurial ecosystems and growth-oriented entrepreneurship.* Background paper for the Entrepreneurial Ecosystems and Growth Oriented Entrepreneurship Workshop, organised by the OECD LEED Programme and the Dutch Ministry of Economic Affairs, The Hague, Netherlands, November 7, 2013. *Final Report, 30*(1), 77–102.

McIntyre-Mills, J. J. M. F. E. A., Kedibone, G. M., Arko-Achemfuor, A., & Njiro, E. (2014). Participatory approach to education: An action learning approach at the University of South Africa. *Participatory Educational Research, 1*(2), 106–132.

Melass, T. (2015). Feminine touch. *JSE Magazine: The Johannesburg Stock Exchange Quarterly Publication.* Retrieved 15 January 2018, from www.jsemagazine.co.za/smes/feminine-touch/

Mujahid, S., Mubarik, S., & Naghavi, N. (2019). Prioritizing dimensions of entrepreneurial ecosystem: A proposed framework. *Journal of Global Entrepreneurship Research, 9*(1), 1–21.

NAFCOC (National African Federated Chamber of Commerce and Industry). (2021). *Nafcoc's Vision 2023.* https://nafcoc.org.za/vision-2023/

Naidoo, M., & Hoque, M. E. (2017). Reducing youth unemployment beyond the youth wage subsidy: A study of Simtech apprentices. *SA Journal of Human Resource Management, 15*(1), 1–10.

Nel, J. A. (2017). Psychological ownership in corporate South Africa: An ubuntu and social identity perspective. In C. Olckers, L. Van Zyl & L. Van der Vaart (Eds.), *Theoretical orientations and practical applications of psychological ownership.* Springer.

Nhleko, Y., & van der Westhuizen, T. (2022). The role of higher education institutions in introducing entrepreneurship education to meet the demands of industry 4.0. *Academy of Entrepreneurship Journal, 28*(1), 1–23.

Nonaka, I., Chia, R., Holt, R., & Peltokorpi, V. (2014). Wisdom, management and organization. *Management Learning, 45*(4), 365–376.

NYDA (National Youth Development Agency). (2021). *What is NYDA? Who are we?* http://www.nyda.gov.za/About-Us/What-is-NYDA

Oyugi, J. (2014). Effectiveness of the methods of teaching entrepreneurship courses to developing self-efficacy and intention among university students in Uganda. *International Journal of Social Sciences and Entrepreneurship, 1*(11), 491–513.

Parsons, T. (1951). *The social system.* The Free Press.

Paton, S., Chia, R., & Burt, G. (2014). Relevance or 'relevate'? How university business schools can add value through reflexively learning from strategic partnerships with business. *Management Learning, 45*(3), 267–288.

Penn, C., & Thomas, P. H. (2017). Bank employees' engagement in corporate social responsibility initiatives at a South African retail bank. *Acta Commercii, 17*(1), 1–10.

Pillay, K. (2015a). *Learning and the illusion of solid and separate things: Troublesome knowledge and the curriculum.* Edge Hill University Centre for Learning and Teaching University Learning and Teaching Day Conference, July 6.

Pillay, K. (2015b). *Unfolding wisdom: Theory U and the magic of nondual perception.* Proceedings of the SAIMS 29th Annual Conference, Bloemfontein, September 10–12.

Preedy, S., Jones, P., Maas, G., & Duckett, H. (2020). Examining the perceived value of extracurricular enterprise activities in relation to entrepreneurial learning processes. *Journal of Small Business and Enterprise Development, 27*(7), 1085–1105.

Rahimi, H., Amini, M., & Jahanbani, F. (2015). The place of entrepreneurial curriculum components in higher education. *International Journal of Academic Research in Business and Social Sciences, 5*(9), 263–279.

Reinhard, K., Pogrzeba, A., Townsend, R., & Pop, C. A. (2016). A comparative study of cooperative education and work-integrated learning in Germany, South Africa, and Namibia. *Asia-Pacific Journal of Cooperative Education, 17*(3), 249–263.

Remenyi, D., Grant, K. A., & Singh, S. (2019). *The university of the future.* Academic Publishing International (ACPIL).

Röpke, J. (1998). *The entrepreneurial university: Innovation, academic knowledge creation and regional development in a globalized economy.* Philipps-Universitat.

Ruba, R. M., Van der Westhuizen, T., & Chiloane- Tsoka, G. E. (2021). Influence of entrepreneurial orientation on organisational performance: Evidence from Congolese Higher Education Institutions. *Journal of Contemporary Management, 18*(1), 243–269.

SA Institute for Entrepreneurship. (2021). *About us: Who are we?* http://www.entrepreneurship.co.za/contents/who-are-we/#OurVision

SACCI (South African Chamber of Commerce and Industry). (2021). *The Voice of Business.* https://sacci.org.za/

Sahay, A., & Nirjar, A. (2006). *Entrepreneurship: Education, research and practice.* Excel Books.

Sahay, A., & Nirjar, A. (2012). *Entrepreneurship: Education, research and practice.* Excel Books.

Scharmer, C. O., & Käufer, K. (2013). *Leading from the emerging future: From ego-system to eco-system economies.* Berrett-Koehler Publishers.

Scharmer, C. O. (2009). *Theory U: Learning from the future as it emerges.* Berrett-Koehler Publishers.

Scharmer, C. O. (2011). *Leading the future as it emerges* (MA thesis). Cambridge, MA: Society of Organizational Learning, University of Cambridge.

SEFA (Small Enterprise Finance Agency). (2021). *About SEFA: Who are we.* https://www.sefa.org.za/about/history

Seta's South Africa. (2021). *About SETA South Africa: What is a SETA?* https://seta-southafrica.com/

Shirokova, G., Tsukanova, T., & Morris, M. (2013). The moderating role of national culture in the relationship between university offerings and students' start-up activities: Embeddedness perspective. *European Journal of International Management, 4,* 2–29.

Van der Westhuizen T. (2016). *Developing individual entrepreneurial orientation: A systemic approach through the lens of Theory U* (PhD thesis). Durban: UKZN.

Van der Westhuizen, T. (2017a). The use of Theory U and individual entrepreneurial orientation to increase low youth entrepreneurship in South Africa. *Journal of Contemporary Management, 14,* 531–553.

Van der Westhuizen, T. (2017b). A systemic approach towards responsible and sustainable economic development: Entrepreneurship, systems theory and socio-economic momentum. In Z. Fields (Ed.), *Collective creativity for responsible and sustainable business practice.* IGI Global.

Van der Westhuizen, T. (2018a). The SHAPE project: Shifting hope, activating potential entrepreneurship. In D. Remenyi & D. A. Grant (Ed.), *Incubators for young entrepreneurs—20 case histories.* ACPIL.

Van der Westhuizen, T. (2018b). *Open heart, open mind and open will in transformative individual entrepreneurial orientation pedagogies.* Academic Conferences and Publishing International Limited. Redding, United Kingdom, 443–448.

Van der Westhuizen, T. (2019). Action! Methods to develop entrepreneurship. In *18th European Conference on Research Methodology for Business and Management Studies* (pp. 331–337).

Van der Westhuizen, T. (2021). Applying Theory U through SHAPE to develop student's individual entrepreneurial orientation in a university eco-system. In O. Gunnlaugson & W. Brendel (Eds.), *Advances in presensing volume III: Collective approaches, in Theory U* (pp. 395–435). Trifoss Business Press.

Van der Westhuizen, T. (2022). *Effective youth entrepreneurship.* Sunbonani. https://omp.sunbonani.co.za/index.php/sunbonani/catalog/book/6

Vuk'uzenzele. (2021). *Support for youth.* https://www.vukuzenzele.gov.za/support-youth

Xavier, S., Kelley, D., Kew, J., Herrington, M., & Vorderwülbecke, A. (2013). *Global entrepreneurship monitor (GEM) 2012 global report.* GERA (Global Entrepreneurship Research Association), London Business School. https://www.gemconsortium.org/file/open?fileId=48545

Yeo, R. K., & Marquardt, M. J. (2015). (Re)interpreting action, learning, and experience: Integrating action learning and experiential learning for HRD. *Human Resource Development Quarterly, 26*(1), 81–107.

Zhao, Y., Llorente, A. M. P., & Gómez, M. C. S. (2021). Digital competence in higher education research: A systematic literature review. *Computers & Education, 168*, 104212.

Zondi, B. (2016). Industry internships gain momentum. *CSIR Science Scope, 9*(1), 104–105.

Part II

An Empirical Case Study from Theory to Practice: Developing, Implementing and Monitoring the SHAPE Youth Entrepreneur Support (YES) Network

4

Architecture of the Case Study: Developing an Ecosystem for Young Entrepreneurs

4.1 Introduction

Before youths engage with entrepreneurship, it is important to have matured internal domain heartset, mindset and handset, further, to have developed external domain support networks. The youth entrepreneurship ecosystem might ensure awareness of business opportunities and risks and how to innovatively manage them Van der Westhuizen (2017a, b), Van der Westhuizen (2018a, b, 2019, 2021). To create initiatives and research that impacts and is effective in a youth entrepreneurship ecosystem, it needs to be approached using a systemic action learning and action research (SALAR) approach in shifting hope activating potential entrepreneurship (SHAPE). This chapter describes the development of a model that details the change needed to facilitate transformation in each of these 'sets', and the establishment of a support system needed to boost IEO among students. The development and validation of the proposed model to transform and sustain change in entrepreneurial activity was done through empirical observation and evaluation of functioning within a group of identified youth.

The research design, methodology and approach positioned the researcher-practitioner to co-create novel and new theoretical models

© University of Kwazulu-Natal 2023
T. van der Westhuizen, *Youth Entrepreneurship*,
https://doi.org/10.1007/978-3-031-44339-8_4

from which youth entrepreneurship ecosystems were developed within a unique and novel context. The research was based in settings not previously appraised for the purposes of evaluation and harnessing entrepreneurial potential. Toward this end, a mixed-method approach was applied to the SALAR case-study design to measure the changes occurring throughout the implementation of the study. Case studies can study single persons or a group of persons or cases relating to a bounded phenomenon in order to relinquish in-depth insights into a particular phenomenon in a descriptive and explorative way. A qualitative approach was adopted for the purposes of allowing the input and exploration of participant experiences, as reported directly from the phenomenological viewpoint of research subjects, and repeated measures, quantitative approach for the purpose of measuring the impact at three subsequent timeframes throughout implementation. The empirical, quantitative dimension allowed for the discernible measuring of the impact of programme delivery and implementation, statistically measuring for the changes occurring within IEO and ESE at various stages of roll-out. Furthermore, measurement allowed for the refinement and consolidation of a theoretical model and refined instrumentation sensitive to measuring change occurring within ESE and IEO throughout implementation.

The practical application and implementation of the SHAPE model using SALAR was viable as it facilitated a boost of youth entrepreneurship. Adopting this approach allowed for research sensitive to empirically measuring changes occurring within entrepreneurial orientation throughout implementation. For example, when SALAR, in combination with SHAPE, were applied to facilitate youths' development of their internal and external domains, there was a noted and measurable initial decrease in youths' ESE and IEO, which thereafter showed steady and sustainable development over time was observed.

To the best of our knowledge, this is the first systematic articulation and implementation of this model and youth ecosystem and contributes original research. This study provides insights into the model, which was effectively applied over time. It can be simulated at other institutes, organisations or youth entrepreneurship development programmes. The model is generic and flexible, providing scope for adaptation and movement.

4.1.1 Systemic Action Learning and Action Research

SALAR can be described as interactive processes between local stake-holders and the researcher-practitioner that enable individuals to bring diverse knowledge and a dialogical process to a problem or challenge that allows the researcher to observe and act upon dynamics at the systemic level. SALAR is the application of interactive processes among youths and a possible support system to enable entrepreneurship. The role of educational institutes, through offering entrepreneurial education, moderates the relationships between in youth entrepreneur ecosystem's internal and external domains Adelakun and Van der Westhuizen (2021), Awotunde and Van der Westhuizen (2021a, b), Nhleko and West-huizen (2022), Ruba et al. (2021). Generic models of action learning (AL) and action research (AR) programmes traditionally include the following phases: (1) problem definition and needs analysis, (2) start-up workshops, (3) project work, (4) midway specialist workshop, (5) continuation of project work, (6) concluding workshop, (7) preparing for presentations and publications and (8) presentation and celebration.

Four phases in a typical AL programme include: (1) diagnosis of the socio-economic challenge that needs to be addressed, (2) six sequential phases to follow (analysing the challenge, developing the programme, procuring items needed for programme facilitation, construction or assembly, application and review), (3) intermediate invigoration and (4) therapeutic feedback. AL in entrepreneurship education centres on the identification of real-life challenges in relation to entrepreneurial venture establishment and operation and provides an opportunity for youths—students at an education institute—to act and reflect on the results. Thus, the AL approach cultivates problem-solving skills and invites students to reflect on solutions. As such, this research consisted of three stages divided into eleven phases. To measure impact, a conceptual instrument measuring IEO and ESE was administered at baseline, thereafter after the Pre-SHAPE, During-SHAPE and Post-SHAPE stages, in order to measure the overall change initiated through participation in the research.

An AR approach combines the generation of theory with changing the social system through the researcher acting as part of the social system.

The act itself is presented as the means of both changing the system and generating critical knowledge about it. AR takes place in a cyclical process.

While action learning and action research (ALAR) is usually applied to the internal environment of an education institute, organisation or initiative, SALAR uses a systems approach to bridge systemic disconnects by bringing together role-players from a larger system, studying the whole.

This research applied a combination of SALAR and SHAPE strategies to boost youths internal and external domains. In applying this combination, the importance of support for the programme participants from full-time professors, lecturers, tutors, researchers, peers and administrative personnel within education institutions, as well as role-players from the youth entrepreneur ecosystem external to the education institute, was emphasised to address the problem of systemic disconnect and lack of all-round support for youth entrepreneurs.

4.1.2 SHAPE Research Methodology Supporting the SALAR Design

The principal research paradigms informing the mixed-method research design is nondualism because it embraces and encompasses the ever-changing notion of human nature, and events, being true within the constraints of that time and context, but notwithstanding metaphysical certainty. This framework was intended to appreciate the nature of change, given the exposure and processes evoked through participation.

The SHAPE research strategy was informed by a mixture of both positivist and interpretivist, phenomenological and sequential mixed-method approaches. The former was employed as a repeated measures survey design to the impact of the programme by empirically measuring the changes in youth entrepreneur internal domains as baseline, mid-line and summatively after programme implementation completion. This questionnaire was re-administered two years post hoc to determine the enablers and barriers of youth entrepreneurship experienced within the entrepreneurial ecosystem.

The phenomenological leg of the study included an inductive thematic analysis of youths' reflections across the three stages of SHAPE implementation to understand the personal changes occurring on each of the three internal domains as personally experienced during SHAPE implementation. The combination of these two approaches allowed for the participants to construct and measure for themselves the development of a perceived reality through participating in SHAPE, where concepts were broken down into categories; participants deconstructed and reconstructed their perceived realities through a reflective writing process where they were required to challenge 'the me' by suspending old mental models and opening up to a possible unfragmented reality. These reflections were analysed thematically to reveal their phenomenological experiences of their lived realities, and in congruence with nondualistic notions of understanding.

Theory U's five stages include: (1) co-initiating, (2) co-sensing, (3) co-inspiring, (4) co-creating and (5) co-evolving. Theory U informed the research's conceptual framework. It allows a focus on the elements of support given to programme participants by instructors, peers and administrative personnel and focuses on the areas and domains across which change occurs and how the change is initiated. At the time of the initial research, the proposed youth entrepreneur ecosystem did not exist. It took almost 18 months of groundwork by the researcher-practitioner to form crucial relationships with role-players in the youths' external domains. It was difficult to determine like-minded, like-hearted and like-willed business friends who were willing to commit to supporting youth entrepreneur development. However, over an extensive period, key role-player buy-in was secured and participated in the SHAPE youth entrepreneur ecosystem. SALAR, informed by SHAPE strategies, provides that development occurs if there is an openness to change on an individual and collective level. However, measuring the change-impact and effectiveness of the intervention takes time as the youths mature within their entrepreneurial ecosystem. In this case, most time was spent forming and maintaining crucial relationships between the youths and their intermediaries where the researcher-practitioner played the facilitating role.

4.1.3 Designing Systemic Action Learning Action Research Phases

The eleven-phase structure of the SHAPE design and methodology components included the following phases (Fig. 4.1).

The detailed roll-out sequence of the eleven-phase structure serves as a research method for the three cycles: Pre-SHAPE, During-SHAPE and Post-SHAPE. Phases one to four took place during the Pre-SHAPE cycle and relate to Theory U aspects of Co-Initiating, Co-Sensing and Co-Inspiring. The During-SHAPE project cycle included phases five to seven and relate to all Theory U aspects. The Post-SHAPE project cycle included phases eight to eleven and relate to Theory U aspects

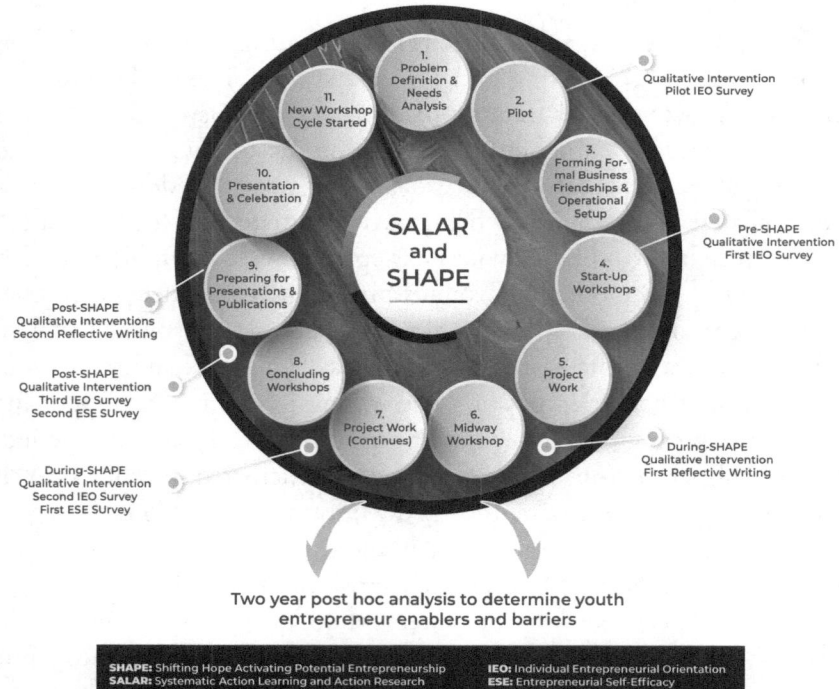

Fig. 4.1 Systemic Action Learning Action Research Phases (*Source* Van der Westhuizen [2022])

of Co-Inspiring, Co-Creating and Co-Evolving. Given the programme structure developed and outlined as above, the questionnaire was administered at baseline (Phase 2), then again during the SHAPE implementation phase, and a third time at Phase 10. This repeated measures design facilitated an empirical analysis of the impact at each of the three implementation stages (Pre-, During- and Post-SHAPE), along the IEO and ESE constructs, and in relation to changes to the innate structures occurring along Theory U.

Given the conceptual and theoretical framework, the adopted SHAPE and SALAR methodology stages were formulated as follows:

1. Pre-SHAPE (phases one to four).
2. During-SHAPE (phases five to seven).
3. Post-SHAPE (phases eight to eleven) (Fig. 4.2).

As the research design and methodological planning occurred theoretically, the researcher-practitioner needed to ask several strategic questions that possibly can guide the practical application, as listed in Fig. 4.3.

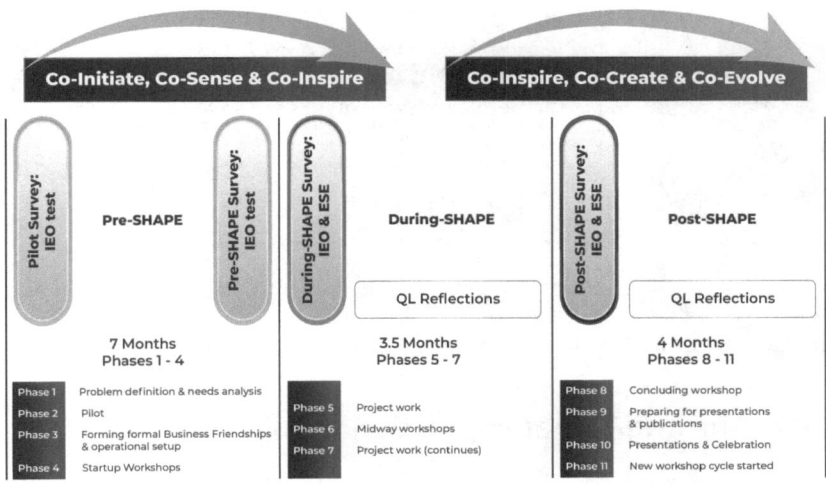

Fig. 4.2 Applying SHAPE and SALAR (*Source* Van der Westhuizen [2022])

PRE-SHAPE: co-initiate, co-sense and co-inspire

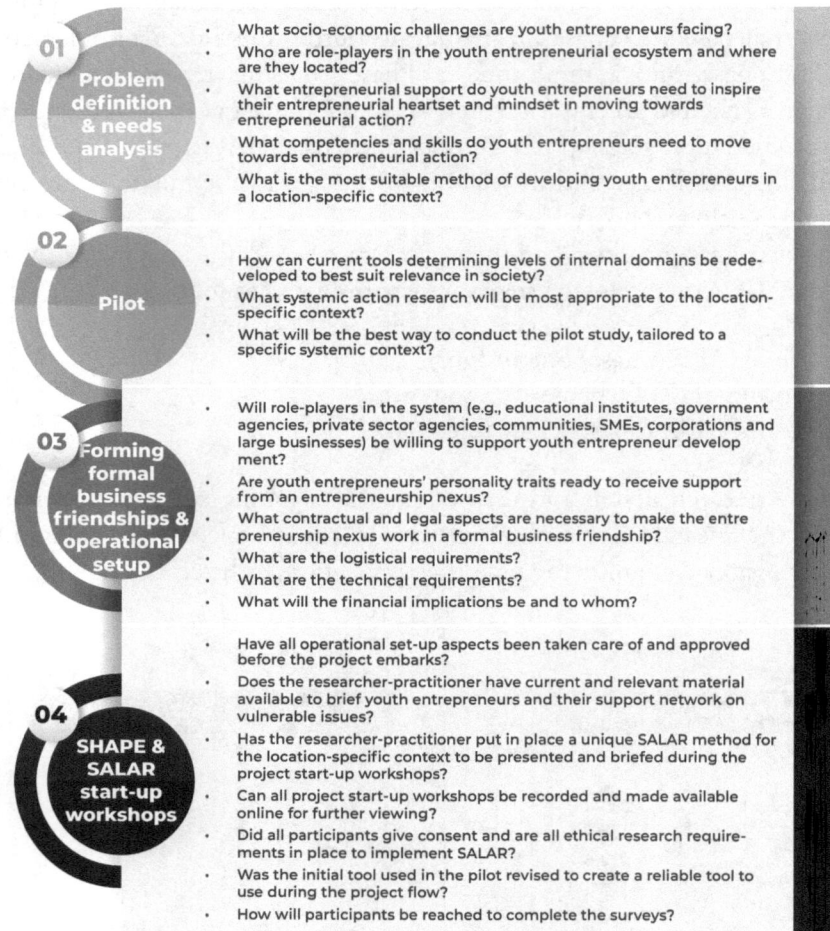

01 Problem definition & needs analysis
- What socio-economic challenges are youth entrepreneurs facing?
- Who are role-players in the youth entrepreneurial ecosystem and where are they located?
- What entrepreneurial support do youth entrepreneurs need to inspire their entrepreneurial heartset and mindset in moving towards entrepreneurial action?
- What competencies and skills do youth entrepreneurs need to move towards entrepreneurial action?
- What is the most suitable method of developing youth entrepreneurs in a location-specific context?

02 Pilot
- How can current tools determining levels of internal domains be redeveloped to best suit relevance in society?
- What systemic action research will be most appropriate to the location-specific context?
- What will be the best way to conduct the pilot study, tailored to a specific systemic context?

03 Forming formal business friendships & operational setup
- Will role-players in the system (e.g., educational institutes, government agencies, private sector agencies, communities, SMEs, corporations and large businesses) be willing to support youth entrepreneur development?
- Are youth entrepreneurs' personality traits ready to receive support from an entrepreneurship nexus?
- What contractual and legal aspects are necessary to make the entrepreneurship nexus work in a formal business friendship?
- What are the logistical requirements?
- What are the technical requirements?
- What will the financial implications be and to whom?

04 SHAPE & SALAR start-up workshops
- Have all operational set-up aspects been taken care of and approved before the project embarks?
- Does the researcher-practitioner have current and relevant material available to brief youth entrepreneurs and their support network on vulnerable issues?
- Has the researcher-practitioner put in place a unique SALAR method for the location-specific context to be presented and briefed during the project start-up workshops?
- Can all project start-up workshops be recorded and made available online for further viewing?
- Did all participants give consent and are all ethical research requirements in place to implement SALAR?
- Was the initial tool used in the pilot revised to create a reliable tool to use during the project flow?
- How will participants be reached to complete the surveys?

Fig. 4.3 Strategic Questions for applying SHAPE AND SALAR

4.1.4 Site and Target Population

To explore, model and validate the SHAPE and SALAR theoretical and conceptual frameworks of contextualised understanding of youth development within the South African entrepreneurial ecosystem, a public

DURING-SHAPE: co-initiate, co-sense, co-inspire, co-create and co-evolve

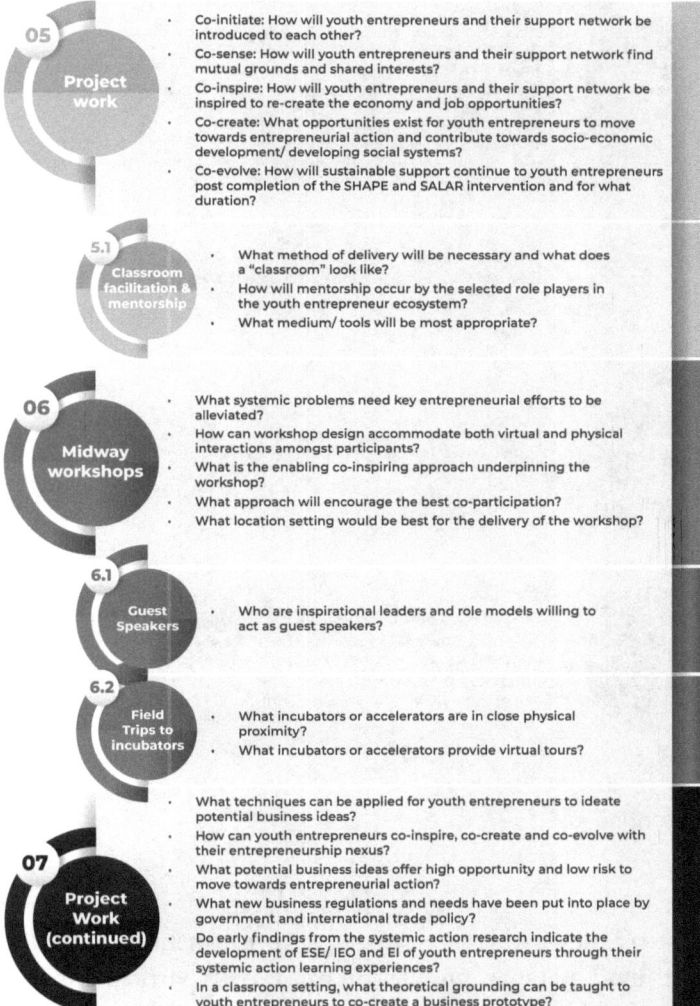

05 Project work

- Co-initiate: How will youth entrepreneurs and their support network be introduced to each other?
- Co-sense: How will youth entrepreneurs and their support network find mutual grounds and shared interests?
- Co-inspire: How will youth entrepreneurs and their support network be inspired to re-create the economy and job opportunities?
- Co-create: What opportunities exist for youth entrepreneurs to move towards entrepreneurial action and contribute towards socio-economic development/ developing social systems?
- Co-evolve: How will sustainable support continue to youth entrepreneurs post completion of the SHAPE and SALAR intervention and for what duration?

5.1 Classroom facilitation & mentorship

- What method of delivery will be necessary and what does a "classroom" look like?
- How will mentorship occur by the selected role players in the youth entrepreneur ecosystem?
- What medium/ tools will be most appropriate?

06 Midway workshops

- What systemic problems need key entrepreneurial efforts to be alleviated?
- How can workshop design accommodate both virtual and physical interactions amongst participants?
- What is the enabling co-inspiring approach underpinning the workshop?
- What approach will encourage the best co-participation?
- What location setting would be best for the delivery of the workshop?

6.1 Guest Speakers

- Who are inspirational leaders and role models willing to act as guest speakers?

6.2 Field Trips to incubators

- What incubators or accelerators are in close physical proximity?
- What incubators or accelerators provide virtual tours?

07 Project Work (continued)

- What techniques can be applied for youth entrepreneurs to ideate potential business ideas?
- How can youth entrepreneurs co-inspire, co-create and co-evolve with their entrepreneurship nexus?
- What potential business ideas offer high opportunity and low risk to move towards entrepreneurial action?
- What new business regulations and needs have been put into place by government and international trade policy?
- Do early findings from the systemic action research indicate the development of ESE/ IEO and EI of youth entrepreneurs through their systemic action learning experiences?
- In a classroom setting, what theoretical grounding can be taught to youth entrepreneurs to co-create a business prototype?
- In a mentorship setting, what strategies will the support network apply to enable the co-evolution of youth entrepreneurs?

Fig. 4.3 (continued)

POST-SHAPE: co-inspire, co-create and co-evolve

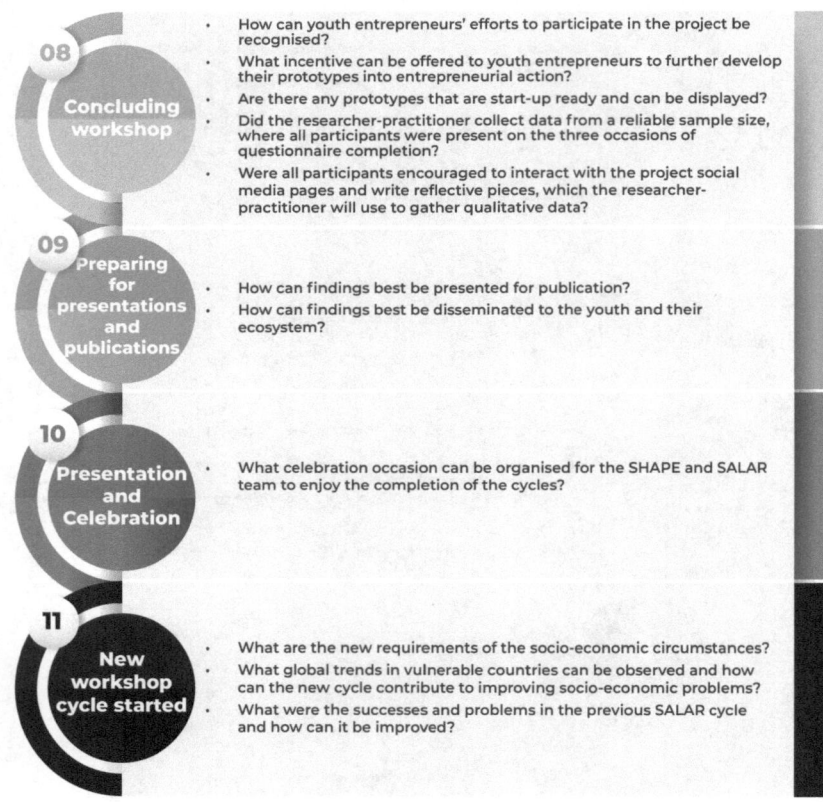

08 Concluding workshop
- How can youth entrepreneurs' efforts to participate in the project be recognised?
- What incentive can be offered to youth entrepreneurs to further develop their prototypes into entrepreneurial action?
- Are there any prototypes that are start-up ready and can be displayed?
- Did the researcher-practitioner collect data from a reliable sample size, where all participants were present on the three occasions of questionnaire completion?
- Were all participants encouraged to interact with the project social media pages and write reflective pieces, which the researcher-practitioner will use to gather qualitative data?

09 Preparing for presentations and publications
- How can findings best be presented for publication?
- How can findings best be disseminated to the youth and their ecosystem?

10 Presentation and Celebration
- What celebration occasion can be organised for the SHAPE and SALAR team to enjoy the completion of the cycles?

11 New workshop cycle started
- What are the new requirements of the socio-economic circumstances?
- What global trends in vulnerable countries can be observed and how can the new cycle contribute to improving socio-economic problems?
- What were the successes and problems in the previous SALAR cycle and how can it be improved?

Fig. 4.3 (continued)

university in South Africa and its ecosystem of youth entrepreneurs and intermediaries within the same city constituted the sample site for the case study. The target population of SHAPE participants comprised second-year students in a three-year higher degree programme at the university, within business and thus indicative of entrepreneurial intent. Non-probability, self-selection sampling was employed in the first round, while a longitudinal, repeated measures validation using the same cohort (factoring in attrition) was conducted as a follow-up two years later. Within the first phase of the study, a pilot test was administered while sample participants were in the first year of their academic studies, followed by an invitation to participate as volunteers in their second year of studies. As part of the Post-SHAPE intervention of support, study participants wished to proceed with entrepreneurial action and start-ups, the student would be supported by the university, and the youth entrepreneur ecosystem, in the third year of study. The goal was that participants graduate from the educational institute with an academic qualification and an entrepreneurial endeavour that will launch them into the world of work after exiting the education institute—hopefully leveraging their youth entrepreneur ecosystem to support further business development.

Once the first iteration of SHAPE was completed, the social technology's strategies were revised and implemented again two years later (SHAPE 2). The second iteration was based on the systemic action research findings of the first iteration's repeated testing measures, adjustments to the questionnaire and validation of previous sections were incorporated into the model of understanding using confirmatory factor analysis. During this time, some of the first iteration participants moved onto postgraduate studies; they were invited to use SHAPE as a focus area for their postgraduate research and assist during SHAPE 2. The potential was thus created for SHAPE to become a Living Theory social technology with continuous cycles of systemic action learning and action research.

4.1.5 Sampling Strategies and Sample Size

Initially, self-selection, non-probability sampling was employed to recruit participants who volunteered to join the programme after seeing the SHAPE flyers on the campus and online. Subsequently, repeated surveys were conducted throughout the SHAPE programme using convenience sampling when questionnaires were administered to the youth participants attending a programme contact session. Use of a non-probability sampling technique has ramifications for the generalisability of the research findings.

This case study presents the findings of the first iteration where 280 participants completed the Pre-SHAPE survey, 160 the During-SHAPE survey and 140 the Post-SHAPE survey. Thus, due to attrition, the final analysis of the full impact and verification of study findings in the development of the model of IEO and ESE in the youths were premised on those youths who completed the baseline, During- and Post-SHAPE phases, and participated fully in the programme. Youth Entrepreneur Ecosystem intermediaries participated during these phases and were investigated, but this data is not presented in this book. The sample size was determined by set criteria as the practitioner-researcher was interested in those participants who had completed three rounds of questionnaires and provided qualitative data, primarily through writing reflections, with the final size of the sample being 60. A census of 60 first iteration who completed the programme fully were surveyed in the post hoc analysis and verification of findings two years after the first iteration to determine the enablers and barriers experienced over time.

4.1.6   Data Collection Methods

Primary data was collected quantitatively through the questionnaire survey method and qualitative data through written reflections from research participants. Quantitative data analytics were performed for each of the three phases to gain a snapshot into cross-sectional segments of student IEO and ESE orientations, and across the three phases as a repeated measure in order to determine temporal changes and areas of impact affected by participation in the programme.

The questionnaire consisted of three sections pertaining to measuring the constructs of IEO and ESE, breaking them down into the theoretically informed sections of Theory U, and consisted of three sections relating to student Individual Entrepreneurial Orientation, Risk-taking, Opportunity Identification, Entrepreneurial Self-Efficacy and Individual Orientation using a 4- and 7-point Likert scale.

Qualitative data was collected through (a) qualitative reflections from the researcher-practitioner (the last chapter of the book) and (b) a blog (www.shapentrepreneurs.com) as administered by the principal investigator and a social media page on Facebook.

The two-year follow-up confirmatory analysis was performed using a telephonic survey to determine enablers and barriers experienced by youths in entrepreneurial activities subsequent to their participation in SHAPE. The survey comprised eight sections, each within the context of being independent variables of the youth entrepreneur ecosystem. Seven sections related to the seven domains of the SHAPE entrepreneurial ecosystem and one section to biographical and demographic details. A seven-point Likert scale was used to capture the participants' responses in two test formats with measure descriptors as 'agree/disagree' and 'extent'. Certain question items were negatively phrased:

#8—I consider my personality traits to hinder my progress in becoming an entrepreneur.

#10—I have experienced difficulty accessing financial support to start my own business.

#11—Coming up with ideas, especially on-the-spot creative thinking, is challenging when planning a business.

#12—Decision-making is challenging for me when planning a new business.

#33—I feel my community does not have an entrepreneurial attitude.

4.1.7 Data Quality Control

Quantitative data measures of quality were achieved in this study. The test/re-test approach achieved reliability because stability was tracked over time, and the extent to which results compare was determined as retesting ensued. Construct validity was also achieved as the tests were designed to reveal, and did reveal, significant associations with the underlying theories. In addition, a high degree of convergent validity as multiple different methods for measuring a construct (IEO, ESE, Theory U concepts) emerged in the youths' reflections and their questionnaire responses. Additionally, data was triangulated utilising multiple sources of data, collected using multiple methods and using multiple investigators. Thus, through the use of data and methodological triangulation (survey responses and student reflections), credibility was assured. Confirmability was achieved through follow-up with participants and reflections and feedback sessions. Dependability was also established through extensive documentation by the practitioner-researcher of all changes and observations over time, firstly, by incorporating the test/re-test in the research design and using the student reflections at multiple points throughout the study. This meant that careful attention was paid to documenting all the raw data generated, assessing the method of data analysis, the way the data was kept and the accuracy of the data. Moreover, to establish confirmability.

4.1.8 Data Analysis

Chapter 5 presents qualitative findings of the youths' reflections in the During-SHAPE stage to better understand the youths' journey with SHAPE and SALAR. Youths were asked to write reflections published on the project website, which was analysed thematically. NVivo 10 Pro was used to analyse the qualitative data generated from student reflections as captured on the SHAPE website and exported into Google Drive. The purpose of investigating the qualitative reflections of participants was to determine whether their entrepreneurial heartset, mindset and handset developed through the co-initiation, co-sensing, co-inspiring, co-creating and co-evolving strategies of SHAPE. A qualitative thematic analysis of data was used where themes were allowed to emerge from the data. From the inductive coding process, themes and nodes emerged from the text and were identified, along with simultaneous sub-themes and sub-nodes, which will be discussed in their entirety in the following chapter.

Chapters 6–9 present findings from the post hoc, follow-up or second iteration relating to the enablers and barriers experienced by youth entrepreneurs in relation to engaging in or initiating any entrepreneurial activities. Quantitative statistical data analysis was conducted to assess and measure respondent IEO, particularly concerning innovation, proactivity and the five factors underpinning Theory U. A test/re-test, repeated measures methodology was followed across the three test conditions (Pre-SHAPE, During-SHAPE and Post-SHAPE). Scores on each dimension were tested statistically utilising a repeated measures ANOVA or, where applicable, the Friedman Test to determine the impact of participation in SHAPE in relation to the test criteria.

Parametric tests are based on theoretical distributions allowing for inferences to be made about populations based on sample data. Data was subjected to testing relating to univariate and multivariate parametric assumptions, and where unsuitable to parametric testing, non-parametric tests (distribution-free tests) were employed to analyse the data. Scores relating to each construct were aggregated to produce continuous outcomes, at times, facilitative of the necessary parametric tests.

4.1.9 Ethical Considerations

Prior to the commencement of the pilot test and the SHAPE project, ethical clearance was obtained from the selected university. Participants to the pilot test signed an informed consent form (ICF) detailing the risks and benefits of participation, prior to administration of the questionnaires. Collaboration agreements on youth development programmes were already in place between the selected university, government agencies and some private sector agencies. Permission for photos to be taken was sought from participants, where applicable. Written consent and indemnity were also obtained from each participant whenever a field trip or workshop took place, and consent was provided for access to participants in the future for potential follow-up studies.

4.1.10 Limitations of the Case Study

The case is presented on a selected site and further research is needed on multiple sites and creating multiple youth entrepreneur ecosystems. The findings can therefore not be generalisable to contexts outside of the embedded study population, truly reflective and characteristic of case-study research but do provide novel and valuable insights. Further limitations are:

- Non-probability sampling took place where youths in their second year chose to voluntarily participate in the project. The result might be different if the youths who did not volunteer to participate were observed and tested.
- The result might be different if the SHAPE were done among different levels of undergraduate (first or third year) or postgraduate (honours, masters, doctorate and beyond).
- Young people enrolled at universities or educational institutions other than the selected site were not taken into consideration.
- Young people in general (employed or unemployed), other than youths enrolled in the selected education institute, were not taken into consideration.
- For the purpose of this book, only the observations, tests and reflections of the youths are presented. Data were, however, also collected (through surveys, reflective report writing and observations) from a wider set of participants who included intermediaries associated with the youth entrepreneur ecosystem. It is recommended that future research should also take these data into account and perhaps compare intermediaries' perceptions to those of the youth.
- All SHAPE processes, procedures and operational aspects were initiated and developed by the practitioner-researcher. The results might have been different had the intervention has been implemented by somebody else.
- More case-study research can be done on deep-learning and other seminal entrepreneurship programmes around the world.

4.2   Conclusion

This chapter described the systemic action learning and action research, case-study design and methodology through presenting a case study where the youth entrepreneur ecosystem was created and assessed over time. It is recommended that more similar case-study research is conducted to provide a better comparative idea of the effective application of theoretical models when creating a youth entrepreneur ecosystem.

References

Adelakun, Y., & Van der Westhuizen, T. (2021). Delineating government policies and individual entrepreneurial orientation. *Journal of Sociology and Social Anthropology, 12*(3–4), 106–117. https://doi.org/10.31901/245 66764.2021/12.3-4.371

Awotunde, O. M., & Van der Westhuizen, T. (2021a). Entrepreneurial self-efficacy development: An effective intervention for sustainable student entrepreneurial intentions. *International Journal of Innovation and Sustainable Development, 15*(4), 475–495.

Awotunde, O. M., & Van der Westhuizen, T. (2021b, September). Entrepreneurial self-efficacy and the SHAPE ideation model for university students. In *ECIE 2021 16th European Conference on Innovation and Entrepreneurship Vol 1* (p. 37).

Nhleko, Y., & van der Westhuizen, T. (2022). The role of higher education institutions in introducing entrepreneurship education to meet the demands of industry 4. 0. *Academy of Entrepreneurship Journal, 28*(1), 1–23.

Ruba, R. M., Van der Westhuizen, T., & Chiloane-Tsoka, G. E. (2021). Influence of entrepreneurial orientation on organisational performance: Evidence from Congolese Higher Education Institutions. *Journal of Contemporary Management, 18*(1), 243–269.

Van der Westhuizen, T. (2017a). The use of Theory U and individual entrepreneurial orientation to increase Low Youth Entrepreneurship in South Africa. *Journal of Contemporary Management, 14*, 531–553.

Van der Westhuizen, T. (2017b). A systemic approach towards responsible and sustainable economic development: entrepreneurship, systems theory and socio-economic momentum. In Z. Fields (Ed.), Collective creativity for responsible and sustainable business practice. IGI Global.

Van der Westhuizen, T. (2018a). The SHAPE Project: Shifting hope, activating potential entrepreneurship. In D. Remenyi & D. A. Grant (Eds.), *Incubators for young entrepreneurs—20 case histories*. ACPIL.

Van der Westhuizen, T. (2018b). *Open heart, open mind and open will in transformative individual entrepreneurial orientation pedagogies* (pp. 443–448). Academic Conferences and Publishing International Limited.

Van der Westhuizen, T. (2019). Action! Methods to develop entrepreneurship. In *18th European Conference on Research Methodology for Business and Management Studies* (pp. 331–337).

Van der Westhuizen, T. (2021). Applying Theory U through SHAPE to develop student's individual entrepreneurial orientation in a university eco-system. In O. Gunnlaugson & W. Brendel (Eds.), *Advances in presensing volume III: Collective approaches, in Theory U* (pp. 395–435). Trifoss Business Press.

Van der Westhuizen, T. (2022). *Effective youth entrepreneurship*. Sunbonani. https://omp.sunbonani.co.za/index.php/sunbonani/catalog/book/6

5

The SHAPE Youth Entrepreneur Support Network to Develop University Students' Individual Entrepreneurial Orientation

Purpose: Before engaging with entrepreneurship, it is important to have an individual entrepreneurial orientation (IEO), which ensures the psychological development of entrepreneurial behaviour. This may be achieved through the shifting hope activating potential entrepreneurship (SHAPE) youth entrepreneur support (YES) network and systemic action learning and action research (SALAR) models.

Design/ Methodology/ Approach: A theoretical framework for SHAPE and SALAR was created as a basis for the development and application of a youth entrepreneur support network for university students. The theoretical framework and empirical model were validated through a series of assessments. A mixed methods approach was applied to the SALAR design.

Findings: Practical implementation of the SHAPE YES Network and SALAR models was viable and allowed us to facilitate student entrepreneurship. An initial decrease in students' individual entrepreneurial orientation with steady sustainable development over time was observed.

This study describes the development of a youth entrepreneur support network to inspire IEO development among students. This support

© University of Kwazulu-Natal 2023
T. van der Westhuizen, *Youth Entrepreneurship*,
https://doi.org/10.1007/978-3-031-44339-8_5

network was validated by observing and evaluating its functioning with a group of students. The purpose of this study was to determine if the combination of SHAPE and SALAR is an effective intervention for improving IEO of students when synthesised into the youth entrepreneur support framework.

Originality: To the best of our knowledge, this is the first systematic articulation and implementation of the framework for the youth entrepreneur support network, and the 11-cycle SALAR model to address the theoretical and practical gaps in our knowledge of IEO development. This study provides insights into the framework and model, which were effectively applied over time. The research can be simulated at other institutes, organisations, or youth entrepreneurship development programmes. The SHAPE youth entrepreneur support framework and SALAR model are generic and flexible, providing scope for adaptation. The research contributes to bridging the theoretical, practical and methodological gaps on SALAR to develop IEO through SHAPE.

5.1　Introduction

Vulnerable populations such as youth entrepreneurs in developing countries are under potential threat from individuals or groups within their larger systemic context.[1] It is fundamental to build a healthy socioeconomic systemic context where youth is facilitated at university level to engage in a youth entrepreneur support (YES) network. Before engaging with entrepreneurship, it is important to have an individual entrepreneurial orientation (IEO), which ensures awareness and innovative management of business opportunities and risks. For university students, this orientation may be achieved through participating in a YES Network where systemic action learning and action research (SALAR) is applied.[2] Creating a tailored location and specific YES Network to

---

[1] SAG (2021) and UNDP (2020).
[2] Schweikert et al. (2013).

support university students,[3] and developing students' IEO are theoretically suggested methods to address systemic challenges in youth entrepreneurship.[4] This significant challenge is taken up in this research.

On the issue of whether public higher education institutions in developing countries can provide necessary skills and learning for entrepreneurial development in emerging economies, Chia's[5] comment is apposite, that a radical change in intellectual and educational priorities is needed. Building on almost two decades of empirical research on entrepreneurship education in developing countries, Scharmer and Kaufer[6] recommended that a deeper dimension to entrepreneurship learning is needed. Gaps in the literature indicate that an experiential learning programme (or action learning programme) in a South African context is needed to enable a paradigm shift among youth entrepreneurs and their support structure (called intermediaries), to advance socio-economic development in pursuit of the National Development Vision.[7]

With pedagogy in the field of entrepreneurship shifting the emphasis from classroom teaching to action learning, static and content-oriented teaching, according to Sahay and Nirjar,[8] is no longer appropriate in South Africa's complex and change-driven society. When it comes to teaching entrepreneurship, traditional educational methods which focus on theory and information are now regarded as inappropriate both for the content and for the pedagogy.[9]

Entrepreneurship curriculum pedagogies based on discovery theory and creation theory provide a basis for shifting from static classroom approaches to an action learning methodology. Most current undergraduate curricula in South African higher education have adopted principles from discovery theory where the emphasis is on creativity,

---

[3] Bezerra et al. (2017) and Miller and Acs (2017).
[4] Scharmer (2018) and Van der Westhuizen (2017a, b).
[5] Chia (2014).
[6] Scharmer and Kaufer (2013).
[7] Chia (2014).
[8] Sahay and Nirjar (2012).
[9] Oyugi (2014).

scanning, shaping ideas and developing business plans.[10] In developing and presenting an entrepreneurship programme, there needs to be a suitable process to help aspirant entrepreneurs assimilate entrepreneurial practice, with action-focused, appealing themes that are student-oriented and encourage reflective thinking.[11] In the constantly evolving South African context, there is also a case for pedagogic approaches that draw on creation theory, where the emphasis is on overall programme process and how ideas transform over time and where programme participants have the opportunity to practise in adapting initial ideas in response to new knowledge and information. Benefits of such an entrepreneurship programme include creation of an environment of experiential learning or action learning. In this way, the programme helps to promote self-direction and adaptability in its participants. It then becomes possible to assess the impact of entrepreneurship, whereas, traditionally, programme participants would merely be allocated a 'pass' or 'fail'. The cyclical approach of the experiential or action learning process thus shapes students into lifelong learners.[12]

Teaching and learning practices adopting Scharmer's Theory U as an enabling vehicle to bring the shift required by the creation theory have had proven success at the Presencing Institute (Harvard) and at a number of its international higher education partners.[13] Entrepreneurship programmes in South Africa face a number of challenges, among which are the following:

- *Making students aware of socio-economic change.* Scharmer[14] believes that society has a blind spot in relation to a deeper dimension of systemic change. This could be attributed to the systems thinking paradigm where systems are seen only as interconnected and interrelated—which might imply fragmentation of systems.[15] The current era calls for innovative cognition processes adopting a nondual

---

[10] Rahimi et al. (2015).
[11] Chia (2014).
[12] Rahimi et al. (2015).
[13] Scharmer and Kaufer (2013).
[14] Scharmer (2009).
[15] Pillay (2014).

perspective where systems are perceived as a whole, with one source.[16] Scharmer[17] notes also that this might allow youth to create a future of greater opportunities.

- *Enhancing levels of individual entrepreneurial orientation.* Strategy-making processes in both public and private sector organisations can provide a basis for entrepreneurial initiatives and create opportunities for young people to be involved in decisions and actions.[18]
- *Developing a youth entrepreneur support network in the university's internal and external environment.* In South Africa, it is difficult for student entrepreneurs to engage with a nexus of supportive inter-mediaries.[19] Not enough corporate, small- or medium-sized business owners are willing to form business friendships with youth entrepreneurs to harness their entrepreneurial drive and help them to develop sustainable entrepreneurial skills.[20] Many government agencies, such as local municipalities and private sector agencies such as local chambers of commerce, provide support programmes for nascent entrepreneurs, but there is an ongoing problem of disconnect between the support agencies and youth entrepreneurs.

Given the context above, the objectives of the study are:

- to develop a theoretical youth entrepreneur support framework for university students in a public university in a developing country;
- to co-create the proposed youth entrepreneur support framework in practice; and
- to determine if the combination of SHAPE and SALAR is an effective intervention for improving IEO of students when synthesised into the youth entrepreneur support framework.

---

[16] Pillay (2014).
[17] Scharmer (2009).
[18] Bolton and Lane (2012).
[19] Dhliwayo (2008).
[20] DTI (2020).

5.2   Theoretical Framework

To fill the research gap identified in the introduction, we focused on building a theoretical framework based on theories of SALAR and IEO.

5.2.1 Systemic Action Learning and Action Research

Systemic Action Research and Action Learning is a conceptual approach to connect university students to their entrepreneurial support network (Fig. 5.1) and impacts systemic levels.[21] The effectiveness of SALAR as a long-term approach is evident in developed countries like Switzerland with its Creative Living Lab,[22] but there little knowledge about tailoring this approach for developing countries such as South Africa. When studying university students' behaviour development within an entrepreneurial ecosystem, SALAR can be applied as both a conceptual approach and research design[23] however leaving a gap in empirical evidence in a South African context.

SALAR comprises interactive processes between local stakeholders and researchers that enable individuals to bring diverse knowledge and a dialogical process to a problem or challenge that allows the researcher to observe and act upon dynamics at the systemic level.[24] Theoretically, SALAR can moderate the relationships among propensities of the IEO, entrepreneurial creativity and entrepreneurial intent, and is an important approach for researchers to use when designing a systemic intervention to support youth entrepreneurship.[25]

Existing literature on SALAR describes its processes and the "how to" of the approach, but to our knowledge, there is no existing framework to position SALAR. There is a strong case to argue that the concepts and theories relating to action learning and action research (ALAR) are

---

[21] Van der Westhuizen (2019a, b).
[22] Schweikert et al. (2013).
[23] Paton (2001) and Burns (2007).
[24] Van der Westhuizen (2019a, b).
[25] Shahab et al. (2019).

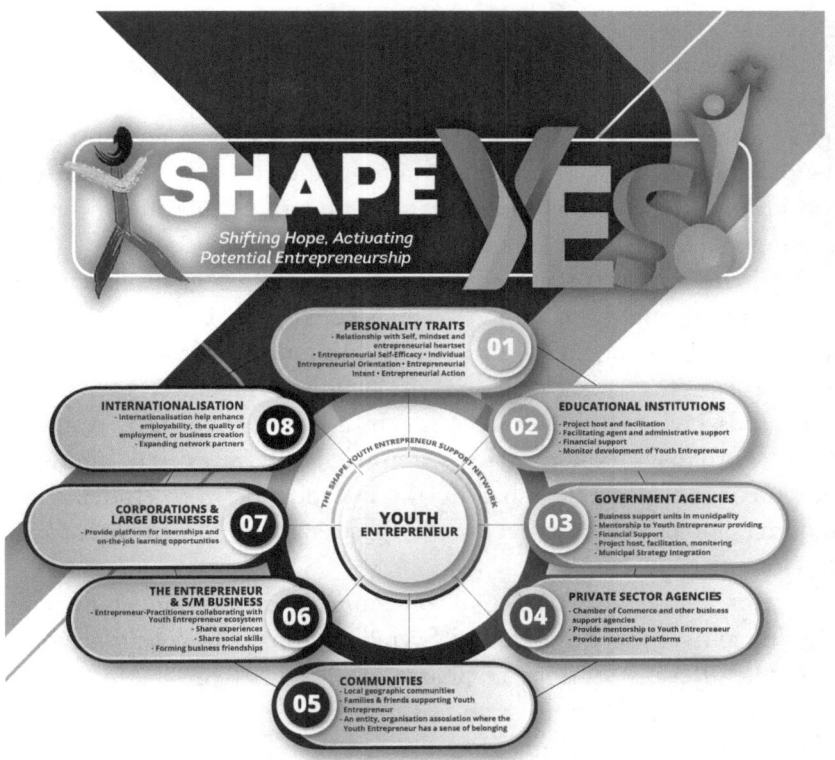

Van der Westhuizen, T. 2023. Effective Youth Entrepreneurship. Sunbonani Scholar. South Africa. 447 pages.

Fig. 5.1   The SHAPE YES Network for youth entrepreneurs (expanded) (*Source* Van der Westhuizen, T. [2023]. Effective youth entrepreneurship. SunBonani Scholar (447 pp.). South Africa)

the foundation of SALAR. Zuber-Skerritt[26] developed generic models of ALAR with the following phases: (1) problem definition and needs analysis; (2) start-up workshops; (3) project work; 4) midway specialist workshop; (5) continuation of project work; (6) concluding workshop; (7) preparing for presentations and publications; and (8) presentation and celebration. These occur systematically and cyclically. Action learning means learning from action or concrete experience, as well as taking action as a result of this learning. Similarly, action research is

---

[26] Zuber-Skerritt (2002).

a cyclical iterative process of action and reflection on and in action.[27] ALAR provides appropriate methodologies and processes for (re)creating change, innovation, leadership and personal, professional and organisational learning. This is because they are more enduring and sustainable than traditional ways of learning, training and research.[28] A theoretical background to ALAR is important as it underpins this study's research methodology.

While ALAR is usually applied to the internal environment of a university, organisation, or initiative, SALAR uses a systems approach to bridge systemic disconnects by bringing together role-players from a larger system, studying the whole. Therefore, the application holds potential to be successful in a systemic context. Ammirato et al.[29] proposed that a systems approach integrates and interrelates entrepreneurial processes, shaping the interplay between students' IEO and the opportunities they pursue to strengthen the socio-economic development system.

In this study, SALAR builds on Zuber-Skerritt's model of action learning and adopts Susman and Evered's[30] approach to action research to further Revans' notion on phases of an ALAR programme.[31] This research applied a further synthesis of the SHAPE YES Network and SALAR to develop students' IEO.

5.2.2 Developing Individual Entrepreneurial Orientation

Bolton and Lane[32] described IEO as a spin-off concept from EO, relating specifically to human behaviour with three propensities: risk-taking, innovativeness and proactivity. The effectiveness of the concept

---

[27] Zuber-Skerritt (2002).
[28] Zuber-Skerritt (2002).
[29] Ammirato et al. (2019).
[30] Susman and Evered's (1978).
[31] Van der Westhuizen (2016).
[32] Bolton and Lane (2012).

of EO has been debated over several decades, and there is disagree-ment on using the terminologies EO and IEO, which are sometime used interchangeably.[33] This study uses Bolton and Lane's definition.

IEO is purported to facilitate effective entrepreneurship among university students through introducing a psychological change,[34] but there is a gap in knowledge on its successful application among students within a South African and African context. IEO is an important psycho-logical component of the entrepreneurial mindset and heartset which can possibly lead to increase entrepreneurial intent and actions through risk-taking, innovation and proactivity.[35] IEO is enhanced by feeling a sense of inspiration which can be caused by internal or external stim-ulae.[36] When feeling inspired, an individual might be able to keep the inner flame or entrepreneurial spirit alive for prolonged periods.[37] Increased feelings of inspiration also lead to higher self-efficacy to engage with risk-taking, innovation and proactivity which in turn results in further processes, practices and decision-making activities that lead to entrepreneurship.[38] Academic programmes at South African universi-ties are not directed at developing the entrepreneurial spirit of students, but rather focus on theoretical commerce aspects. Mediating the effect of IEO might provide students with an opportunity to redesign their envisioned business value chain and effectively connect to their support entrepreneurial system.[39] Franke and Lüthje[40] have noted that the entrepreneurial decision-making process is influenced by external and internal factors. Internal domain factors for IEO include risk-taking, innovation and proactivity while external domain factors relate to society, the economy, technology, competition and politics.[41] IEO leads the way for an individual's innovative actions, and reactiveness is associated with

---

[33] Mondal and Chakrabarti (2021).

[34] Van der Westhuizen (2017a, b).

[35] Teles et al. (2021) and Nhleko and Van der Westhuizen (2022).

[36] Weinberg (2011).

[37] Steenberg (2017).

[38] Bolton and Lane (2012).

[39] Urban and Galawe (2019).

[40] Franke and Lüthje (2004).

[41] Ljungkvist et al. (2019) and Nhleko and Van der Westhuizen (2022).

an individual's response to competitors or external stimuli.[42] Mahrous and Genedy[43] emphasised the importance of systemically connecting the dots to develop IEO, which might lead to increased socio-economic success in developing countries.

Theory U processes of co-initiation, co-sensing, co-inspiring and co-creation were applied in this study to connect stakeholders with one another in the SHAPE YES Network and boost IEO for both youths and their possible support systems.[44] The IEO propensity of risk-taking relates to co-initiating and co-sensing by enabling interpersonal and intrapersonal discussions between youths and their possible support systems (Fig. 5.2).

The enabling vehicle in this case is the SHAPE intervention, through entrepreneurship education at a South African public university. During the SHAPE intervention, the IEO propensity of innovation correlates with co-inspiring students and role-players in their support system by ideating collectively to bring their entrepreneurial dreams into action and designing a model or business prototype.[45] The IEO propensity of proactivity correlates with co-creating and co-evolving by supporting students to take entrepreneurial action during the intervention proposed in this case study. During co-creation of the intervention, students develop an expanded business model canvas and strengthen their value chain of future entrepreneurial support. They enable themselves to start up their business and demonstrate an increase in the developmental maturity of their IEO, becoming capable of re-powering themselves to lead their entrepreneurial endeavours with the support of the system they create.[46]

Theoretically, it is possible to develop students' IEO when SHAPE and SALAR are applied interactively, but there is little empirical evidence to prove success. Addressing this gap led to the research design of this case study.

---

[42] Lumpkin and Dess (2001).
[43] Mahrous and Genedy (2019).
[44] Van der Westhuizen (2017a, b).
[45] Scharmer (2018).
[46] Van der Westhuizen (2017a, b).

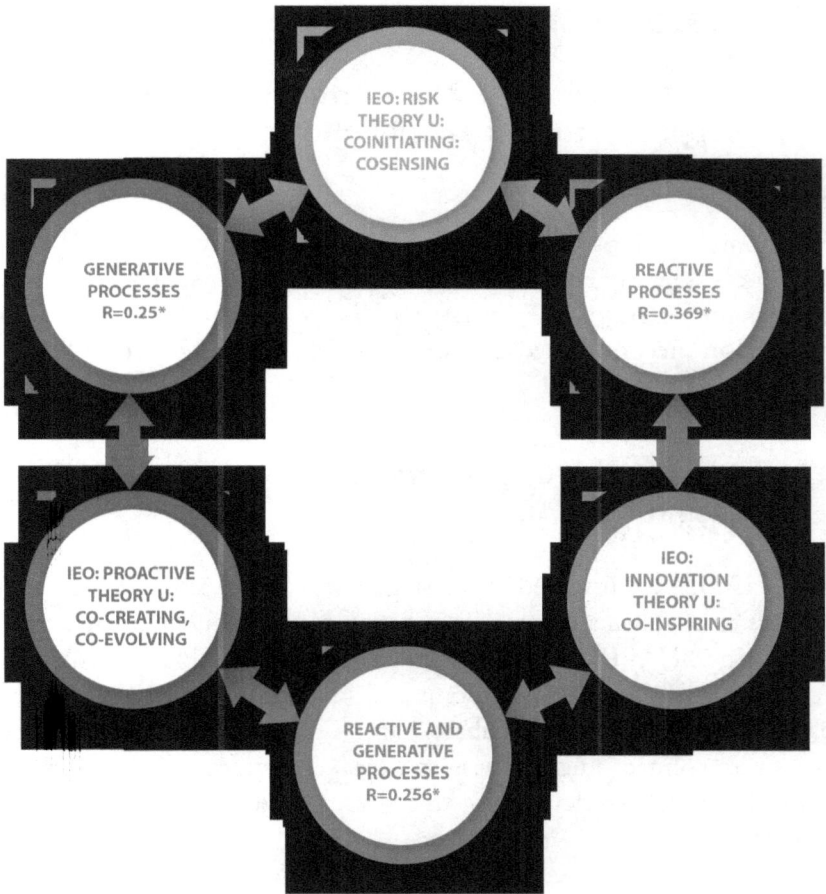

Fig. 5.2 Individual Entrepreneurial Orientation and Theory U

5.3   Research Methods

5.3.1 Developing the SHAPE Youth Entrepreneur Support Network and Tailoring the SALAR Model

The research design's first step was to practically form the SHAPE YES Network by identifying role-players from each of the segments in Fig. 5.1 and bringing them together to agree on the purpose and vision. Creating the support network needed seven months of groundwork, which is referred to as 'pre-SHAPE'.

5.3.2 Architecture of the Three Stages of the SHAPE Case for SALAR

The SHAPE case involved three stages: (i) Pre-SHAPE, in which the aim was to establish a strategic foundation for subsequent enhancement; (ii) During-SHAPE, in which the aim was to provide students with facilitated workshops (in classrooms and small-group guided mentorship sessions) and field trips to incubators and (iii) Post-SHAPE, in which the aim was to connect students with strategic, ecosystemic role-players who might contribute to developing their business idea or prototype into a start-up.

5.3.3 Architecture of the 11 Phases in the Different SHAPE Stages

The pre-SHAPE stage relates to Phases 1–4, while during-SHAPE relates to Phases 5–7 and post-SHAPE relates to Phases 8–11 (Fig. 5.3).

Phase 1: Problem definition and needs analysis. The empirical literature review, (or theory), suggested establishing what was appropriate and feasible for the collective to work on in the upcoming ALAR. The practical application of the theory, that is, the praxis, included an additional literature review and several stakeholder colloquia with role-players in the support system for youth entrepreneurs. The colloquia involved

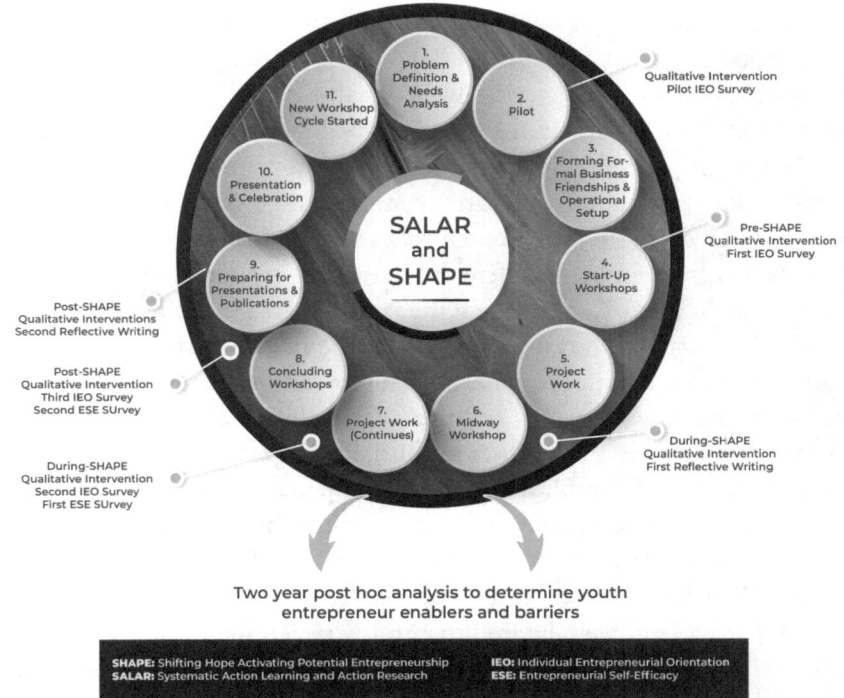

Fig. 5.3   SHAPE and SALAR

extensive discussions on the problem of high youth unemployment and ideation on possible measures to boost youth entrepreneurship.

After the problem definition and needs analysis, the researchers decided that the target population was students who volunteered to participate in the SHAPE initiative. The selection criteria were full-time enrolment in the selected university and good academic standing.

Phase 2: Pilot. The theory suggested that a pilot systemic AL workshop be developed if there was a need among youths for this. The praxis initially deployed purposive sampling to recruit participants. This involved circulation of an invitation to youths who met the following criteria: they were (1) enrolled in the selected university; (2) registered full-time in a commerce-related field; (3) in good academic standing and (4) in their second year of studies. This was executed through public information session presentations, direct emails and university-wide notices, posters and flyers. Public invitations on social media platforms were created specifically to enable SHAPE to attract youth participants in and beyond the KwaZulu-Natal province of South Africa. Those wishing to participate needed to submit an online registration form so the likely number of participants could be estimated. All youths who registered online were invited to a co-initiation session in a facility equipped with computers, where the researcher explained the purpose of SHAPE with SALAR, after which the youths were given the opportunity to withdraw or proceed to participate in the first quantitative intervention, i.e. the completion of the IEO survey online in the facility, with the researcher present. This occurred three times in one week, owing to the large number of youths who initially expressed interest. From an initial group of 255 applicants, 120 participated in the IEO survey. As the group might still have been too large to effectively apply SHAPE and SALAR to boost IEO, a further criterion was added: the ability to attend class on Tuesdays between 12:00 and 14:00. Of the 120 youths, 80 who were able to attend were invited to enrol with 60 finally enrolling.

Phase 3: Forming formal business friendships and operational setup. The theory emphasised the importance of forming and maintaining crucial relationships with systemic role-players who can support youth IEO development. In praxis, this phase built on the actions taken in Phase 1, continuing over seven months of continuous co-initiating, co-sensing and co-inspiring. The needs analysis and findings from Phases 1 and 2 served as the building blocks of this phase. After it was ideated, initial stakeholder engagements took place over 18 months before the SHAPE stages commenced. This was favourably received by the local municipality business support unit, local chamber of commerce and local economic development unit for KwaZulu-Natal, which volunteered to make mentors available weekly to support youths during-SHAPE and to contribute in kind; e.g. by including youths in email databases that disseminated news and opportunities for entrepreneurship, by waiving fees for using facilities and by expanding systemic support networks.

Phase 4: Start-up workshop. The theory recommended that this phase include the initiation of teamwork, preferably at an independent venue, away from participants' usual locations. Focal points could include principles of systemic action learning, methods, design and further project planning. The praxis involved deploying further co-initiating, co-sensing and co-inspiring strategies to explore the expectations, intent and vision behind the students' participation in SHAPE. This was done through a facilitated session during which youths were introduced to the support system they would have while participating in SHAPE: facilitators; administrators; operational staff; mentors from the local municipality, the local chamber of commerce, the local economic development unit and successful entrepreneurs from the private sector. Youths were required to attend a weekly formal facilitated session presented by the researcher and specialist guest presenters, as well as additional sessions presented by the mentors.

Phase 5: Project work. The theory suggested that this phase should include data collection, analysis, feedback, interpretation, ongoing literature review and regular SHAPE meetings to monitor progress. In praxis, the methodology includes the continuation of the co-initiating, co-sensing and co-inspiring strategies. The thirteen-workshop sequence associated with these applied strategies is available on YouTube: https://youtube.com/playlist?list=PLaDa69Xxxbv2Rw4-3kD8UnhG95PxDpqCP.

Phase 6: Midway specialist workshop. The theory recommended that this phase include a review of and reflection on progress by the researcher and stakeholders, bringing in outside experts whose input could help focus the discussion and thinking. The praxis involved introducing youths in Week 8 to successful entrepreneurs, innovators, investors and international sportspersons. The specialists spoke about the challenges and successes in their own entrepreneurial journeys and our discussions explored the importance of ethics in business and entrepreneurship. Youth IEO was purposefully boosted through the encouragement of network formation with the business sector.

Phase 7: Project work (continued). The theory suggested that in this phase, fieldwork should be resumed and focused on in the light of ongoing reflection. The praxis included a field trip, co-ordinated by municipality mentors and the researcher. The field trip came about as an intervention after the youths indicated, in previous phases, their desire to visit incubators. The municipality mentor took them to three municipal-supported incubators located in different areas in Durban, a city in KwaZulu-Natal. Youths observed how other entrepreneurs, with little or no savings to invest in getting their businesses off the ground, had engaged with the entrepreneurial conceptual process. Further, the trip enabled them to see how government entrepreneurship support programmes had helped entrepreneurs start-up their businesses. Thereafter, the youths were introduced to creating their own business model canvas. Strategies of co-initiating, co-sensing, co-inspiring and co-creating were applied. Youths were required to complete the IEO surveys for a second time.

Phase 8: Concluding workshop. The theory proposed that, in this stage, project teams should come together to present and discuss their learnings and solutions. The praxis unfolded in the form of 'Meet Your Business Friend Day', organised and attended by youths; systemic role-players who could potentially support youth entrepreneurship were also invited. SHAPE mentors sent invitations to their extended networks of successful entrepreneurs located in KwaZulu-Natal; 73 agreed to attend. This one-day workshop aimed to introduce youths to business professionals to explore possibilities of further entrepreneurial action through co-inspiring, co-creating and co-evolving, and forming business friendships with these professionals. The programme included six sessions which were photo documented on the SHAPE website: https://shapen trepreneurs.com/gallery/meet-your-business-friend-day/.

Phase 9: Preparation for presentations and publications. The theory recommended that this phase include oral and written presentations as a key element in the individual and team learning processes, as well as for documentation and accountability. The praxis involved furthering the co-inspiring, co-creating and co-evolving. Youths were given more time to work on their business prototypes or to start up their businesses. Mentors prepared reports for their respective workplaces on activities performed to support youth entrepreneurship through participation in SHAPE and how they aligned with organisational systemic visions and missions. The researcher prepared different types of research outputs, including a thesis, journal article and conference presentation and proceedings.

Phase 10: Presentation and celebration. The theory described a presentation day as the culmination of the project, bringing together participants, stakeholders, media and interested parties for a public overview of objectives and attainments. In praxis, youths with existing business prototypes or start-ups were invited by the local municipality to participate in the Durban Business Fair, where there was a sponsored official exhibition space for the youths from SHAPE. Photo documentation of this intervention is available: https://shapentrepreneurs.com/gallery/durban-business-fair/. SHAPE was nominated for the KwaZulu-Natal Young Achievers award and won in the category of best youth development organisation. For the researcher, a conference paper and preliminary case-study paper were accepted into the 6th International Conference on Innovation and Entrepreneurship in Washington DC. The case of SALAR and SHAPE was internationally presented at 'The Innovative Youth Incubator Awards' and was awarded 'Winner, Excellence in reaching out to the community' (van der Westhuizen, 2018).

Phase 11: New workshop cycle starts. The theoretical assumption for Phase 11 was that the original systemic support system for youth entrepreneurs remained open for participation, but natural attrition occurred. Many of the role-players changed between the original negotiations and the agreements, and between programme completion and re-introduction. In praxis, after analysing the findings from Phases 1–10, adjustments were made to the architecture of applying SALAR and SHAPE, and the instruments were refined. A new cycle started in 2018.

The time frame was seven months for the pre-SHAPE stage, four months for the during-SHAPE stage, and four months for the post-SHAPE stage. Introducing Phase 11 took almost two years because the data from the SALAR needed to be analysed, and new methods for introducing Phase 11 needed to be created. Therefore, the cycle took 15 months from the start of Phase 1 to the end of Phase 10. In applying this combination of SALAR, SHAPE and IEO, the importance of support for the programme participants from full-time professors, lecturers, tutors, researchers, peers and administrative personnel within academic institutions, as well as role-players from systems external to the university, was emphasised to address the systemic disconnect and lack of all-round support for youth entrepreneurs.

5.4   Measures

5.4.1 Quantitative measures

A 4-point Likert scale questionnaire was developed, in which 1 = disagree; 2 = somewhat disagree; 3 = somewhat agree; and 4 = agree. Multiple items were set for each of the three major constructs: risk, innovation and proactiveness. The aim of the questionnaire was to determine the development of IEO of the participants and identify any changes brought about by the SHAPE programme. A repeated measures process was adopted where the survey was applied at three different stages of SHAPE—pre-SHAPE, during-SHAPE and post-SHAPE.

Data was statistically analysed using SPSS 22. Inferential analysis used Friedman's test to determine significant changes in facets of risk-taking, innovation and proactivity across the three phases of the study. The Wilcoxon signed-rank test was applied to determine significant changes within each pair of the time intervals.

5.4.2 Qualitative Measures

Participants were asked to produce a reflective writing piece on the project website around their entrepreneurial behaviour in relation to IEO propensities. A qualitative thematic analysis of textual data was done by means of inductive coding to determine themes, sub-themes and sub-nodes. Word frequencies, word tag clouds and word trees were identified in the during-SHAPE and post-SHAPE stages from participants' reflections to support the thematic analysis.

5.5   Results and Discussion

The study took gender into consideration, as 70% of the participants were male, and 30% were female. Furdas and Kohn[47] found that it is common in developing countries for more men to start up new businesses than women. They maintained that differing personality traits between men and women and socio-economic aspects affected gendered decision-making. An interesting finding from the gender distribution for SHAPE was that men were more likely to volunteer than women. Of the student participants, 95% were African, 3.3% Indian, and 1.7% Caucasian. This matched the participating university's overall racial distribution at the time. Of the student participants, 98.3% resided in KwaZulu-Natal, and 1.7% resided outside this province.

5.5.1   Changes in IEO Across the Stages of SHAPE

Results from the analysis to determine changes in aspects of IEO across the three stages of SHAPE are summarised in Tables 5.1, 5.2, and 5.3.

5.5.2   Changes in Risk-Taking

Participants were more likely to disagree post-SHAPE than in other stages about their willingness to work full-time for themselves. This might be owing to a more realistic perception regarding risk-taking in becoming a young entrepreneur post-SHAPE. Participants were more likely to agree pre-SHAPE, compared to subsequent stages that they were willing to invest their own money in a new business. A reason for this might be that most aspiring young entrepreneurs indicated that they had no savings and had financial obligations after completing their studies. Therefore, they had no money of their own to invest in starting a new business. This reinforces the view of Krieger[48] that the barriers to entrepreneurship, especially in the young African population, include

---

[47] Furdas and Kohn (2010).
[48] Krieger (2018).

minimal financial support and the high cost of starting up a business.[49] Innocenti and Zampi[50] emphasised the importance of bridging these barriers, as start-ups need systemic synergy to grow (Table 5.1).

Respondents showed more agreement in the pre-SHAPE stage that they would prefer to start a business in partnership with an established business in the private sector. This was validated with the result that they were less likely to start a business alone rather than in partnership pre-SHAPE than in subsequent stages. The increased agreement of preferring to start a business alone (as opposed to starting a business in partnership) from pre-SHAPE to post-SHAPE, could arise from the realisation about the importance of business friendships and various support structures for entrepreneurs within systemic levels. This confirms Dhliwayo's[51] theory that an array of intermediaries is necessary to support students in action learning approaches. Exposure to a combination of experiences and actions during-SHAPE made them realise that if they wanted to move forward in business as individuals, they would need positive relationships with the collective system around them. This also implies that they felt supported by the intermediaries that the SHAPE structure provided them. The realisation of the importance of others in ensuring entrepreneurial success undermines the entrepreneurial thrust to start a business alone, be self-employed, or work for themselves.[52] This links to the trait of proactiveness, which was emergent in these participants. However, the nature of proactivity in the post-SHAPE stage was not that of seeking opportunities by embracing the programme, but rather looking for new opportunities to promote themselves by securing access to finance, and more importantly, partnerships.[53] This drive to form partnerships is particularly relevant in instances where students do not have the necessary practical skills or the finance to start their businesses. The practical aspects of entrepreneurship, as recognised by

---

[49] Brixiova and Kangoye (2014).
[50] Innocenti and Zampi (2019).
[51] Dhliwayo (2008).
[52] Lumpkin and Dess (2001).
[53] Noel (2014).

Table 5.1 Changes in risk-taking

Item	Mean rank			X^2	p-value	Pre to During		During to Post		Pre to Post	
	PRE-SHAPE	DURING-SHAPE	POST-SHAPE			Z	p-value	Z	p-value	Z	p-value
Risk-taking											
I am willing to work full-time for myself	2.23	1.91	1.87	7.473	0.024	−1.945	0.052	−0.905	0.366	−2.310	0.021
I am willing to invest my own money into a new business	2.22	1.88	1.91	6.724	0.035	−1.677	0.093	−0.879	0.380	−1.549	0.121
I can handle risky situations with confidence	1.86	2.05	2.09	3.439	0.179	−0.332	0.740	−0.816	0.414	−0.675	0.500
It is a safe career choice to work for an organisation that offers a good salary	2.25	1.84	1.91	11.421	0.003	−2.491	0.013	−1.732	0.083	−2.211	0.027
I prefer to have job security through working full-time for a well-established business	2.25	1.88	1.87	12.519	0.002	−2.195	0.028	−0.577	0.564	−2.085	0.037
I rather want to start up a business alone than in partnership	1.58	2.24	2.18	33.271	<0.001	−2.955	0.003	−1.134	0.257	−2.670	0.008
I prefer to start a business in partnership with an established business in the private sector	2.24	1.84	1.92	11.835	0.003	−3.248	0.001	−0.791	0.429	−2.842	0.004
Overall Risk-taking	2.23	1.88	1.89	6.655	0.036	−1.883	0.060	0.000	1.000	−2.017	0.044

Significant change was evidenced in several aspects of risk-taking

Spinelli and Adams,[54] often exceed the limits of what can be taught in entrepreneurship education.

Participants were more likely to agree in the pre-SHAPE stage than in subsequent stages, that it is safer to work for an organisation that offers a good salary. A possible reason is that the students observed other entrepreneurs, systemic interactions, and the realities and challenges that go with the new venture creation process. Most participants also indicated that they had no capital to start a new venture and had direct financial obligations to meet after completing their studies, a challenge many South African students face that hinders their engagement in nascent entrepreneurialism.[55] They perhaps preferred to have a steady income from an additional source while working part-time for themselves.

Participants were more likely to disagree during-SHAPE and post-SHAPE that they preferred to have job security through working full-time for a well-established business. The reason for this choice might be the same as discussed above. In addition, job security in South Africa is very rare and thus valued.[56]

Reliable composite scores were formed for overall risk-taking at each stage (Cronbach's alpha = 0.778; 0.765 and 0.716, respectively) from items 1 and 2. Overall risk levels changed across the three stages with a significant change being experienced from Pre- to Post-stages. A possible reason for this is that the students' knowledge and experiences regarding what it takes to become an entrepreneur developed as they needed to make major decisions and pursue new opportunities.[57]

Responses from the qualitative analysis indicated that some students began to grasp that there were real risks involved in realising their identified opportunities, as the following verbatim responses indicate:

Yes, I feel afraid to take risk but I always try to take risks because for me taking risks can reveal my abilities which I did not know about before

---

[54] Spinelli and Adams (2012).
[55] Herrington et al. (2015).
[56] Herrington et al. (2015) and Xavier et al. (2013).
[57] Fiebig (2015).

and I believe winning is [a] close friend of failing, that [is] what make[s] me take risk[s] [to gain] new opportunities.
That you can go from having all the money in the world to being bankrupt, and in debt. That risks are part of business should be seen as motivation to defy the odds.
Taking risks [is] are part of the characteristics of an entrepreneur.
Yes, I don 't like taking risks. However, I do under-stand that the life of an entrepreneur is largely based on risk-taking.

Some students commented that they did not like taking risks, but they also realised that deciding to take some entrepreneurial risks was important if one wanted to start a new business. Lumpkin and Dess[58] consider that lack of experience in taking real entrepreneurial risks and that performing entrepreneurially under risky situations, like those faced by participants, contributes significantly to how problem-solving is conceptually framed. This implies that the students now needed to apply their newly framed entrepreneurial behaviour to solve challenges at hand in taking entrepreneurial action.

5.5.3 Changes in Innovation

There was a significant decrease in agreement from pre-SHAPE to post-SHAPE that they needed help to come up with new ideas. This might imply that the participants felt supported by the intermediaries SHAPE provided, or that through co-inspiring[59] in the during-SHAPE stage (as indicated in the previous section), they now had a renewed creative vision for themselves and their new ventures. Hannon et al.[60] emphasised the need for teaching and learning practices to be radically transformed and suggested that deep-learning practices be embedded in

---

[58] Lumpkin and Dess (2001).
[59] Scharmer (2018).
[60] Hannon et al. (2013).

entrepreneurship education to successfully address contemporary socio-economic development challenges. The findings indicate transformation—a change in developmental maturity[61]—of the participant through learning to think more creatively. Therefore, transformative learning, a process where students deconstruct past mental models through new experiences, fundamentally changed the way they saw themselves and the world they lived in.[62] Shahab et al.[63] emphasised the importance of applying creativity in all forms of education to develop students' IEO propensities (Table 5.2).

These participants were less likely to agree in the post-SHAPE stage than in the pre-SHAPE stage that they were comfortable moving into new situations. At the post-SHAPE stage, the future the students wished to see emerge in the during-SHAPE stage became a reality. The process of internal change was challenging, but as Scharmer and Kaufer[64] put it, 'It's as if something is dying and something else is waiting to be born' (p. 19). This analogy describes the sometimes-painful process that change brings to individuals. However, change is necessary to create the future they desire. They eventually become more comfortable when facing new situations.

There was significantly more agreement in the pre-SHAPE stage that B-BBEE would help them get their business started. In particular, there was no change between the during- and post-SHAPE stages. Again, the students wanted to take responsibility for creating their own futures, although there were political support systems available to them. Senge et al.[65] indicated that societies have moved beyond post-modernism, and Naudé[66] indicated that government policies, especially on innovation, fail to account for the new types of entrepreneurs that are emerging. Black economic empowerment and affirmative action are political policies in South Africa developed by the country's democratic government, which, in the

---

[61] Fitch and O'Fallon (2013).

[62] Korthaugen et al. (2013).

[63] Shahab et al. (2019).

[64] Scharmer and Kaufer (2013).

[65] Senge et al. (2008).

[66] Naudé (2013).

Table 5.2 Changes in innovation

Item	Mean Rank			X^2	p-value	Pre to During		During to Post		Pre to Post	
	PRE-SHAPE	DURING-SHAPE	POST-SHAPE			Z	p-value	Z	p-value	Z	p-value
Innovation											
I am comfortable moving into new situations	2.22	1.83	1.95	7.943	0.019	−2.313	0.021	−1.436	0.151	−1.611	0.107
I have already experienced very big changes in my life	2.33	1.85	1.83	13.939	0.001	−1.176	0.239	−0.816	0.414	−1.307	0.191
I sometimes like to try new and unusual activities	2.26	1.91	1.83	10.818	0.004	−1.969	0.049	−0.877	0.380	−2.345	0.019
I like order and routine	2.25	1.86	1.88	9.589	0.008	−0.809	0.418	−0.757	0.449	−0.447	0.655
I think that government should provide me with new business ideas	2.27	1.88	1.86	10.831	0.004	−1.473	0.141	−3.903	<0.001	−1.532	0.126
The government must tell me where new business opportunities will arise	2.62	1.72	1.67	61.433	< 0.001	−4.742	< 0.001	−0.356	0.722	−4.803	<0.001
Black Economic Empowerment and affirmative action will help me getting my business started	2.29	1.86	1.86	11.796	0.003	−2.678	0.007	−1.342	0.180	−2.426	0.015

(continued)

Table 5.2 (continued)

Item	Mean Rank			X^2	p-value	Pre to During		During to Post		Pre to Post	
	PRE-SHAPE	DURING-SHAPE	POST-SHAPE			Z	p-value	Z	p-value	Z	p-value
I am creative and new business ideas come easily to me	2.02	2.02	1.97	0.178	0.915	−0.826	0.409	−0.816	0.414	−1.166	0.244
I need help to come up with new ideas	2.54	1.72	1.74	54.875	<0.001	−4.515	<0.001	−0.966	0.334	−4.428	< 0.001
I prefer to experiment and use original approaches to solve challenges rather than using methods that others generally apply	2.09	1.97	1.94	1.676	0.433	−0.732	0.464	−1.890	0.059	−1.059	0.290
I spend hours and hours finding out more about new business ideas	2.42	1.75	1.83	25.000	<0.001	−4.127	< 0.001	−0.378	0.705	−3.684	<0.001
Overall Innovation	2.43	1.81	1.76	25.949	<0.001	−3.661	< 0.001	−1.406	0.160	−3.715	<0.001

Significant change was evident in most of the items measuring innovation current era, might not be sufficient to address student entrepreneurship challenges.[67] Again, this might imply that the students developed the ability to deconstruct their mental models, developing the ability to move beyond political shackles and dogma from the past.[68]

There was a decrease in agreement from pre-SHAPE to post-SHAPE that they sometimes liked to try out new and unusual activities. This occurred as students developed their multiple intelligences[69] and deconstructed their experiential learning processes,[70] enabling new knowledge through generating new learning experiences and taking action towards potential entrepreneurship.[71] Again, this question item related to their experiences with change and transformation. A possible explanation for this result is that the question item itself was worded vaguely: *I sometimes like to try out new and unusual activities. It might have had a different result if worded as follows: I always like to try out new and unusual activities, or I do not like to try out new and unusual activities.*

There was a decrease in agreement among these participants from pre-SHAPE to post-SHAPE that they liked order and routine. This contradicts the result that shows the decrease in agreement that they sometimes like to try new and unusual activities. The findings indicate that the students preferred the 'chaos' of the changes that the SALAR project brought, and that they liked new experiences and actions. Practically, it might imply that they needed to become more organised, as they now had added responsibilities owing to their participation in SHAPE, and in becoming more organised, they became more mature. Creating life order and some form of routine, but simultaneously staying flexible to change can also be seen as personality traits of successful entrepreneurs.[72]

Pre-SHAPE students seemed to agree more with the statement that they had had some major changes in their lives, while responses remained almost the same between the during- and post-SHAPE stages. A possible

---

[67] Naudé (2013).

[68] Pillay (2014).

[69] Gardner (2003).

[70] Kolb (1984).

[71] Revans (2011).

[72] Quintillán and Peña-Legazkue (2019).

reason for the mean rank decrease is that the students did not yet realise they had experienced major changes in personal development during-SHAPE. They were still in the process of co-creating and co-evolving and might not yet have had the opportunity to reflect on their personal development.

Three items related to researching new business ideas. Agreement that they spend hours finding out more about new business ideas decreased as students moved from pre-SHAPE to post-SHAPE. A possible reason for this might be that the participants took an initial risk in investing their time in researching innovative business ideas, despite the pressures of the regular academic programme. Therefore, in attempting to innovate new entrepreneurial concepts, they demonstrated initial IEO proactivity propensities.

A decrease in agreement was also seen as students moved from pre-SHAPE to post-SHAPE regarding the suggestions that government should tell them about new business opportunities and provide them with new business ideas. These findings imply that there is a shift away from relying only on government structures to provide them with business opportunities. Although the municipality mentors played an integral part in the students' developmental process, the latter seem to have developed the ability to research business opportunities and proactively reach out to role-players in their system to explore opportunities. The students increasingly started thinking about the future they wanted to create for themselves to live up to their highest personal aspirations for their entrepreneurial endeavours, therefore holding themselves accountable for their future in the world of work.

Scharmer and Kaufer[73] indicate that for personal innovation as a behavioural trait to occur, an individual needs to connect to a source, or Source, of inspiration. This connection might spark the inner place from which an individual acts, which might lead to sustained entrepreneurial action. Some students expressed direct experiences of inspiration:

Many great business ideas have started flood[ing] my mind.
The joy and happiness started to move inside me.

---

[73] Scharmer and Kaufer (2013).

Let the brain, muscles, nerves, every part of your body, be full of that idea it time ... to shift hope and to activate the young entrepreneur inside me.

These reflections indicated that some students felt strongly that transformation was happening within them. Following Pillay,[74] it would be fair to say that the U-process enabled students to deconstruct their mental models, explore their entrepreneurial fears and find ways to overcome the fears.

Composite scores were formed for overall innovation at each stage (Cronbach's alpha = 0.568; 0.801 and 0.851 respectively) from items 5 and 6. Overall propensity for innovation levels differed significantly across the three stages with changes being experienced specifically between the first and second interventions and between the first and third interventions. A possible reason for these changes is that the application of SALAR and SHAPE assisted the participants to deconstruct their mental models and develop new ways of seeing things through new experiences.[75]

5.5.4 Changes in Proactivity

It must be considered that the participants had different cognitive capacities in the pre-SHAPE, during-SHAPE and post-SHAPE stages. Proactivity in the pre-SHAPE stage implied that there were prospective students who wanted to become entrepreneurs and acted accordingly by identifying opportunities and acting upon them. These high levels of opportunity identification are indicative of high levels of IEO.[76] In the during-SHAPE stage, the emphasis was on business idea development and individual development, whereas in the post-SHAPE stage, the students moved forward to take entrepreneurial action (Table 5.3).

There was greater agreement in the pre-SHAPE phase that they usually plan ahead. In particular, there was no change between the during- and post-SHAPE stages. As the SALAR and SHAPE proceeded, the students

---

[74] Pillay (2014).
[75] Pillay (2014).
[76] Callaghan (2009).

Table 5.3 Changes on proactivity

Item	Mean Rank			X^2	p-value	Pre to During		During to Post		Pre to Post	
	PRE-SHAPE	DURING-SHAPE	POST-SHAPE			Z	p-value	Z	p-value	Z	p-value
Proactivity											
I usually plan ahead	2.31	1.85	1.84	18.339	< 0.001	−2.984	0.003	−0.962	0.336	−3.280	0.001
I already have a business plan	2.69	1.65	1.66	61.880	< 0.001	−5.663	< 0.001	−1.000	0.317	−5.284	< 0.001
I submit my assignments before time	2.23	1.89	1.88	7.471	0.024	−1.590	0.112	−0.447	0.655	−1.646	0.100
When working in a team, I often found myself doing more work than the others just to get the tasks done on time	2.13	1.94	1.93	3.607	0.165	−0.715	0.475	−0.378	0.705	−0.738	0.461
I have lots of experience working in teams	1.82	2.10	2.08	4.608	0.100	−1.924	0.054	−1.414	0.157	−1.905	0.057
I am regarded by my friends as a person who makes things happen	2.12	1.97	1.92	2.811	0.245	−1.187	0.235	−1.000	0.317	−1.374	0.170
Usually when I start with a new idea, I follow it through	1.92	2.06	2.03	1.137	0.566	−0.838	0.402	−1.000	0.317	−0.964	0.335
Overall Proactivity	2.19	1.93	1.88	5.681	0.058	−1.072	0.284	−1.134	0.257	−1.460	0.144

Three of the seven items measuring proactivity showed significant changes across the phases of SHAPE came to realise that things do not always go according to plan. They were confronted with changes within themselves, possibly because they were deconstructing past mental models, and changes in developmental maturity (transformation) occurred.[77] They also changed their business ideas and potential business friends several times. These changes were indicative of personality traits associated with successful IEO proceeding towards potential new entrepreneurial action.[78] Therefore, the plans they made needed to be continually adapted. This is in line with the nature of ALAR.[79] The SALAR and SHAPE stages and phases also taught the students to learn from the future as it emerges and that the emerging future does not always arrive as planned.[80]

These students showed more agreement in the pre-SHAPE stage if they submitted assignments before time. A possible reason for this is that the students were not entirely truthful in the pre-SHAPE survey, as they might have wanted to make a positive impression on the practitioner-researcher by making her think they were diligent students. Agreement that they already had a business plan decreased after the pre-SHAPE stage, with no change occurring between the during- and post-SHAPE stages. This is understandable because, when the survey was conducted, the participants were still in the process of writing a business plan. However, they had all completed business model canvases.

Composite scores were formed for overall proactivity at each stage (Cronbach's alpha = 0.622; 0.737 and 0.721, respectively) from items 4 and 6. Proactivity IEO level did not differ statistically between pre-, during- and post-SHAPE. If the construct of proactivity is similar to the construct of opportunity identification,[81] a possible reason could be that different types of opportunities were identified and pursued by the participants at different SHAPE stages. For example, in pre-SHAPE, opportunity and proactivity were linked to choosing to participate in the programme, whereas in during-SHAPE, the participation process brought opportunities through interactions with intermediaries.

---

[77] Fitch and O'Fallon (2013).

[78] Stephenson (2015).

[79] Zuber-Skerritt (2002).

[80] Scharmer (2018).

[81] Callaghan (2009).

In post-SHAPE, opportunity identification and proactivity were linked to pursuing possible entrepreneurial action.

Students needed to be well aware of the opportunities available to them to ensure that they were proactive:

> Being proactive as a young entrepreneur requires a lot of time and commitment, requires you to be well-versed about the opportunities available around you.

For the aspiring student entrepreneurs to be proactive, they needed to have accessible knowledge and information. Without support of the entrepreneurial ecosystem, or educational information, the aspiring student entrepreneurs felt unable to see their way in implementing, anticipating and acquiring the necessary tolerance in business activity. Being proactive allowed the aspiring entrepreneurs to anticipate risks, and as previously discussed, when a risk can be anticipated, its effect can be mitigated, increasing the aspiring entrepreneur's capacity for tolerance:

> I learn[ed] that [to] be proactive enable[s] entrepreneur[s] to anticipate challenges that she/he did not know about before and also [to] bring about confidence in entrepreneurship.

Thus, the link between proactivity, innovation and tolerance was made, often in relation to risk.

5.6 Contributions

The study's theoretical contribution is the SHAPE YES framework as illustrated in Fig. 5.1. The methodological contribution is the model as illustrated in Fig. 5.3: The SALAR and SHAPE model for developing IEO. The empirical contribution is that applying the SHAPE intervention synthesised to the SALAR methodology, significantly increases university students' IEO.

5.6.1 The SHAPE Youth Entrepreneur Support Network

The acronym SHAPE refers to the intervention under investigation in this research. The acronym was used this research's novel framework that illustrates the intervention's youth entrepreneur support network (Fig. 5.1). There is a lack of knowledge about whether existing frameworks for South African and African youth entrepreneur support (YES) networks, when applied, facilitate effective youth entrepreneurship and increase youths' IEO. This research contributes to closing this knowledge gap. SHAPE is grounded in the principles of Theory U[82] and is a descriptor for the processes and strategies to shifting hope and activating potential entrepreneurship of students. This process involves the strategy of guiding students through Theory U's five cycles, moving them from reactive thought processes to generative behavioural processes, where ideation of entrepreneurial opportunities can be brought into action.[83] The application of Theory U processes has been reported as successful in many cases, both in developing and developed countries where the notion of co-inspiring also referred to as presencing is key to bring the desired transformation.[84]

Transformation in this context is interpreted as growth in developmental maturity[85] and is a possible indicator that there is a change in the students' mindset, namely a change of thinking, feeling, acting and being.[86] If co-inspiring or entrepreneurial transformation occurs within the motivation of a student entrepreneur, such a microsystemic change could result in socio-economic change at other systemic levels. This study uses the terms 'entrepreneurial mindset' as a concept relating to the end-product of thought, 'entrepreneurial heartset' as the neurological process of creating a mindset and 'entrepreneurial handset' as behavioural action. Simply put, is it possible that a transformation in a young entrepreneur's

---

[82] Scharmer (2018).
[83] Van der Westhuizen (2016).
[84] Van der Westhuizen (2021).
[85] Fitch and O'Fallon (2013).
[86] Leaf (2013).

mindset, heartset and handset is the key to changing the larger local ecosystem of the student?

Deep learning and growth in developmental maturity of student entrepreneurs occur when they are connected to a support network from the university's internal and external environment. This support network is known as the students' entrepreneurial ecosystem. It is, therefore, essential for an intervention like SHAPE to create relationships and to connect students with intermediaries within this support network. There are further gaps in knowledge within the context of South African public universities on effective application of such programmes where YES Networks are introduced to students and continue to provide long-term support. Literature addressing entrepreneurial ecosystems and entrepreneurial behaviour in the African continent is sparse.[87] There is a lack of current knowledge about whether South African and African YES frameworks, when applied, facilitate effective youth entrepreneurship. Current research is inconclusive about the long-term success of university entrepreneurship programmes, and controversies remain about long-term effectiveness of entrepreneurship interventions to university students. This research proposes a framework where seven categories of intermediaries are identified to form a YES Network: (1) personality traits; (2) educational institutes; (3) government agencies; (4) private sector agencies; (5) communities; (6) the entrepreneur and small & medium businesses; and (7) corporations and large businesses. An eighth aspect, Internationalisation, was identified after concluding the study as an integral part of the ecosystem. The research addresses gaps in literature because studies on YES Networks in South Africa such as Dhliwayo[88] proposed theoretical models but were not empirically validated.

In addressing the literature gap on YES Networks, the SHAPE YES Network was developed as a framework to increase and inspire effective individual entrepreneurial orientation among university students.

It was created to connect students with entrepreneurial aspirations to a support system and inspire them to become successful young

---

[87] Jones et al. (2018).
[88] Dhliwayo (2008).

entrepreneurs, consistently motivated to take business risks, be innovative, and overcome challenges by being proactive.[89]

The SHAPE YES Network illustrated in Fig. 5.1 describes possible roles of the intermediaries. In our proposed framework, the youth's personality traits are considered key to developing their relationship with themselves, their mindset and entrepreneurial heartset.[90] Educational institutions, in this case, a university, host and lead the initiative and provide administrative support. The university facilitates the learning and research aspects. Government agencies are the third intermediary in the ecosystem and contribute by connecting youth to entrepreneurship services and infrastructure; for example, business support units and mentorship programmes.[91] Private sector agencies like the local chambers of commerce act as the fourth intermediary by providing platforms to youth entrepreneurs to connect with the private sector. Communities comprising families and friends of the youth play a supporting role in their entrepreneurial growth. Entrepreneurs and small and medium business owners are the sixth intermediary in the ecosystem. Their role is to collaborate with youth entrepreneurs and absorb the youth into the economy.[92] Corporations and large businesses are the seventh intermediary in the ecosystem and function to provide a platform for internships and on-the-job learning opportunities. The framework for the SHAPE YES Network is generic and flexible and can be used by other universities in South Africa or other African countries although it needs to be contextualised.

The framework was implemented, applied, validated and is presented as a case study. We must add that the framework was illustrated only after the last intervention, because the methodology underwent several changes during the multiple cycles of application. There was no formal ecosystemic support system for aspiring or existing student entrepreneurs in place at the case site before the intervention was applied. Over time,

---

[89] Van der Westhuizen and Krieger (2018).
[90] Krieger (2018) and Van der Westhuizen (2016).
[91] Van der Westhuizen (2016).
[92] Van der Westhuizen (2016).

the framework was adapted to accommodate the socio-economic, political, technological and cultural changes sweeping South Africa. The SHAPE intervention and the YES Network were practically applied in combination with SALAR in this study to develop students' IEO.

5.7   Conclusion

The creation of the framework for the SHAPE YES Network to facilitate applying SALAR to enhance youth IEO development, followed by the practical application of the intervention over a period of 15 months, is important, novel and contributes to the current debate on ways to boost youth entrepreneurship in developing nations. The findings show that significant changes to and development of youth IEO occurred over time. Thus, synthesising SHAPE, SALAR and IEO development within the context of a youth entrepreneur support network is an important consideration for policymakers and the academe.

This study identified six key factors for developing youths' IEO: (1) teamwork and proactivity; (2) individual entrepreneurial contributions; (3) business friendships to facilitate new venture creation; (4) business friendships and individual innovation; (5) experience with change management; and (6) researching new business ideas.

It was also noted that a strong systemic support network (ecosystem) is necessary to develop youths' IEO, therefore justifying a case where policymakers and the academe can collaborate to increase effective youth entrepreneurship. The findings indicate that while youths have initial IEO, it needs further development to move them towards taking entrepreneurial action. The findings further confirmed that the SHAPE model, with its three stages and 11 phases, is effective when practically applied through SALAR.

The study was limited to one geographic area in South Africa and confined to a selected case study; therefore, the results are not generalisable. However, the study reflects on a case where the model was effectively applied over time, and if repeated in other institutions or youth entrepreneurship development programmes, could yield valuable results. Further analysis is needed on the second iteration of applying

SHAPE and SALAR and how the results differ from the first iteration. This study could also be expanded to multiple sites in other developing countries.

References

Adelakun, Y., & Van der Westhuizen, T. (2021). Delineating government policies and individual entrepreneurial orientation. *Journal of Sociology and Social Anthropology, 12*(3–4), 106–117. https://doi.org/10.31901/245 66764.2021/12.3-4.371

Ammirato, S., Sofo, F., Felicetti, A. M., Helander, N., & Aramo-Immonen, H. (2019). A new typology to characterize Italian digital entrepreneurs. *International Journal of Entrepreneurial Behavior & Research, 26*(2), 224–245. https://doi.org/10.1108/ijebr-02-2019-0105

Awotunde, O. M., & Van der Westhuizen, T. (2021a). Entrepreneurial self-efficacy development: An effective intervention for sustainable student entrepreneurial intentions. *International Journal of Innovation and Sustainable Development, 15*(4), 475–495.

Awotunde, O. M., & Van der Westhuizen, T. (2021b, September). Entrepreneurial self-efficacy and the SHAPE ideation model for university students. In *ECIE 2021 16th European Conference on Innovation and Entrepreneurship Vol 1* (p. 37).

Bezerra, É. D., Borges, C., & Andreassi, T. (2017). Universities, local partnerships and the promotion of youth entrepreneurship. *International Review of Education, 63*(5), 703–724.

Bolton, D. L., & Lane, M. D. (2012). Individual entrepreneurial orientation: Development of a measurement instrument. *Education and Training, 54*(2–3), 219–233. https://doi.org/10.1108/00400911211210314

Brixiova, Z., & Kangoye, T. (2014). Youth employment in Africa: New evidence and policies from Swaziland. In M. Á. Malo & D. Sciulli (Eds.), *Disadvantaged workers* (pp. 181–202). Springer. https://doi.org/10.1007/978-3-319-04376-0_9

Burns, D. (2007). *Systemic action research: A strategy for whole system change.* Policy Press.

Callaghan, C. W. (2009). *Entrepreneurial orientation and entrepreneurial performance of central Johannesburg informal sector street traders* (Master's Thesis, University of the Witwatersrand).

Chia, R. (2014). From relevance to relevate: How university-based business school can remain seats of "higher" learning and still contribute effectively to business. *Journal of Management Development, 33*(5), 443–455. https://doi.org/10.1108/jmd-02-2014-0013

Dhliwayo, S. (2008). Experiential learning in entrepreneurship education: A prospective model for South African tertiary institutions. *Education + Training, 50*(4), 329–340. https://doi.org/10.1108/00400910810880560

DTI. (2020). *Coronavirus COVID-19 economic and social measures.* Department of Trade and Industry.

Fiebig, J. C. (2015). *When angels fly—Identification, activation and integration of potential business angels in Denmark* (Master's Thesis, Aarhus University).

Fitch, G., & O'Fallon, T. (2013). Theory U applied in transformation development. In O. Gunnlaugson, C. Baron, & M. Cayer (Eds.), *Perspectives on theory U: Insights from the field* (pp. 114–127). https://doi.org/10.4018/978-1-4666-4793-0.ch008

Franke, N., & Lüthje, C. (2004). Entrepreneurial intentions of business students—A benchmarking study. *International Journal of Innovation and Technology Management, 1*(3), 269–288. https://doi.org/10.1142/s0219877004000209

Furdas, M. D., & Kohn, K. (2010). *What's the difference?! Gender, personality, and the propensity to start a business* (IZA Discussion Paper [No. 4778]). Social Science Research Network.

Gardner, H. (2003). *Multiple intelligences after twenty years.* American Educational Research Association.

Hannon, V., Gillinson, S., & Shanks, L. (2013). *Learning a living: Radical innovation in education for work.* Bloomsbury.

Herrington, M., Kew, J., & Kew, P. 2015. *GEM South Africa Report. South Africa: The crossroads—A goldmine or a time bomb?* Department of Economic Development and Tourism.

Innocenti, N., & Zampi, V. (2019). What does a start-up need to grow? An empirical approach for Italian innovative start-ups. *International Journal of Entrepreneurial Behavior & Research, 25*(2), 376–393. https://doi.org/10.1108/ijebr-04-2018-0194

Jones, P., Maas, G., Dobson, S., Newbery, R., Agyapong, D., & Matlay, H. (2018). Entrepreneurship in Africa, part 1: Entrepreneurial dynamics in Africa. *Journal of Small Business and Enterprise Development, 25*(3), 346–348. https://doi.org/10.1108/JSBED-06-2018-399

Kolb, D. A. (1984). *Experiential learning: Experience as the source of learning and development.* Prentice Hall.

Korthaugen, F. A. J., Hoekstra, A., & Meijer, P. C. 2013. Promoting presence in professional practice: A core reflection approach for moving through the U. In O. Gunnlaugson, C. Baron, & M. Cayer (Eds.), *Perspectives on theory U: Insights from the field.* (pp. 77–96). Business Science Reference. https://doi.org/10.4018/978-1-4666-4793-0.ch006

Krieger, W. (2018). *Barriers to youth entrepreneurship—a systemic approach. Masters Dissertation.* University of KwaZulu-Natal.

Leaf, C. (2013). *Switch on your brain: The key to peak happiness, thinking, and health.* Baker Books.

Ljungkvist, T., Boers, B., & Samuelsson, J. (2019). Three stages of entrepreneurial orientation: The founder's role. *International Journal of Entrepreneurial Behavior & Research, 26*(2), 285–306. https://doi.org/10.1108/ijebr-10-2018-0630

Lumpkin, G. T., & Dess, G. G. (2001). Linking two dimensions of entrepreneurial orientation to firm performance: The moderating role of environment and industry life cycle. *Journal of Business Venturing, 16*(5), 429–451. https://doi.org/10.1016/s0883-9026(00)00048-3

Mahrous, A. A., & Genedy, M. A. (2019). Connecting the dots: The relationship among intra-organizational environment, entrepreneurial orientation, market orientation and organizational performance. *Journal of Entrepreneurship in Emerging Economies, 11*(1), 2–21. https://doi.org/10.1108/jeee-09-2016-0036

Miller, D. J., & Acs, Z. J. (2017). The campus as entrepreneurial ecosystem: The University of Chicago. *Small Business Economics, 49*(1), 75–95.

Mondal, A., & Chakrabarti, A. B. (2021). Entrepreneurial orientation during adversity: Differences across ownership categories. *International Journal of Entrepreneurial Behavior & Research, 27*(4), 845–865. https://doi.org/10.1108/IJEBR-10-2019-0593

Naudé, W. (2013). *Entrepreneurship and economic development: theory, evidence and policy* (IZA Discussion Paper [No. 7507]). Social Science Research Network (SSRN).

Nhleko, Y., & van der Westhuizen, T. (2022). The role of higher education institutions in introducing entrepreneurship education to meet the demands of industry 4.0. *Academy of Entrepreneurship Journal, 28*(1), 1–23.

Noel, L. J. (2014). Do business angels have an entrepreneurial orientation? *Venture Capital, 6*(2–3), 197–210. https://doi.org/10.1080/136910604200 01675983

Oyugi, J. L. (2014). Effectiveness of the methods of teaching entrepreneurship courses to developing self-efficacy and intention among university students in Uganda. *International Journal of Social Sciences and Entrepreneurship, 1*(11), 491–513.

Paton, G. (2001). A systemic action learning cycle as the key element of an ongoing spiral of analyses. *Systemic Practice and Action Research, 14*(1), 95–111.

Pillay, K. (2014). Learning, the whole and theory U: Reflections on creating a space for deep learning. *Problems and Perspectives in Management, 12*(4), 340–346.

Quintillán, I., & Peña-Legazkue, I. (2019). Emotional intelligence and venture internationalization during economic recession. *International Journal of Entrepreneurial Behavior & Research, 26*(2), 246–265. https://doi.org/10.1108/ijebr-08-2018-0521

Rahimi, E., van den Berg, J., & Veen, W. (2015). A learning model for enhancing the student's control in educational process using Web 2.0 personal learning environments. *British Journal of Educational Technology, 46*(4), 780–792.

Revans, R. (2011). *ABC of action learning*. Gower.

Ruba, R. M., Van der Westhuizen, T., & Chiloane-Tsoka, G. E. (2021). Influence of entrepreneurial orientation on organisational performance: Evidence from Congolese Higher Education Institutions. *Journal of Contemporary Management, 18*(1), 243–269.

SAG. (2021). *President Cyril Ramaphosa: Virtual engagement with SMMEs and cooperatives.* https://www.gov.za/speeches/president-cyril-ramaphosa-vir tual-engagement-smmes-and-cooperatives-25-feb-2021-0000

Sahay, A., & Nirjar, A. (2012). *Entrepreneurship: Education, research and practice*. Excel Books.

Scharmer, C. O. (2009). *Theory U: Learning from the future as it emerges*. Berrett-Koehler.

Scharmer, C. O., & Kaufer, K. (2013). *Leading from the emerging future: From ego-system to eco-system economies*. Berrett-Koehler.

Scharmer, O. (2018). *The essentials of theory U: Core principles and applications*. Berrett-Koehler.

Schweikert, S., Meissen, J. O., & Wolf, P. (2013). Applying theory U: The case of the creative living lab. In O. Gunnlaugson, C. Baron, & M. Cayer (Eds.), *Perspectives on theory U: Insights from the field* (pp. 193–206). Business Science Reference. https://doi.org/10.4018/978-1-4666-4793-0.ch013

Senge, P., Scharmer, C. O., Jaworski, J., & Flowers, B. S. (2008). *Presence: Human purpose and the field of the future*. Doubleday.

Shahab, Y., Chengang, Y., Arbizu, A. D., & Haider, M. J. (2019). Entrepreneurial self-efficacy and intention: Do entrepreneurial creativity and education matter? *International Journal of Entrepreneurial Behavior & Research, 25*(2), 259–280. https://doi.org/10.1108/ijebr-12-2017-0522

Spinelli, S., & Adams, R. (2012). *New venture creation: Entrepreneurship for the 21st century*. McGraw-Hill/Irwin.

Steenberg, R. (2017). *The entrepreneurial spirit—towards an education model for entrepreneurial success in South Africa* (Doctoral Thesis, Texila American University in association with University of Central Nicaragua).

Stephenson, J. (2015). *25 common characteristics of successful entrepreneurs*. http://www.entrepreneur.com/article/200730

Susman, G. I., & Evered, R. D. (1978). An assessment of the scientific merits of action research. *Administrative Science Quarterly, 23*, 582–603.

Teles, D. D. S., Nieuwenhuizen, C., & Schachtebeck, C. (2021). Entrepreneurial education and individual entrepreneurial orientation: An experts' perspective. An empirical Delphi study. An empirical Delphi Study. *EUREKA: Social and Humanities, 4*, 46–56.

United Nations Development Programme. (2020). *COVID-19: looming crisis in developing countries threatens to devastate economies and ramp up inequality.* https://www.undp.org/content/undp/en/home/news-centre/news/2020/COVID19_Crisis_in_developing_countries_threatens_devast ate_economies.html

Urban, B., & Galawe, J. (2019). The mediating effect of self-efficacy on the relationship between moral judgement, empathy and social opportunity recognition in South Africa. *International Journal of Entrepreneurial*

Behavior & Research, 26(2), 349–372. https://doi.org/10.1108/ijebr-05-2019-0271

Van der Westhuizen, T. (2016). *Developing individual entrepreneurial orientation: A systemic approach through the lens of theory U* (Doctoral thesis, University of KwaZulu-Natal).

Van der Westhuizen, T. (2017a). A systemic approach towards responsible and sustainable economic development: Entrepreneurship, systems theory and socio-economic momentum. In Z. Fields (Ed.), *Collective creativity for responsible and sustainable business practice*. IGI Global.

Van der Westhuizen, T. (2017b). The use of theory U and individual entrepreneurial orientation to increase low youth entrepreneurship in South Africa. *Journal of Contemporary Management, 14*, 531–553.

Van der Westhuizen, T. (2018a). The SHAPE Project: Shifting hope, activating potential entrepreneurship. In D. Remenyi & D. A. Grant (Eds.), *Incubators for young entrepreneurs—20 case histories*. ACPIL.

Van der Westhuizen, T. (2018b). *Open heart, open mind and open will in transformative individual entrepreneurial orientation pedagogies* (pp. 443–448). Academic Conferences and Publishing International Limited.

Van der Westhuizen, T. (2019a). *Action! Methods to develop entrepreneurship.* In 18th European Conference on Research Methodology for Business and Management Studies (pp. 331–337).

Van der Westhuizen, T. (2019b). South African undergraduate students' access to entrepreneurial education and its influence on career choice: Global considerations for developing countries. In *Global considerations in entrepreneurship education and training* (pp. 232–252). IGI Global.

Van der Westhuizen, T. (2021). Applying theory U through SHAPE to develop student's individual entrepreneurial orientation in a university eco-system. In O. Gunnlaugson & W. Brendel (Eds.), *Advances in presencing Volume III: Collective approaches in theory U* (pp. 395–435). Trifoss Business Press.

Van der Westhuizen, T. (2022). *Effective youth entrepreneurship.* Sunbonani. https://omp.sunbonani.co.za/index.php/sunbonani/catalog/book/6

Van Der Westhuizen, T., & Krieger, W. (2018). The SHAPE project: Shifting hope, activating potential entrepreneurship. Incubators for young entrepreneurs. https://ukzn-dspace.ukzn.ac.za/handle/10413/16538

Weinberg, I. (2011). *Neurophysics: Exploring the multiple dimensions of consciousness.* http://www.pninet.com/articles/Neurophysics.pdf

Xavier, S., Kelley, D., Kew, J., Herrington, M., & Vorderwülbecke, A. (2013). *Global entrepreneurship monitor 2012 global report*. GEM Consortia.

Zuber-Skerritt, O. (2002). The concept of action learning. *The Learning Organization, 9*(3), 114–124. https://doi.org/10.1108/09696470210428831

6

Applying Theory U Through SHAPE to Develop Student's Individual Entrepreneurial Orientation in a University Ecosystem

6.1   Introduction

The focus in the first half of this chapter is a single, brief, but a very powerful moment in an 11-week Theory U-inspired initiative for aspiring young entrepreneurs at the University of KwaZulu-Natal in Durban (UKZN), South Africa.[1] Presencing occurred during Meet Your Business Friend Day, where student entrepreneurs co-initiated, co-sensed, co-inspired, co-created and setting the tone co-evolve with possible Business Friends, in the spark of forming an ecosystem of deep support. Student entrepreneurs interacted during Meet Your Business Friend Day with peers, private sector entrepreneurs, mentors from the local municipality, mentors from the local chamber of commerce and mentors from the provincial Local Economic Development Unit. The aim of bringing them together was to co-initiate a potential future

---

[1] This article was previously published as follows: Van der Westhuizen, T. (2021). Applying Theory U through SHAPE to develop student's individual entrepreneurial orientation in a university eco-system. In O. Gunnlaugson & W. Brendel (Eds.), *Advances in pre-sensing volume III: Collective approaches, in Theory U* (pp. 395–435). Trifoss Business Press.

© University of Kwazulu-Natal 2023
T. van der Westhuizen, *Youth Entrepreneurship*,
https://doi.org/10.1007/978-3-031-44339-8_6

ecosystem for students, through co-sensing and co-inspiring, to enable them to be more entrepreneurial. At the time of the event, such an actual ecosystem of Business Friends and the interrelationships between role players didn't exist. After this powerful moment, students were requested to write reflections on their experiences building up to this day and during this day. As they've been *en route* through the U-journey, their reflections at this stage were ripe for analysis. Utilising participant's account in a survey and reflective writing, I will be exploring the thematic relationships between Theory U levels and IEO dimensions.

SHAPE (Shifting Hope, Activating Potential Entrepreneurship) is a social technology that draws its participants from students with entrepreneurial aspirations who are registered for undergraduate and postgraduate degrees in business studies at UKZN. SHAPE, at the time of writing, has run successfully for four years. In this chapter, we provide an account theoretical overview groundwork, planning and implementation for a one-day event called 'Meet Your Business Friend Day'. With 60 student participants and 20 mentors, this meeting took place in October 2014 as part of the inaugural cycle of the SHAPE social technology. SHAPE, in turn, was, and continues to be, part of a larger systemic action learning and action research project in which the cycles and phases of the project build on the cycles of Theory U. This project also specifically considers whether a positive correlation exists between aspects of Theory U and dimensions of a participant's individual entrepreneurial orientation, namely risk-taking, innovation and proactivity.

Seen systemically, each individual constitutes a microsystem closely linked to various processes at differing levels of systemic development. The 2015 Global Entrepreneurship Monitor notes that a person's heartset and mindset, and his or her entrepreneurial profile, attitudes, activities and aspirations, are directly linked to national and indeed global socio-economic development.[2] If entrepreneurialism is to spur socio-economic development, one possible starting point could be to develop those internal domains of aspirant individuals—the individual microsystem—by tapping into resources that are reachable at other

---

[2] Herrington and Kew (2016).

systemic levels.[3] These resources can include intermediaries from: (a) universities, (b) municipality business support units, (c) communities, (d) private sector practitioners who support youth entrepreneurs, (e) parastatals and agencies set out to develop commerce or (f) a Local Economic Development Unit embedded within a government entity.[4]

6.2   Connection with Theory U

Theory U identifies four fundamental meta-processes of the systemic levels, which we speculate, develop different dimensions of one's IEO. Systemic levels include micro-field processes (individual thinking and orientation), meso-field processes (group conversing), macro-field processes (institutional structuring) and 'mundo-field' processes (global ecosystem coordination).[5] For Scharmer[6] and Hannon, Gillinson and Shanks,[7] the development of the micro-field starts at a deep level of an individual's connection to knowledge, then reacts to internal and external domains, generating new thought and opportunities and creating new possibilities to tackle challenges. The Theory U trajectory resonates with an entrepreneurship training shift from classroom teaching to action learning—static and content-oriented teaching no longer matching the needs of change-driven economies.[8]

This chapter explores the systemic levels that influence the development of IEO propensities present in the SHAPE social technology, outlines how it evolved theoretically and draws on Theory U during the illustrative moment of 'Meet Your Business Friend Day'. Our study demonstrates that applying Theory U as a social technology, theoretical framework and research methodology, can play a significant

---

[3] Van der Westhuizen (2016).
[4] Van der Westhuizen (2016).
[5] Scharmer and Kaufer (2013).
[6] Scharmer (2008).
[7] Hannon et al. (2013).
[8] Bodhanya (2014), Goodman (2014), and Oyugi (2014).

role in boosting youth entrepreneurship in South Africa and lead to the significant and radically-positive transformation of young people's aspirations.

6.3   Theoretical Framework

The elements of IEO and Theory U relate to one another in the entrepreneurial process in the following ways[9]:

6.3.1   IEO Risk and Theory U Co-initiation

Risk-taking propensity is a behavioural dimension of IEO which may drive the pursuit of opportunities. Broadly, IEO leads the way for innovative action on the part of an individual, and reactiveness is associated with an individual's response to competitors or external stimuli.[10] Co-initiation of IEO occurs on an intrapersonal level and an interpersonal level.[11] Individuals find resources within themselves that inspire them to initiate the entrepreneurial process, and they also engage with others in various environments and in the public domain to explore entrepreneurial options and possibilities.

6.3.2   IEO Risk and Theory U Co-sensing

The co-sensing stage is paramount because entrepreneurs can break through old patterns by stepping into different but relevant experiences.[12] The co-sensing stage helps the would-be entrepreneur to build relationships with key stakeholders, acquiring a widened perspective of the environment as an undivided reality where fragmented social realities

---

[9] Van der Westhuizen (2016).
[10] Lumpkin and Dess (1996) and Ramkissor and Cassim (2013).
[11] Gardner (2003).
[12] Van der Westhuizen (2016).

are deconstructed, and collective growth is encouraged.[13] According to Scharmer and Kaufer,[14] individuals observe and are influenced by actions and interactions in various systems around them, and there are four levels of system that influence IEO: (a) the *micro system,* synonymous with an individual's mindset; (b) the *meso-system,* or direct environment where the individual is co-sensing the entrepreneurial process; (c) the *macro-system,* including local economic development field in which the individual is located; and (d) the *mundo-system,* the bigger economic picture on a national and global scale.[15]

6.3.3 IEO Innovation and Theory U Co-inspiring

One definition of entrepreneurial innovation cited by Lumpkin and Dess[16] is a 'willingness to support creativity and experimentation in introducing new products/services, and novelty, technological leadership and research and development in developing new processes. In an earlier paper,[17] the same authors note that, as an IEO propensity', 'innovation is an important means of pursuing opportunities'.

Intrapersonal and interpersonal integration potentially makes individuals more receptive to a source of inspiration,[18] and more likely to reach an 'aha' moment of insight.[19]

In the Theory U process, co-inspiring is synonymous with pre-sensing.[20] With this alternative term, the emphasis is on the birth of a creative and novel idea, or an 'aha' moment that can lead to innovation. The link between successful innovations in entrepreneurship and

---

[13] Pillay (2016).
[14] Scharmer and Kaufer (2013).
[15] Jackson (2003) and Scharmer and Kaufer (2013).
[16] Van der Westhuizen (2016).
[17] Lumpkin and Dess 1996).
[18] Scharmer and Kaufer (2013).
[19] Jung-Beeman et al. (2004) and Weinberg (2014).
[20] Scharmer and Kaufer (2013).

the interrelationship between Theory U co-inspiring and IEO innovation is therefore crucial not only to boost entrepreneurship but also to transform entrepreneurial thinking among individuals.

6.3.4 IEO Proactivity and Theory U Co-creating

For Callaghan,[21] 'proactiveness is related to initiative and first-mover advantages' through the pursuit of new opportunities and acting in anticipation of future problems. For Lumpkin and Dess,[22] the importance of proactiveness is its 'forward-looking perspective' for entrepreneurial activity and innovation. Fiebig[23] describes proactiveness as a behavioural trait where individuals constantly seek opportunities and have a forward-looking perspective.

When IEO leads to entrepreneurial intention, the individuals concerned are engaging in the process of co-creation. This process can occur on an intrapersonal level, where the individual moves towards entrepreneurial activity. Interpersonal co-creations occur, where the individual moves towards more formal business friendships or entrepreneurial activities. Scharmer and Kaufer[24] indicate that these co-creations often lead to prototyping, where one creates ideas, innovatively develops them and tests them in the market. Prototyping of entrepreneurial intention may thus result in entrepreneurial activity. Prototyping that stems from entrepreneurial intention thus may result in entrepreneurial activity.[25]

6.3.5 IEO Proactivity and Theory U Co-evolving

After developing a prototype, individuals might move into entrepreneurial activity either alone or through partnerships. According

---

[21] Callaghan (2009).
[22] Lumpkin and Dess 1996).
[23] Fiebig (2015).
[24] Scharmer and Kaufer (2013).
[25] Weinberg (2014).

to Scharmer and Kaufer,[26] the extent of entrepreneurial activity marks the outflow intensity of the U process.

The literature suggests that a possible way to boost youth entrepreneurship in South Africa is to develop levels of IEO. The processes outlined in Theory U offer a potential pathway for individuals to move from a reactive response field to a generative response field, with the potential enhancement of IEO.

6.4   Empirical Investigation: Correlation Between IEO and Theory U Factors

As part of a pilot for the SHAPE social technology, we investigated the potential correlation of IEO and Theory U factors using a structured questionnaire with 27 question items. Examples of question items that are associated with IEO and U factors are: '*I can handle risky situations with confidence*'; '*I am creative and new business ideas comes easily to me*'; and '*I am comfortable moving into new situations*'. The questionnaire was administered to 380 second-year students at UKZN. The data we collected gave us a baseline for the SHAPE development. Differences in IEO and Theory U factor scores were examined between male and female participants. Since none of the scores were normal, a non-parametric test supports that, overall, IEO and Theory U scores of male and female participants were similar. Both genders indicated similarities in moving from a reactive to a generative response field. We found that no significant differences exist in scores on IEP and Theory U dimensions for participants of different ages. However, there was a statistically significant correlation ($p < 0.01$) between IEO scores and Theory U scores. Theory U suggests that there should be a positive correlation between co-inspiring and co-initiating or co-sensing.

In addition, co-inspiring should be correlated positively with co-creating and co-evolving. Our results showed that risk factors, which are part of Theory U's reactive processes of co-initiating and co-sensing, were significantly related to innovation as a co-inspiring factor in Theory

---

[26] Scharmer and Kaufer (2013).

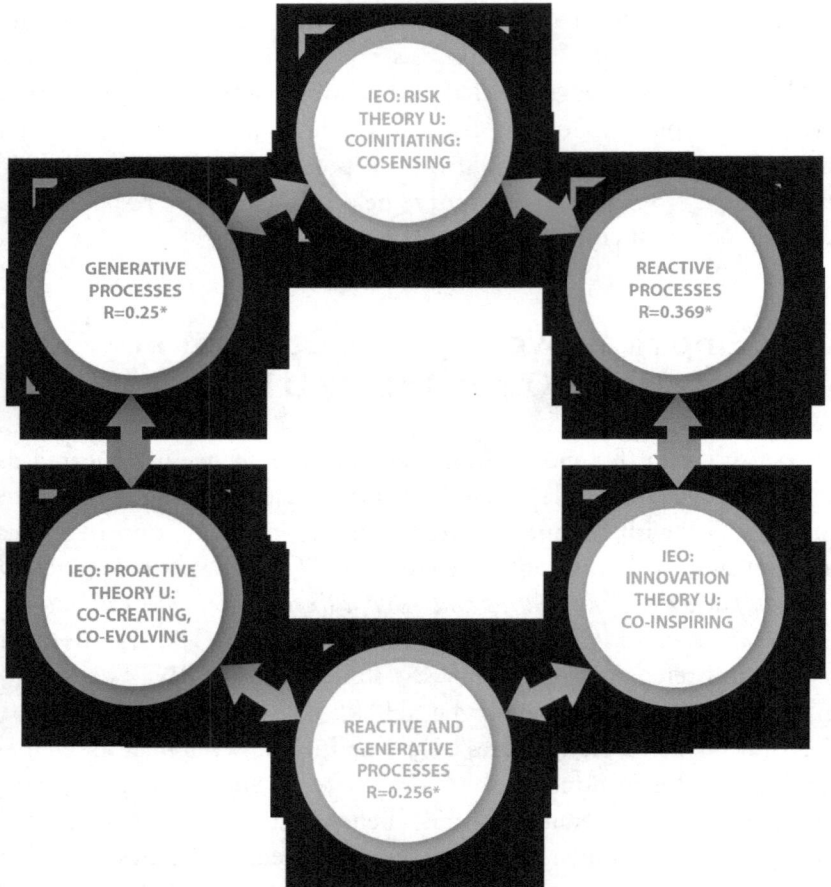

Fig. 6.1 Correlations between IEO propensities and Theory U (*Source* Van der Westhuizen [2016])

U, confirming Theory U's interrelationships.[27] We also found that co-inspiring was significantly related to co-creating or co-evolving likewise confirming Theory U's interrelationships and correlations between Theory U and IEO factors (Fig. 6.1) were used to plot the sequence of events and activities for Meet Your Business Friend Day.

---

[27] Van der Westhuizen (2017a, b, c).

6.5   Background to Practice

We give an account here of the systemic action learning and action research that preceded Meet Your Business Friend Day which enabled it to become an event for enhancement of co-inspiring/presencing.

6.6   Enhance Co-inspiring/Presencing

Building on the notion of action learning and action research as outlined by Revans,[28] Schweikert, Meissen and Wolf[29] propose a *systemic* extension of this approach, which they describe as an interactive process between local stakeholders and the researcher that enable individuals involved to bring diverse knowledge and a dialogical process to a problem or challenge [and] that allows the researcher to observe and act upon dynamics at the systemic level. The SHAPE social technology involves systemic interactivity between student entrepreneurs, their intermediaries from the business world and the practitioner-researcher to (jointly) investigate and find solutions to challenges that young entrepreneurs inevitably encounter. Van der Westhuizen[30] identified systemic intermediaries to support student entrepreneurs. However, within the process of intermediaries supporting student entrepreneurs, several barriers prevented successful and sustainable interaction. These stem mostly form personal barriers that student entrepreneurs have with their interrelationships to intermediaries. IEO as a personality trait can therefore be seen as either a barrier of an enabler to entrepreneurial action. Developed levels of IEO from student entrepreneurs might lead to improved relationships and collaboration with various systemic role-players and eventually result into socio-economic development, as a result of entrepreneurial momentum gained throughout systemic levels.

---

[28] Revans (2011).

[29] Schweikert et al. (2013).

[30] Van der Westhuizen (2016).

6.7   Meet Your Business Friend Day

Meet Your Business Friend Day was a concluding workshop for SHAPE participants, representing Phase 8, of the overall SHAPE social technology. Figure 6.2 shows a full outline of the phases and timelines in the SHAPE cycles, as guided by overarching stages in the Theory U cycle. In this case, Theory U was used as both a framework for the project social technology and as a research methodology.

In the Meet Your Business Friend Day event, student entrepreneurs engaged with business professionals to explore possibilities for further entrepreneurial action through mutual co-inspiration, co-creation and co-evolution in 'Business Friendships' potentially formed between them. The event was also facilitated by intermediaries for the student entrepreneurs previously engaged for the project (municipality mentors, government mentors, Local Economic Development tutors; UKZN practitioner-researcher), who helped to bring in the experienced entrepreneurs and business professionals. At this point in the programme, students arrived at a full experience of the U process, encountering what Scharmer calls 'Economies of Creation'. In 'Meet

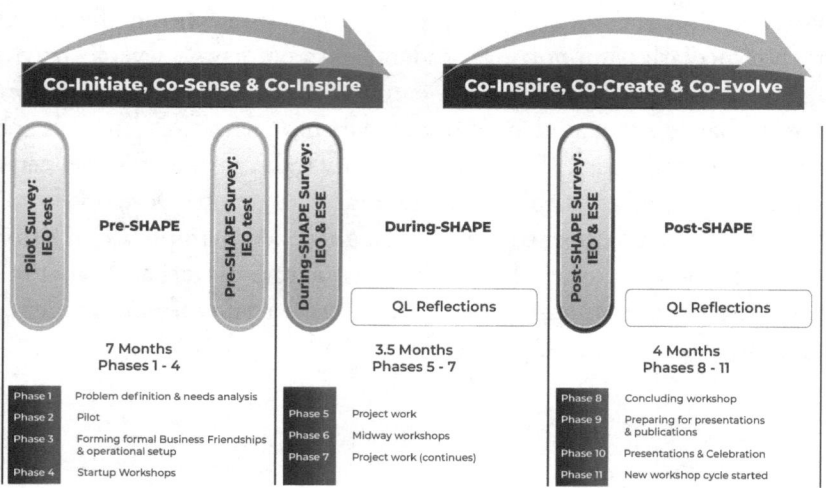

Fig. 6.2 Phases and timelines in the SHAPE social technology/research methodology (*Source* Van der Westhuizen [2016])

Your Business Friend Day' the spiral cycles of the SHAPE systemic action learning and action research methodology materialised as looped experiences and actions: firstly, through the student entrepreneurs' inner experiences, secondly through relationships experienced with their peers and thirdly through reflection upon the supporting structure involving the university, municipality mentors, Chamber of Commerce mentors and tutors from the UKZN Local Economic Development unit.

6.8 Logistics for 'Meet Your Business Friend Day'

Meet Your Business Friend Day activities: beginning action learning and action research methods.

The overall objective of the workshop was to match student entrepreneurs with business mentors to stimulate possible partnerships between them. Each student entrepreneur had a nascent business idea— a basic and novel idea for creating a new venture to be shared with a business mentor who would be a sounding board, helping them with advice, counsel and networking opportunities to shape the raw and underdeveloped ideas into a viable business opportunity.

The planned sequence of sessions was designed to match each young entrepreneur with a business mentor not necessarily on the strength and detail of the business idea but on the 'chemistry' and resonance between the two parties. This objective was based on the Theory U principle of having an Open Heart, where participants in a systemic action learning and action research project develop capabilities to listen emphatically to one another and try to see the world, and their entrepreneurial passions, through the eyes of somebody else.[31] This called for a workshop design that would allow participants to explore their characteristics and attributes more holistically, going beyond just conceptual and intellectual issues.

Session 2, 'Building the Network', was designed as a self-reflexive exercise for holistic exploration by each participant of the various facets of

---

[31] Schweikert et al. (2013).

their identity and construction of self, taking account of the following dimensions:

- emotional;
- mind/cognitive;
- harmony/musical/balance;
- active/kinesthetic;
- spiritual/religious;
- other information/general.

These helped participants explore and illustrate important facets of their identity and arrive at a concise self-description; they were each given an identity board and asked to allocate 18 points among these six dimensions.

Using the identity boards, 'speed-dating' then took place with two concentric circles facing each other; young entrepreneurs in the inner circle and business mentors in the outer circle. Three minutes were given to share identity boards and to engage in discussions, after which the outer circle rotated by one space and the process repeated itself until all those in the inner circle had shared identity boards with all those in the outer circle.

The next step was for participants to self-organise in a way that matched business mentors (business friends) with young entrepreneurs. With the number of student entrepreneurs exceeding the number of business mentors, this meant that each business mentor was allocated a group of student entrepreneurs. Once this allocation was completed, participants began sharing business concepts.

For Session 3, 'Beach Activity', participants were divided into ten groups, each including business mentors and young entrepreneurs, competing in team-building activities on the beach (or sometimes in the water) designed in various ways to elicit and model fact-finding, business intelligence, decision-making, skills assessment, information sharing, resource allocation, motivation, skill, stamina and leadership.

Session 4 was devoted to developing a business canvass model for each of the business ideas. Business mentors assisted their young entrepreneurs with 'teasing out' their business concepts in more detail, focusing explicitly on key attributes of their business concept as set out in a template covering eight broad categories:

- resources;
- funding;
- costs;
- revenues;
- value chain activities;
- competencies;
- value proposition;
- team members.

In addition, the business teams considered issues of competitiveness and engaged in a creative activity to design an appropriate tag line.

The business canvass used at this point was a more elaborate form of the basic business model canvass that had been used during contact sessions in the preceding phase (Phase 7) of SHAPE. It was accordingly familiar to the student entrepreneurs but new to the business friends.

In Session 5, the beach-clubhouse venue was turned into an Arabian-style 'Souk' marketplace. Each of the business teams was allocated space and an assortment of materials (play dough, foil, crayons, old magazines, empty toilet rolls, etc.) to exhibit and demonstrate their business concept at a stand in the Souk. The objective was to develop a prototype or some other kind of presentation of the core business concept that gave 'visitors' a convincing impression of the value of the proposition. The exhibit could be a physical replica of a product or a symbolic and metaphorical depiction of the underlying business concept. Once the exhibits were constructed, some teams remained behind as exhibitors and others became visitors to the Souk. This continued through a few cycles until all participants had been both an exhibitor and a 'visitor' to view and engage with the other exhibits. This was followed by a debriefing to extract the lessons and make connections between the activities and the way they related to the overall purpose of the workshop.

Connection on an emotional level was a continuous thread linking all sessions, with the initial emphasis on entrepreneurial 'heartset' rather than mindset, followed by shared reflections on personal identity, then team beach activities, putting both student entrepreneurs and their potential business friends in a more receptive frame of mind for co-creating and co-evolving possible entrepreneurial activity.

The workshop ended with a feedback activity, coordinated by the lead researcher, in which all participants made music for themselves with tapping and drumming to accompany words and singing. This served as an object lesson showing how it was possible for all to arrive at a point of coherence and synchronisation (Figs. 6.3, 6.4, 6.5, 6.6, 6.7, and 6.8).

In a follow-up analysis of the workshop event, the following categories emerged:

- Student entrepreneurs who wished to co-create and co-evolve solo with their business ideas;
- Business professionals who wished to co-create and co-evolve solo with their business ideas;
- Student entrepreneurs who wished to co-create and co-evolve together with other student entrepreneurs with their business ideas;

The clubhouse venue

Fig. 6.3 The clubhouse venue (*Source* Van der Westhuizen [2016])

Discovering team member skills

Fig. 6.4 Discovering team member skills (*Source* Van der Westhuizen [2016])

- Student entrepreneurs who wished to co-create and co-evolve together with other student entrepreneurs and business professionals with their business ideas; and
- Business professionals who wished to co-create and co-evolve together with other business professionals.

Prototyping and co-creating a new business concept

Fig. 6.5 Prototyping and co-creating a new business concept (*Source* Van der Westhuizen [2016])

6.9   Qualitative Methodology

Participants (sample size $N = 60$) were volunteering second-year B.Comm undergraduates at the University of KwaZulu-Natal. Students were asked to write reflections which were published on the project website. A qualitative thematic analysis of data was used where themes were allowed to emerge from the data. From the inductive coding process, themes and nodes emerged from the text and were identified, along with simultaneous sub-themes and sub-nodes. Word frequencies, word tag clouds and word trees were identified in the During-SHAPE and Post-SHAPE stage from participants' reflections to support the thematic analysis.

All indicated that they would like further support from systemic structures that were in place to assist the student entrepreneurs such as the University, the Municipality, the Chamber of Commerce and

Speed dating: identifying entrepreneurial heartset before
building entrepreneurial mindset

Fig. 6.6 Speed dating: Identifying entrepreneurial heartset before building
entrepreneurial mindset (*Source* Van der Westhuizen [2016])

the Local Economic Development Unit. They also indicated that they
would welcome further business development support from financial
institutions such as banks.

A number of subsequent student comments on what they had gained
from Meet Your Business Friend Day and from the SHAPE social technology overall, reflected the aptness of the Theory U social technology
underlying the concept of Business Friendship and the broad design of
SHAPE.

The Business Friendships not only made possible actualisation of the
student entrepreneur's aspirations for a higher state of Self and Work, but
also created opportunities for expressing these aspirations. One comment
made clear the need of co-development with others to realise inner
aspirations:

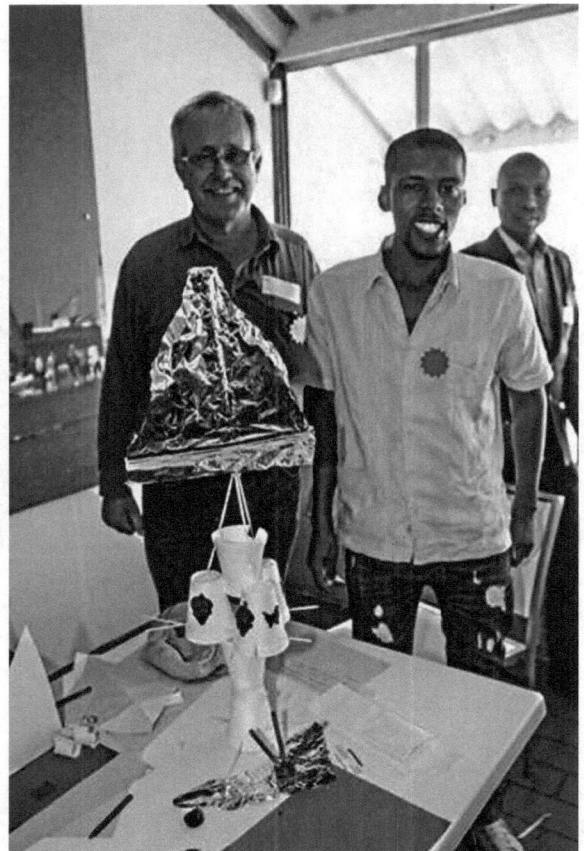

**Student entrepreneurs and business friends
ready to co-create and co-evolve**

Fig. 6.7 Student entrepreneurs and business friends ready to co-create and co-evolve (*Source* Van der Westhuizen [2016])

Having my own business was definitely on the top of my list of goals but I just didn't know how to get there, who were the right people I had to talk to, and how to go about getting everything that I needed.

Working on the business canvass

Fig. 6.8 Working on the business canvass (*Source* Van der Westhuizen [2016])

SHAPE used Theory U as (a) research methodology, (b) an applied social technology and (c) a theoretical framework. The role that relationships and Business Friendships plays in developing IEO for the student entrepreneur are evident in the following:

Another comment captured the broad advantage for IEO of a Business Friendship:

> Relationships, networking, and just generally interacting with multiple stakeholders serve multiple purposes.

As another student remarked,

> When you are young, the concept of networking is very alien and you don't know how to go about raising capital. SHAPE decides to close that gap, so exciting!

The first Business Friendship or partnership identified by the students was indeed SHAPE itself, which students saw as a means to reach their previously internal aspirations:

Partnerships with team leaders and facilitators serve the purpose of allowing us to think beyond our own realm of thought – and start thinking about other sources of infor- mation necessary for further growth.

The next set of Business Friendships or partnerships they identified were with their peers. For the first time, they had met and interacted with like-minded individuals:

Relationships with classmates and other people on the program serves to encourage them, and help to think and discuss matters on deeper levels.

Meet Your Business Friend Day highlighted the benefit offered by external stakeholders creating important opportunities in the external environment, where students gave expression to their ideas and ultimately achieved both personal and societal-level goals.

Partnering with [representatives of] UKZN/Municipalities, etc.— make opportunities for practicing and implementing ideas a reality.

Two common themes emerged in the discourse around Business Friendships: interaction with: like-minded individuals, and interaction with people seen as key role-players in helping the young entrepreneur achieve goals and come to terms with Self and Work aspirations.

The first theme—the ability to interact with like-minded individuals—demonstrates that the ability to have an Open Heart often develops simultaneously and not as a separate or fragmented process, since it is important to listen emphatically to other individuals and to be receptive to their ideas in order to adjust their own mental models to identify and connect with those of others.[32] This evidently happened with the SEs, as is also shown in the following quote:

It has been such an eye-opening experience when I got the chance to interact with peers who also share the same thoughts about what society needs and what we as individuals need.

---

[32] Southern (2013).

The second theme is identifying people to assist in realising aspirations for Self and Work to create more business opportunities, thereby demonstrating the development of entrepreneurial mindset about opportunity identification[33] and proactivity.[34] This was also evident in the reflections from SEs:

> I believe [that] for my business to grow I will need to have people to advise me. I feel honored to get into SHAPE because we will get to meet other successful entrepreneurs who might be interested to join forces in the field I'm interested to get [in]to.

The next quote refers to the second type of Business Friendship (partnership)—ability to partner with like-minded individuals, or peers, allowing for a deeper discussion and understanding of common matters of interest. Reflections correspond with the argument put forward by Hannon et al.,[35] that deep-learning practices such as the U process can enable individuals to develop collectively a Bigger Picture in their pursuit of socio-economic development:

In addition, another student entrepreneur notes that their common ground relates back to having common interests, ideas and goals:

> knowing that there are young people that are as ambitious and dedicated to fulfilling their dreams of being successful entrepreneurs.

Being able to talk to like-minded peers about matters of shared concern suggests there is something common to this group of people—something that will need to be explored first: inherent differences between applicants and non-applicants for SHAPE, or conversely, inherently similarities between all applicants.

Responses such as these indicated that three aspects of Theory U were taking place:

---

[33] Cox et al. (2002).
[34] Callaghan (2009).
[35] Hannon et al. (2013).

- Student participants recognised like-mindedness with other SHAPE applicants.
- Student participants shared a common sense of like-heartedness.
- Student participants saw SHAPE as a means to link like-minded and like-hearted people for goal actualisation.

As one student put it, if a little ungrammatically: SHAPE *came in a right time to right people.*

However, the enhanced socio-economic developmental attitudes, aspirations and activity bring forward challenges and obstacles as the journey to potential entrepreneurial action continues,[36] and these are discussed in the remainder of this chapter.

6.10 Applying Theory U to Develop Individual Entrepreneurial Orientation

The objectives of this research included investigating how using the Theory U conceptual framework as a social technology develops the risk-taking, innovation and proactivity propensities of IEO.

6.10.1 IEO Risk-Taking Propensity

The aspirant student entrepreneurs were now looking at the potential risks involved in becoming an actual entrepreneur. They had no previous experience with entrepreneurship before participating in SHAPE, so taking risks as an entrepreneur now took on a new reality for them. The risk-taking propensity of IEO is also related to the construct of opportunity identification.[37] The students began to grasp that there are real risks involved in realising their identified opportunities:

> Yes, I feel afraid to take risk but I always try to take risks because for me taking risks can reveal my abilities which I did not know about [them]

---

[36] Xavier et al. (2013).
[37] Callaghan (2009).

before and I believe winning is[a] close friend of failing that [is] what make[s] me take risk[s] [to gain] new opportunities.

That you can go from having all the money in the world to being bankrupt, and in debt. That risks are part of business should be seen as motivation to defy the odds.

Taking risks [is] are part of the characteristics of an entrepreneur.

Yes, I don 't like taking risks. However, I do under- stand that the life of an entrepreneur is largely based on risk-taking.

Taking risks is a big part of being a young entrepreneur. One cannot embark on starting a business without taking any risks. From financing the business, to marketing and even deciding what kind of business to start up, every single decision is risky.

I am aware of the many risks involved in business now, and I feel that one has to be teachable and use opportunities available to try and overcome all the risks involved.

Thus, although some students commented that they did not like taking risks, they also realised that deciding to take some entrepreneurial risks is crucial if one wants to start a new business. Lumpkin and Dess[38] consider that lack of experience in taking real entrepreneurial risks and in performing entrepreneurially under risky situations, as faced by these students, contributes significantly to how problem-solving is conceptually framed. This implies that the students now need to apply their newly framed entrepreneurial mental models to address challenges at hand in taking entrepreneurial action.

The reflections cited below suggest that by taking risks and embracing opportunities available to them; the students will unlock their aspirations for Self and Work that are vital if they hope to sustain their businesses. Hays[39] notes that developing a higher sense of Being through questioning the Self and Work is quite difficult, as it was for the students because in a sense, risk forces you to get to know yourself better:

---

[38] Lumpkin and Dess (1996).
[39] Hays (2013).

> Yes, I feel afraid to take risk but I always try to take risks because for me taking risks can reveal my abilities which I did not know about [them] before.

The risk-taking propensity was also perceived as necessary in order to advance personally and professionally:

> Yes. I believe risks occurs when you do not know what you are doing and unless you are willing to go the extra mile and find out, risks will always affect your thinking. And with that said, I believe taking risks is part of what it takes to get ahead and that is what I plan on doing. I realized that without taking risks, you like doing nothing to move forward. You 'll never know about something unless you try, investigate or pursue it.

And ultimately to reach the best possible future they envision for themselves, there is much risk in the entrepreneurial environment, but you have to be able to take risk, because risk is one of the aspects of entrepreneurs. You have to take risks in life to achieve a certain goal. Yes, I feel like being successful requires you to take risks. You cannot win a war with your gun on safety.

Risks are seen as an inevitable consequence of starting up a business.[40] The strategies of SHAPE enabled them to observe other entrepreneurs in real-life situations and also to interact with these entrepreneurs. Every respondent reflected on risks and the role of risk in developing their entrepreneurial abilities.

I feel as I can take these risks because the businessmen have taken this risk.

In becoming young entrepreneurs, they perceive themselves as more resilient, able to pick themselves up after failure, and to realise opportunities that arise as a consequence.

It is much easier to take risk as a young entrepreneur than when you [are] old and have a lot of responsibilities. So, if the[re] was a right time to take risks, I'd say that time is now.

---

[40] Lumpkin and Dess (1996).

Therefore, they see that being a young entrepreneur in South Africa sets them apart from older generations, confirming a similar observation made by Mitchell and Harris.[41] In a way, they, as youngsters, have more of an Open Will than older entrepreneurs do, possibly because opportunity costs for young entrepreneurs are relatively low.[42]

Risk is seen as something that can be understood and managed if 'calculated'[43]:

> I as a young entrepreneur need to be able to calculate the risks at hand and [to] evaluate which is better for my business and myself.

Risk, when it is 'calculated' seems to become less likely to disable the young entrepreneurs' ability to pick themselves up in the event of failure. Here a risk is calculated, based on:

- anticipating risks and their consequences involves the ability to predict and to take the appropriate action to prevent or to minimise its eventuality;
- a cost-benefit ratio that requires awareness of the consequences of risk; weighing up the benefits associated with the risks; and
- an internal locus of control that is the extent to which the individual sees the risk as manageable.

6.10.2 Anticipating Risks and Their Consequences

The ability to anticipate risks is linked closely to the proactivity propensity in IEO[44] and it is also an essential factor in willingness to take risks, which implies that the aspiring young entrepreneurs were able to identify possible risks and to do something about them in an attempt to control the risk.

---

[41] Mitchell and Harris (2012).
[42] Hulsink and Koek (2014).
[43] Poole (2014).
[44] Lumpkin and Dess (1996).

Student entrepreneurs reflected on their vision for themselves as young entrepreneurs in the emerging future. What was the future then, is the current now,[45] and a new future had started to emerge in which they saw themselves now faced with needing to take potential risks to make their vision a reality.

I learned that being proactive helps you with avoiding problems in your business. You can expect them and start planning early how to solve them or [to] avoid them. I learned a lot about being in business and handling the pressure of it.

It is important as an entrepreneur to see things before they can or will actually happen and try to alleviate problems from happening or growing even bigger than what they are.

I [have] come a long way. Risk is a very broad word. I realised that taking risks needs a lot of thinking and having to be aware of the consequences of your risky decisions.

From these reflections, it seems as if the aspiring young entrepreneurs learned from their interaction and experiences with other entrepreneurs—an opportunity that the SHAPE social technology made possible for them. It also seems as if they began to think about possible solutions to the potential risks that they might encounter, as well as the potential costs and benefits to them.

6.10.3 Cost-Benefit Ratio

The aspiring young entrepreneurs, in starting to anticipate entrepreneurial risks, also started to calculate the social and economic cost-benefit ratio—which again required them to look critically at their financial, social and environmental wealth.[46] The aspiring young entrepreneurs seem to have developed an awareness of the consequences of taking risks as an entrepreneur:

I realized that you have to take calculated risks. Not every risk is worth taking. You have to look at your opportunity cost. Taking risks is a big

---

[45] Korthaugen et al. (2013).
[46] Zahra et al. (2014).

deal and is something that has to [be] thought [about] carefully and weighed against all benefits. Risks can turn out unsuccessful or successful but the aim is to get what you want done, so it is worth it to take a risk and have alternative plans in-case [this] doesn't work out. The life of an entrepreneur is largely based on risk taking; therefore I am willing to do so but making every necessary provision for alternative outcomes. Yes, I am more aware of taking risks. Initially I thought I was fine with taking risks but when taking such huge risks there 's always that possibility that the risk will not pay off.

These reflections suggest how students were acquiring the ability, or strengthening their ability to weigh the potential benefits and losses associated with entrepreneurial risk—benefits and losses that Zahra et al.,[47] distinguish as (a) financial, (b) social and (c) environmental. In Theory U terms, this is critical thinking and introspective learning, which the aspiring young entrepreneurs develop in the course of their transformative journey in the U-Curve.[48]

6.10.4 Internal Locus of Control

Internal locus of control relates to the extent to which the aspiring young entrepreneurs see the risk as manageable and relates closely to their levels of Entrepreneurial Self-Efficacy and Individual Entrepreneurial Orientation.[49] The aspiring young entrepreneurs began to think about how they would handle potential entrepreneurial risks:

It is better to take a calculated risk, one that I know I can manage as an individual. There are a lot of risks that occur in the process but the ability to manage and tolerate those risks is important. Yes, I am aware[of] the risk of having a fail[ed] business. What if your business idea doesn't work out and what if it does work out and doesn't make any profit? I am aware of all these risks and I feel like [that] I still need to assess myself if I can [be able to] handle them. Personally, I think that taking a risk is

---

[47] Zahra et al. (2014).
[48] Korthaugen et al. (2013).
[49] Dunwoody and Griffin (2014).

dangerous but it is better to take a calculated risk, one that I know I can manage as an individual or one that I know will not affect other people.

The aspiring young entrepreneurs reflected that they might be able to mitigate the 'riskiness' of risk by taking things whence they came. This shows an element of the self-tolerance factor in Entrepreneurial Self-Efficacy,[50] which will be discussed as a further theme in this chapter. In a way, tolerance mitigates the extent of the risk, and risk can also be mitigated by taking advantage of appropriate opportunities and being proactive. Through reflection on how they saw themselves managing risks as an aspiring young entrepreneur, they also developed a problem-solving capacity concerning the entrepreneurial risks that might arise.

This questioning of problem-solving and anticipation of entrepreneurial risks might, therefore, lead them to generate new knowledge and thus come up with some form of individual innovation—thereby undergoing transformation, which implies a change in developmental maturity.[51]

6.10.5   IEO Innovation Propensity

In moving to become actual entrepreneurs, the students were still developing their business concepts. There was no evidence of reflections about product innovation in the Post-SHAPE stage, but intrinsic individual transformation and innovation were strongly evident in the During-SHAPE stage—which implied a change in developmental maturity.[52] A possible explanation for this is that students had already moved beyond the co-inspiring or presencing phase of the U-Curve as they now began to co-create and co-evolve as aspirant young entrepreneurs.

---

[50] Dunwoody and Griffin (2014).
[51] Fitch and O'Fallon (2013).
[52] Fitch and O'Fallon (2013).

6.10.6 IEO Proactivity Propensity

Intrinsic to innovation is an element of proactivity in that the individual acts on an idea or pushes further when an opportunity arises. This relates back to the empirical findings that an individual who is proactive acts from both the reactive and the generative response fields. Dealing with the problem reflexively requires both innovation and being proactive.

It is crucial to be innovative as an entrepreneur because the obstacles that come up sometimes requires there to be change.

Also, individuals need to be well aware of the opportunities available to them to ensure that they are proactive:

> Being proactive as a young entrepreneur requires a lot of time and commitment. It requires you to be well versed about the opportunities available around you.

For the aspiring young entrepreneurs to be proactive they need to have knowledge and information available to them. Without the support of intermediaries, or educational information, the ambitious young entrepreneurs feel unable to see their way to implementing and anticipating and acquiring the necessary tolerance in business activity.

Yes, as a new entrepreneur almost every move is a risk, as you would be new and would be literally blindly feeling your way through business.

Again the role of the 'other' becomes explicit in knowledge generation, management and self-awareness and confidence. When sufficient entrepreneurial skills are developed, and information is available and has been absorbed, the aspiring young entrepreneur is in a better position to anticipate and calculate risks and to take the necessary steps to mitigate them and improve the chances of success:

> Yes, I feel risk-taking is a good thing because it's always 50/50 either you pass or fail, but you can ensure that you go into a risk with enough information that might aid in getting a business success rather than a failure.

In the beginning my biggest challenge was doubt and not having that much belief in my ability to be a successful entrepreneur. one of the bigger challenges is not having information or enough of it.

Information is of such importance to the aspiring young entrepreneurs that they feel unable to take risks until they are sufficiently informed:

I think I will not be able to take risk[s] at the moment, at least I will learn more about business before I start my own.

Anticipating risks implies proactivity:

Being proactive as an entrepreneur is about taking charge and knowing that if things do go wrong along the way that you will take full responsibility and move on from there.

Being proactive allows the aspiring young entrepreneur to anticipate risks, and as previously discussed, when a risk can be anticipated, its effect can be mitigated, increasing the aspiring young entrepreneur's capacity for tolerance:

I learn[ed] that [to] be proactive enable[s] entrepreneur[s] to anticipate challenges that she/he did not know about before and also [to] bring about confidence in entrepreneurship.

Again, the link between proactivity, innovation and tolerance is made, and often in relation to risk.

6.11 Enablers of Actualising Entrepreneurial Vision: Open Mind, Heart and Will

6.11.1 Open Mind

Open Mind refers to an individual's capacity to suspend old patterns of thought and listen to what others are saying. In this case, 'others' alludes to previous discussions on relations with other people, including peers and intermediaries, giving support to the aspiring young entrepreneurs. Through these interactions, they listen to the 'other' and internalise what has been said to bring about changes within themselves. Guttenstein, Lindsay and Baron[53] believe that these collective processes enable individuals to cross thresholds together, therefore to change collectively in developmental maturity.

Here, the participants acknowledge how SHAPE and the intermediaries they have been exposed to, assisted in their individual development and further assisted them to have an open mind:

> I have been exposed to many different people from different walks of life who have planted ideas in my mind which has made me think more intensively.

It is evident here that through interactions with others the participants acknowledge differences in perspectives and different ways of thinking, and instead of shutting them out they allow their minds to be opened to new ways of thinking and doing things.

This is the first programme, [sic] I have actually been part of. Through this programme [sic] I have actually realized that I am a dedicated person, I given 100% to whatever I sign up for This has been myself finding myself through being part of the programme. [sic] This new way of thinking and doing things is further evident in the next statement:

> I learned about how to listen attentively and [about] breathing exercises.

---

[53] Guttenstein et al. (2013).

By allowing themselves space within which to reflect on what others, with different opinions, have imparted to them, they begin to interrogate their own self-concept and belief, and introspectively gain a better understanding of who they are. Peschl and Fundneider[54] suggest that primary or deep knowledge, which is related to the notion of wisdom, might the result of an observation process that is conducted with a highly open mind. Therefore, one might say that transformation, or a change in developmental maturity occurred.[55]

As they come to know and develop themselves better and their self-concept [grows], so too their way of thinking around business changes.

> I learned that it is important to invest in a business idea that is your niche. It surprised me [at] how many times my business idea changed because of the lessons I was taught.

This change in developmental maturity, which enables the student entrepreneur to move from an old self to a new Self might be an indication of movement through the U-Curve from a reactive to a generative response field.[56] Therefore, the reactive propensity of IEO Risk, the generative propensity of IEO Innovation and the reactive/generative propensity of IEO Proactivity (opportunity identification) has developed.[57]

6.11.2 Open Heart

Having an Open Heart refers to an individual's capacity to empathise or to see a situation through the eyes of somebody else. Unlike the Pre-SHAPE and During-SHAPE phases, where expression of empathy was chiefly aimed at bringing about positive change in society as a whole (feelings of ubuntu78), there now seems to have been an acknowledgement of the role of self in relation to the whole. In other words, when

---

[54] Peschl and Fundneider (2013).
[55] Fitch and O'Fallon (2013).
[56] Gunnlaugson and Walker (2013).
[57] Van der Westhuizen (2017a, b, c).

the participants first embarked on SHAPE, they were only aware of change that needed to take place on a systemic level to bring about socio-economic improvement. Thus they were aware of transformation that needs to happen in communities where they live, or in South Africa as a whole. However, the blind spot seems to have been an inward journey towards their own Entrepreneurial Self-Efficacy and IEO abilities and capabilities to bring about entrepreneurial action needed for systemic change. In other words, they failed to acknowledge their own innovative entrepreneurial action that leads to the change they want to see within the external whole. This echoes Pillay's[58] comment that correlates with the view that as the entrepreneurial mindset develops there is more cognisance of internal orientation in relation to the external whole. This acknowledgement of both individualistic and collective ways of thinking and acting is indicative of a developing entrepreneurial mind.[59]

Seeing situations afresh through the eyes of a newly developed Self is indicated in the following quote:

> I learned doing things that will make you happy at the end. I learned that I should do things that are from the bottom of my heart. first thing[s] first is to find yourself and what you like. I learned to be innovative and creative. It has been amazing.

This might imply that the students had a change in developmental maturity in the way they see entrepreneurship and making money. They suggest they are beginning to realise the importance of 'learning a living' rather than 'earning a living'[60] where living creatively and positively means that you are living for more than just financial gain.

6.11.3 Open Will

Having an Open Will (the ability to let go and let come), the young entrepreneurs come to realise how little they previously knew; therefore,

---

[58] Pillay (2014).
[59] Richardson and Hynes (2008) and Kickul et al. (2009).
[60] Hannon et al. (2013).

change has occurred in their developmental maturity. Moving from a reactive response field, where individuals let go of past preconceptions and personal experiences, a certain internal realisation needs first to take place—this is also referred to as 'Presencing', 'co-inspiring' or 'connecting to the Source'.[61] This Presencing moment results in a generative response field, where an individual enables the emerging future. Thus an individual's Open Mind and Open Heart enables the Open Will to let go of past ways of thinking and doing, resulting in receptiveness to letting into their entrepreneurial mindset new ways of feeling, thinking and acting.[62]

Evidence of first letting go to allow for letting come:

> As optimistic as you should be as an entrepreneur, the first step always takes blind faith and the belief that what you doing is right. I've learned to be free, more open minded especially of my surroundings and not (to) be negligent.

Letting come often created meaningful interactions with others whereby new things were learned:

> I have learned so many things including to have a good relationship with mates, working together with groups, we combined many different new ideas with others and listen to other ideas.

By letting go, participants could allow assimilation of new perspectives, and these new perspectives ultimately allowed the new Self to emerge.

Coming up with new ideas has grown me physically and mentally, being innovative gives you more opportunities/alternatives to succeed in building your future or career.

And in letting go, participants created the space to allow learning new experiences, and this emergent knowledge allowed them to also learn new things about themselves:

> I have learned about myself the following: Self-Confidence, Communication Skills and Being around Peers with Business Minds.

---

[61] Scharmer (2009).
[62] Fitch and O'Fallon (2013).

In the context of this research, the 'somebody else' can be interpreted as the participant in relation to other individuals, and also as the participant as transformative human being.

> I have learned a lot from SHAPE, including how import- ant perseverance is, what it takes to be successful and I also learned that everything that you want to pursue do it with your love, heart and be passionate about it. I also learned you shouldn 't rush at things just give [it] time and relax.

These reflections on Open Will might indicate that transformative learning took place—since the student now sees both themselves and the Whole (the systems or the world they live in) differently.[63] It also might imply that they developed the ability to deconstruct their own mental models (their preconceived realities) and open up to new knowledge and new realities, not only about entrepreneurship but about themselves as well.[64] Therefore, a transformation of the entrepreneurial mindset occurred—contributing positively to sparking socio-economic development in South Africa, starting on a microscale where a change in developmental maturity occurred in entrepreneurial hearts and entrepreneurial minds of this youthful group.

6.12 Systems Perspective

Seen systemically, each individual constitutes a microsystem closely linked to various processes at differing levels of systemic development. The 2015 Global Entrepreneurship Monitor notes that a person's heartset and mindset, and his or her entrepreneurial profile, attitudes, activities and aspirations, are directly linked to national and indeed global socio-economic development.[65] If entrepreneurialism is to spur socio-economic development, one possible starting point could be to develop those internal domains of aspirant individuals—the individual

---

[63] Korthaugen et al. (2013).
[64] Schweikert et al. (2013).
[65] Herrington and Kew (2016).

microsystem—by tapping into resources that are reachable at other systemic levels.[66] These resources can include intermediaries from: (a) universities, (b) municipality business support units, (c) communities, (d) private sector practitioners who support youth entrepreneurs, (e) parastatals and agencies set out to develop commerce or (f) a Local Economic Development Unit embedded within a government entity.[67]

6.13 Conclusion

Taking the happenings of 'Meet Your Business Friend Day' a few years into the future as in November 2017, we surveyed the 2014–2015 cycle participants to investigate how they progressed in their lives as young entrepreneurs and potential graduates. The results showed that nearly all of them were strongly committed to continuing their education and to improving their academic qualifications: 49% were now in their honours year at university and 36% were doing post graduate courses such as a Master's degree. What's more, of those still at university, 36% were in part-time employment, well above the national employment rate for this age group, and an incredible 59% were engaged part-time with an entrepreneurial activity.

Also, the SHAPE cycle of 2014–2015 was repeated in 2017 with amendments made from past lessons learned from both action learning and action research perspectives. During the 2017 cycle, 200 participants completer the 'renewed' version of 'Meet Your Business Friend Day' and the cycle resulted in 73 new business concepts that were prototyped and are ready for the next incubation phase. The research reported on in this chapter showed that cultivation of the Individual Entrepreneurial Orientation in terms of Theory U can indeed enhance the level of entrepreneurship among students in South Africa with positive consequences for youth entrepreneurship in general. Specific connections between Theory U and Individual Entrepreneurial Orientation were identified. These connections were between risk-taking in IEO

[66] Van der Westhuizen (2016).
[67] Van der Westhuizen (2016).

and the co-initiating/co-sensing factors of Theory U, between innovation in IEO and the co-inspiring factor of Theory U), and between proactiveness in IEO and the co-creating/co-evolving factors of Theory U. It can be concluded that through observing and investigating over a period of time; the application of Theory U and Individual Entrepreneurial Orientation can be used to boost youth entrepreneurship Adelakun and Van der Westhuizen (2021), Awotunde and Van der Westhuizen (2021a, b), Franke and Lüthje (2004), Goss (2005), Kickul and D'Intino (2005), Kolb and Kolb (2005), Nhleko and Van der Westhuizen (2022), Ruba et al. (2021), Van der Westhuizen (2018a, b, 2019, 2022).

Acknowledgements This chapter, in part, is derived from the PhD thesis, supervised by Professor Kriben Pillay:

Van der Westhuizen. (2016). *Developing individual entrepreneurial orientation: A systemic approach through the lens of Theory U* (Unpublished PhD thesis). Durban: University of KwaZulu-Natal. South Africa.

Professor Kriben Pillay for mentoring the author in writing this chapter.

This work is based on the research supported in part by the National Research Foundation of South Africa (Grant Numbers: 122002).

Photo credits: Jon Ivins.

References

Adelakun, Y., & Van der Westhuizen, T. (2021). Delineating government policies and individual entrepreneurial orientation. *Journal of Sociology and Social Anthropology, 12*(3–4), 106–117. https://doi.org/10.31901/245 66764.2021/12.3-4.371

Awotunde, O. M., & Van der Westhuizen, T. (2021a). Entrepreneurial self-efficacy development: An effective intervention for sustainable student entrepreneurial intentions. *International Journal of Innovation and Sustainable Development, 15*(4), 475–495.

Awotunde, O. M., & Van der Westhuizen, T. (2021b, September). Entrepreneurial self-efficacy and the SHAPE ideation model for university students. In *ECIE 2021 16th European Conference on Innovation and Entrepreneurship Vol 1* (p. 37).

Bodhanya, S. (2014). The nexus model for local economic development. *Problems and Perspectives in Management, 12*(3), 7–15.

Callaghan, C. W. (2009). *Entrepreneurial orientation and entrepreneurial performance of central Johannesburg informal sector street traders* (Unpublished M Comm thesis). University of the Witwatersrand, South Africa.

Dunwoody, S., & Griffin, R. J. (2014). Risk information seeking and processing model. In H. Cho, T. Reimer, & K. McComas (Eds.), *The SAGE handbook of risk communication*. Sage.

Fitch, G., & O'Fallon, T. (2013). Theory U applied in transformation development. In O. Gunnlaugson, C. Baron, & M. Cayer (Eds.), *Perspectives on Theory U: Insights from the field* (pp. 114–127). Business Science Reference.

Franke, N., & Lüthje, C. (2004). Entrepreneurial intentions of business students—A benchmarking study. *International Journal of Innovation and Technology Management, 1*(03), 269–288.

Gardner, H. (2003). *Multiple intelligences after twenty years*. Paper presented at American Educational Research Association, Chicago, Illinois, USA.

Goodman, M. (2014). *South African presencing foundation course* [Workshop]. Cape Town, South Africa.

Goss, D. (2005). Schumpeter's legacy? Interactions and emotions in the society of entrepreneurship. *Entrepreneurship Theory & Practice, 29*(2), 205–218.

Gunnlaugson, O., & Walker, W. (2013). Deep presencing leadership coaching: Building capacity for sensing, enhancing, and embodying emerging selves and futures in the face of organizational crisis. In O. Gunnlaugson, C. Baron, & M. Cayer (Eds.), *Perspectives on Theory U: Insights from the field*. Business Science Reference.

Guttenstein, S., Lindsay, J., & Baron, C. (2013). Aligning with the emergent future. In O. Gunnlaugson, C. Baron, & M. Cayer (Eds.), *Perspectives on Theory U: Insights from the field*. Business Science Reference.

Hannon, V., Gillinson, S., & Shanks, L. (2013). *Learning a living: Radical innovation in education for work*. Bloomsbury.

Hays, J. (2013). Theory U and team performance: Presence, participation and productivity. In O. Gunnlaugson, C. Baron, & M. Cayer (Eds.), *Perspectives on Theory U: Insights from the field*. Business Science Reference.

Herrington, M., & Kew, P. (2016). *Global entrepreneurship monitor: South African Report 2016. Is Sa Heading for an Economic Meltdown?*

Hulsink, W., & Koek, D. (2014). The young, the fast and the furious: A study about the triggers and impediments of youth entrepreneur-ship. *International Journal of Entrepreneurship and Innovation Management, 18*(2–3), 182–209.

Jackson, M. C. (2003). *Systems thinking: Creative holism for managers*. Wiley.

Jung-Beeman, M., Bowden, E. M., Haberman, J., Frymiare, J. L., Arambel-Liu, S., Greenblatt, R., Reber, P. J., & Kounios, J. (2004). Neural activity when people solve verbal problems with insight. *PLoS Biology, 2*(4), 500–510.

Kickul, J., & D'Intino, R. S. (2005). Measure for measure: Modeling entrepreneurial self-efficacy onto instrumental tasks within the new venture creation process. *New England Journal of Entrepreneurship, 8*(2), 6.

Kolb, A. Y., & Kolb, D. A. (2005). Learning styles and learning spaces: Enhancing experiential learning in higher education. *Academy of Management Learning & Education, 4*(2), 193–212.

Korthaugen, F. A. J., Hoekstra, A., & Meijer, P. C. (2013). Promoting presence in professional practice: A core reflection approach for moving through the U. In O. Gunnlaugson, C. Baron, & M. Cayer (Eds.), *Perspectives on Theory U: Insights from the field*. Business Science Reference.

Lumpkin, G. T., & Dess, G. G. (1996). Clarifying the entrepreneurial orientation construct and linking it to performance. *Academy of Management Review, 21*(1), 135–172.

Mitchell, T., & Harris, K. (2012). *Resilience: A risk management approach*. http://www.odi.org/publications/6271-resilience-risk-management-climate-change.

Oyugi, J. (2014). Effectiveness of the methods of teaching entrepreneurship courses to developing self-Efficacy and intention among university students in Uganda. *International Journal of Social Sciences and Entrepreneurship, 1*(11), 491–513.

Nhleko, Y., & Van der Westhuizen, T. (2022). The role of higher education institutions in introducing entrepreneurship education to meet the demands of industry 4.0. *Academy of Entrepreneurship Journal, 28*(1), 1–23.

Peschl, M. F., & Fundneider, T. (2013). Theory U and emergent innovation: Presencing as a method of bringing forth profoundly new knowledge and realities. In O. Gunnlaugson, C. Baron, & M. Cayer (Eds.), *Perspectives on Theory U: Insights from the field*. Business Science Reference.

Pillay, K. (2014). Learning, the whole and Theory U: Reflections on creating a space for deep learning. *Problems and Perspectives in Management, 12*(4), 340–346.

Pillay, K. (2016). Learning and the illusion of solid and separate things: Troublesome knowledge and the curriculum. In M. A. Samuel, R. Dhunpath, & N. Amin (Eds.), *Disrupting higher education: Undoing cognitive damage* (pp. 81–92). Sense Publishers.

Poole, L. (2014). *A calculated risk: How donors should engage with risk financing and transfer mechanisms*. OECD Publishing.

Ramkissor, M., & Cassim, S. (2013). *The entrepreneurial orientation and intention of UKZN MBA students* (Unpublished MComm thesis). University of KwaZulu-Natal, South Africa.

Revans, R. (2011). *ABC of action learning*. Gower Publishing, Ltd.

Richardson, I., & Hynes, B. (2008). Entrepreneurship education: Towards an industry sector approach. *Education & Training, 50*(3), 188–198.

Ruba, R. M., Van der Westhuizen, T., & Chiloane-Tsoka, G. E. (2021). Influence of entrepreneurial orientation on organisational performance: Evidence from Congolese Higher Education Institutions. *Journal of Contemporary Management, 18*(1), 243–269.

Scharmer, C. O. (2008). Uncovering the blind spot of leadership. *Leader to Leader, 47*, 52–59.

Scharmer, C. O. (2009). *Theory U: Learning from the future as it emerges*. Berrett-Koehler Publishers.

Scharmer, C. O., & Kaufer, K. (2013). *Leading from the emerging future: From ego-system to ecosystem economies*. Berrett- Koehler Publishers.

Schweikert, S., Meissen, J. O., & Wolf, P. (2013). Applying Theory U: The case of the Creative Living Lab. In O. Gunnlaugson, C. Baron, & H. Cayer (Eds.), *Perspectives on Theory U: Insights from the field*. Business Science Reference.

Southern, N. (2013). Presencing as being in care: Extending Theory U in a relational framework. In O. Gunnlaugson, C. Baron, & M. Cayer (Eds.), *Perspectives on Theory U: Insights from the field*. Business Science Reference.

Van der Westhuizen, T. (2016). *Developing individual entrepreneurial orientation: A systemic approach through the lens of Theory U* (Unpublished PhD thesis). University of KwaZulu-Natal, South Africa.

Van der Westhuizen, T. (2017a). The use of Theory U and individual entrepreneurial orientation to increase low youth entrepreneurship in South Africa. *Journal of Contemporary Management, 14*, 531–553.

Van der Westhuizen, T. (2017b). A systemic approach towards responsible and sustainable economic development: entrepreneurship, systems theory and socio-economic momentum. In Z. Fields (Ed.), *Collective creativity for responsible and sustainable business practice*. IGI Global.

Van der Westhuizen, T. (2017c). Theory U and individual entrepreneurial orientation in developing youth entrepreneurship in South Africa. *Journal of Contemporary Management, 14*(1), 531–553.

Van der Westhuizen, T. (2018a). The SHAPE project: Shifting hope, activating potential entrepreneurship In D. Remenyi & D. A. Grant (Eds.), *Incubators for young entrepreneurs—20 case histories*. ACPIL.

Van der Westhuizen, T. (2018b). *Open heart, open mind and open will in transformative individual entrepreneurial orientation pedagogies* (pp. 443–448). Academic Conferences and Publishing International Limited.

Van der Westhuizen, T. (2019). Action! Methods to develop entrepreneurship. In *18th European Conference on Research Methodology for Business and Management Studies* (pp. 331–337).

Van der Westhuizen, T. (2021). Applying Theory U through SHAPE to develop student's individual entrepreneurial orientation in a university eco-system. In O. Gunnlaugson & W. Brendel (Eds.), *Advances in presensing volume III: Collective approaches, in Theory U* (pp. 395–435). Trifoss Business Press.

Van der Westhuizen, T. (2022). *Effective Youth Entrepreneurship*. Sunbonani. https://omp.sunbonani.co.za/index.php/sunbonani/catalog/book/6

Weinberg, I. (2014). *The complete triangles model. Pninet*. http://www.pninet.com/articles/Memory.pdf

Xavier, S., Kelley, D., Kew, J., Herrington, M., & Vorderwülbecke, A. (2013). *Global Entrepreneurship Monitor (GEM) 2012*. Global Report. GERA/GEM.

Zahra, S. A., Newey, L. R., & Li, Y. (2014). On the frontiers: The implications of social entrepreneurship for international entrepreneurship. *Entrepreneurship Theory and Practice, 38*(1), 137–158.

7

Mapping Momentum in Youth Entrepreneurship

7.1 Introduction

The research described earlier in this book suggests that the core, or starting point, in socio-economic development is enabling and co-inspiring an individual's mind, heart and will. This is the very essence of the microsystem. This implies that fundamental to developing entrepreneurial momentum is the ability to first inspire individuals before seeking to teach them skills. When individuals are inspired, it is more likely that they will think innovatively about business potential rather than merely react to experiences and actions around them. Continuing co-inspiration will help sustain entrepreneurial action and build entrepreneurial momentum on each systemic level, countering the fears and anxieties that a young person might have about being an entrepreneur or being entrepreneurial in South Africa. This co-inspiration will come from the co-caring support system of business friends, business friendships and intermediaries drawn from mesosystemic organisations.

This chapter will review the three enemies (barriers) that obstruct effective youth entrepreneurship and detail the internal states or voices—Voice of Judgement, Voice of Cynicism and Voice of Fear—required of youths to overcome in order to initiate and sustain successful youth entrepreneurship and deal with new situations and changes. It is these three "enemies" that needed to be overcome, informed the SHAPE methodology, the structure of programme contents and order. To promote an Open Will, Open Mind and Open Heart within the youth entrepreneurs, these "enemies" were needed to move them into new situations.

7.1.1 Enabling Entrepreneurial Action in the Case Study

SHAPE—Shifting Hope, Activating Potential Entrepreneurship—constitutes a process in which an overall facilitator—either an individual or a team—will have a key role to play, especially in enabling linkages between youth entrepreneurs and business friends, and with various mesosystemic players such as government organisations, non-government organisations, the private sector and the community.

Through deep-learning practices, youth entrepreneurs can positively change (transform) in developmental maturity in their mental models and their experiences and actions in being entrepreneurs in South Africa. However, they will need both support from a nexus of intermediaries based in mesosystemic organisations and co-caring from like-minded, like-hearted and like-willed business friends. The importance of intermediaries cannot be understated in sustaining entrepreneurial action for the reason that, and as will be discussed later, they require a Source of inspiration outside of themselves to inspire thought potential.

Ideally, these business friends, as an ecosystem or support nexus to the youth entrepreneurs, should undergo the same sequence of experiences, in step with the youth entrepreneurs themselves. Therefore, different role-players in the system undergo the same type of entrepreneurial heart, mind and hand development—parallel skills development on different systemic levels occur.

During the different iterations of SHAPE, participants included both youth entrepreneurs and potential business friends to the youth entrepreneurs. These business friends could be:

- youth entrepreneurs who wish to co-create and co-evolve solo with their business ideas—thus, the youth entrepreneur could become his or her business friend;
- business professionals who wish to draw on their participation in SHAPE to co-create and co-evolve solo with their business ideas;
- youth entrepreneurs who wish to co-create and co-evolve together with other youth entrepreneurs with their business ideas;
- youth entrepreneurs who wish to co-create and co-evolve together with other youth entrepreneurs and business professionals with their business ideas; and
- business professionals who wish to co-create and co-evolve together with other business professionals.

However, no matter which groups emerge in co-caring about entrepreneurship, continuous co-inspiring will be necessary for new ideas and new possibilities to come into view. The continuous process of co-inspiring and co-caring from the Source (see the centre of the systematic map at Fig. 7.1) can potentially generate entrepreneurial momentum for socio-economic development.

7.2   Youth Entrepreneurs *En Route* to Action

Before a youth entrepreneur mobilises to entrepreneurial action, many psychological, neurological and physiological processes occur. From a nondual perspective, one might argue that all are connected to Source, and therefore, this is the epicentre to co-inspire action. If youth entrepreneurs cannot find ways to co-initiate and co-sense within Self to spark action, sources of inspiration will need to come from else-where. Therefore, to bring the youth from no entrepreneurial action into a process of taking entrepreneurial action, a personal innovation or personal transformation occurs. The term 'transformation' in this sense can be defined as 'growth in developmental maturity'.

For personal innovation (also seen as transformation) as a behavioural trait to occur, an individual needs to connect to a source, or Source, of inspiration. This connection might spark the inner place from which a

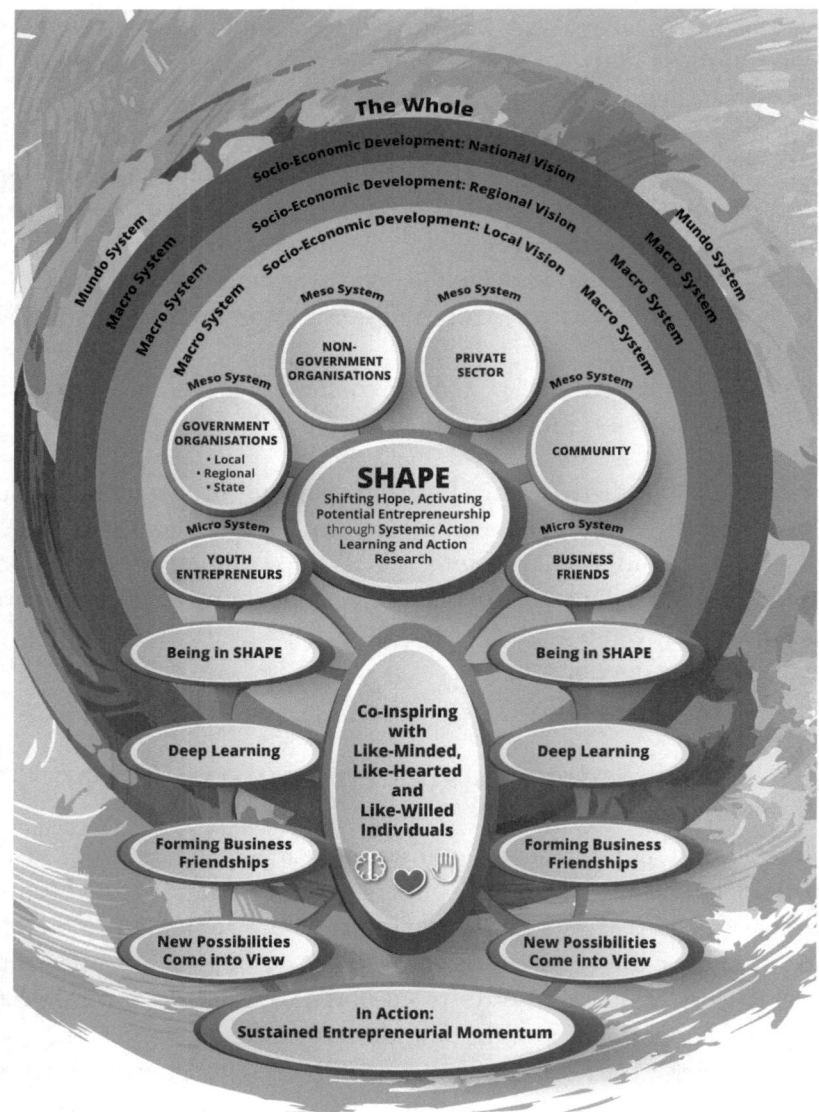

Fig. 7.1 Entrepreneurial momentum: A systemic map (*Source* Van der West-huizen, 2022)

person acts, which could lead to a potentially sustained entrepreneurial act. Connecting to the source or Source of inspiration presents several synonyms, such as co-inspiring or presencing, through a Theory U lens.[1] Co-inspiring formed part of the SHAPE five-phase programme methodology using the Theory U conceptual framework. When co-inspiring, presencing or connecting to the source or Source of inspiration occurs, an individual is likely to move from a reactive to a generative response field of thought due to transformation (growth in developmental maturity) of their internal and external domains. This process might subsequently develop and stimulate the ability to produce new thoughts, ideas or actions that they had not shown before.[2] No literature on Theory U mentions what the Source of inspiration—when written with a capital S—exactly implies, except that the Source implies the 'Whole'.

Chapters 2 and 3 identify the internal domain development of the microsystem as fundamental determinants of their interactions with their external domains. Therefore, it is important to identify and investigate the sources of inspiration that enabled them to gain momentum in entrepreneurial action and inspired mind before brain:

- the vision of Self and work;
- spirituality; and
- intermediaries (youth entrepreneur ecosystem).

7.2.1 Vision of Self and Work as a Source of Inspiration

The aspects being discussed on sources of inspiration are fundamental and essential for the development of the SHAPE ecosystem for youth entrepreneurship because they drive the desired shift.

The process of co-inspiring or presencing in an entrepreneurial ecosystem has been described as the vision phase.[3] Youth entrepreneurs

---

[1] Scharmer and Käufer (2013).

[2] Scharmer (2009).

[3] Schweikert et al. (2013).

start envisioning the future they want to see and act on. Here youth entrepreneurs might experience direct expressions of feeling inspired, feelings of positivity and enthusiasm and imaginings of how they envisioned their emerging future.

7.2.1.1 Direct Expressions of Inspiration

Some youth entrepreneurs might experience strong feelings as they start thinking about future possibilities, which might indicate an initial source of would have been self-inspiration by proactively taking a risk to participants and sustaining the participation of the participants. During the participation, multiple transformations happen within them. It would be fair to say that the processes of social technologies such as SHAPE and Theory U enable youths to deconstruct their mental models, explore their entrepreneurial fears and find ways to overcome the fears. When these fears are overcome, these youths are increasingly open to new possibilities and can take entrepreneurial actions without being as scared. The notion of South African youths being scared of becoming young entrepreneurs, and conquering personal barriers, was highlighted in the research findings as a major challenge in youth entrepreneurship.

7.2.1.2 Feelings of Positivity and Enthusiasm

When participating in developmental programmes from education institutes, youth entrepreneurs often feel positive and enthusiastic about their journey and the potential entrepreneurial opportunities that might await them in the future. If youths choose to participate in an entrepreneurship development programme offered by an education institute, they demonstrate the proactivity propensity in their entrepreneurial orientation, which is also an indicator of progressing towards entrepreneurial action.

Although such programmes might spark a 'good feeling' and leave youths inspired after a session, this feeling might not last and is, therefore, not enough on its own to sustain entrepreneurial action, and thus, mechanisms for sustained change and momentum maintenance are necessary.[4] Positive emotions are associated with coherent, ordered brain waves in individuals, whereas negative emotions are associated with more chaotic brain waves. Positive feelings might increase the likelihood that individuals will come into a coherent state together and, therefore, be more receptive to information from the 'Whole' system. This corresponds with the psycho-neuro-endocrinological principles,[5] which note that the head, heart and hand of individuals are interlinked to the external environment, thereby forming a system as a 'Whole'. Should this occur as a result of youths attending entrepreneurship development programmes, it might indicate that they have started to create entrepreneurial potential where it did not previously exist. It might also indicate that they developed the enthusiastic ability to detect in the present moment those positive elements they envision in the future—perhaps a future without being afraid of taking entrepreneurial actions.

7.2.2 Envisioning the Future as It Emerges

The future is an extension of the past. Innovators and creative people see the emerging future as 'an advent, a coming-into-being of something profoundly new'.[6] This resonates with the argument that what people experience as time is a construct of thought; that time is a movement happening in the timeless now. Therefore, envisioning the future as it emerges can be interpreted as detecting, in the present moment, that which is yet to come.[7]

The youths started to demonstrate positive and enthusiastic feelings when they began to see themselves as 'Young Entrepreneurs'. A generative process or 'aha' moment of co-inspiring can be interpreted as having occurred because the youths seem to be in a state of being in which they are fully aware of what is happening in the here and now, both in their

---

[4] Guttenstein et al. (2013).
[5] Weinberg (2014).
[6] Scharmer and Käufer (2010, 32).
[7] Scharmer (2011).

environment and within themselves.[8] They engage in a continuous cycle of reinventing vision for themselves, whereby they envisage themselves as becoming more innovative and more entrepreneurial in the future and therefore adaptable and resilient to change to socio-economic situations and create value-adding solutions to ecosystemic problems.

In the process of envisioning a future of entrepreneurial possibilities, another technique is for youths to associate themselves with already successful entrepreneurs. A problem in this association is that youths might not have an actual notion of what it means to innovate, and how to be innovative in the 'real world'—how to be a youth entrepreneur. Though youths might be associating themselves with 'game changers' and 'world shapers', there is little 'how' or personal internalisation of the effort required to realise these dreams or the actions that need to be taken to actualise the Self and Work they want to see in their future. After the youths' envisioning process, they need to crystallise, prototype and perform further entrepreneurial actions. It is, therefore, key for youths to realise that although they have a vision of becoming an innovator; they need to be proactive and take actions to make these visions a reality.

Learning about entrepreneurship occurs through interpersonal interactions. Interpersonal learning characteristically involves understanding how to communicate with and understand other people when working collaboratively. This relates to the Theory U notion of an open heart, where youths are listening empathetically to others. Demonstrating an open heart is also one of the enabling elements for co-inspiring.[9] If youths are receptive to socio-economic problems around them, they might envisage themselves as a change agent for bringing about transformation within their external domains. Therefore, the attitude, activity and aspirations of the microsystem constitute the baseline of socio-economic development from a systems perspective.[10]

This notion was emphasised in SHAPE practices when the project work commenced and was reinforced in discussions on 'The Why of Doing Business'. The teaching practices, therefore, assisted the youths to

---

[8] Korthaugen et al. (2013).
[9] Schweikert et al. (2013).
[10] Xavier et al. (2013).

explore 'Why' they want to engage in entrepreneurial activity—they felt inspired through the practices of SHAPE.

7.2.3 SHAPE as a Source of Inspiration for Vision and Work

This chapter describes the responses and reactions of the participants in the SHAPE social technology. Therefore, this phenomenon was perceived by youth as a source of inspiration to radically influence and facilitate vision. Entrepreneurship courses that focus only on developing the management and planning skills of youth entrepreneurs are insufficient to truly develop the entrepreneurial mindset and heartset since these two components are only fragmentations of the elements that spark entrepreneurial action.[11] Traditional entrepreneurship programmes tend to teach technical skills with little or no focus on the cognitive or belief systems, which might underpin youth entrepreneurial attitudes and perceptions.[12]

A radical change in teaching practices is necessary to address the cognitive belief system and reshape the youth's mental models. This was what the SHAPE social technology aspired to achieve through the U-processes and through linking it to propensities of IEO development.[13]

Youth who choose to participate in entrepreneurship development programmes see the programmes as a tool or instrument to support them in reaching their highest possible Self, therefore, as enablers of entrepreneurial action.

7.2.4 Spirituality as a Source of Inspiration

Reflections from youth entrepreneurs who participated in SHAPE indicated that they link new knowledge they acquire with a sense of divine purpose and inspiration: this is what God wishes them to know. This

---

[11] Kickul and D'Intino (2005).

[12] Ibid.

[13] Hannon et al. (2013).

is what God wishes for them. But it is unclear how they perceive 'God' and who it is that they refer to as 'God'. Within the Christian religion paradigm, the Source of inspiration or Whole—when written with a capital letter, implies 'God Divine' and that an individual's intellect is a source of knowledge because God is the Source of knowledge.[14] The concept of 'God' and 'God's will for an individual'—in this context, a youth entrepreneur's life—is strongly evident as a source of inspiration that can lead to inner transformation.

Youth entrepreneurs might feel inspired when they believe they have had a higher calling to entrepreneurial action. Also, youths who adopt the concept of God show faith that they will receive Divine guidance through their journey of becoming successful youth entrepreneurs. For those who adopt this 'lens', the way God interacts with them inspires the inner source from which they act. Here the Source of inspiration is both God and the action that follows because they believe that God is steering their Reality. Therefore, to these student entrepreneurs, the sources of inspiration from God are both Truth and Reality.[15]

In addition, youths taking part in the SHAPE social technology indicated that they felt inspired through the intermediaries they interacted with—thus building their interpersonal knowledge.

7.2.5 Intermediaries to the Youth Entrepreneurs as a Source of Inspiration

The research and activities recounted in this book demonstrate the important role intermediaries play in developing youth entrepreneurs' entrepreneurial orientation. A radical change in teaching and learning practices was necessary for youth entrepreneurs to experience deep learning. Interpersonal interactions with intermediaries hold the potential to radically transform youth entrepreneurs as an outflow of their

---

[14] Popper (2014).
[15] Ibid.

experiences. Therefore, co-initiation and co-sensing practices with inter-mediaries resulted in the co-inspiring of the youth entrepreneur—confirming the reason for applying social technology to develop indi-vidual entrepreneurial orientation and entrepreneurial self-efficacy. These interactions might lead youths to have inspirational thoughts about entrepreneurship and thus take entrepreneurial actions that they had not considered before.

In addition, it seems that, through the development of their inter-personal and intrapersonal intelligence, the youth entrepreneurs develop an open mind, open heart and open will to not only develop them-selves into young entrepreneurs but also develop their community or society. This development of attitudes and aspirations is much needed for socio-economic development to occur.

7.3 A Theory U Lens on Obstacles *En Route* to Entrepreneurial Action

Theory U introduces three enablers to youth entrepreneurship to support the five processes in the U curve. These are an open heart, open mind and open will. Further, Theory U warns against three barriers to youth entrepreneurship in relation to the U process and these are called Voices of Judgement (VoJ), Voices of Cynicism (VoC) and Voice of Fear (VoF). According to Theory U, an individual encounters three enemies, which serve as potential blocks *en route* to entrepreneurial action. The first of these is the Voice of Judgement (VoJ), which shuts down the open mind; the second is the Voice of Cynicism (VoC), which shuts down the open heart; and the third is Voice of Fear (VoF) which shuts down the open will.[16]

These three enemies are very important aspects of entrepreneurial heartset and mindset since they might be the root cause of obstruc-tions in the development of youth entrepreneurship in South Africa, as well as obstructing the development of the microsystem as part of the greater socio-economic developmental process. These are the core

---

[16] Scharmer (2011).

internal domain barriers. These barriers are also referred to as the three enemies of the youth. These three enemies relate directly to core components of and act as barriers to the mindset and heartset because they obstruct their attitudes, spirit and aspirations towards themselves as well as towards collective socio-economic development.

When youth entrepreneurs perceive personal obstacles as the biggest hindrance to their actualisation of entrepreneurial action, the deconstruction of their mental models becomes necessary. Mental structures are heavily influenced by the socialisation of ideals—and in African perspectives—this is a very much community-based structure focusing on pluralism over individuation. These non-material values in South Africa place emphasis on communal living—thus and the people as having an interdependent view of the self. Sense of belonging can become so strong that it makes sense to think of the relationship instead of the self as the functional unit of conscious reflection. It would make sense to be sensitive to context when identifying barriers, especially when leveraging the co-creation aspect of initiating activity. Social technologies such as SHAPE and Theory U might be enabling vehicles, not only in bringing forward new knowledge about entrepreneurship but also in developing entrepreneurial 'gut feeling' or intuitive knowledge.

The literature on Theory U mentions the omnipresence of these three enemies and postulates that they can be conquered through open-minded, open-hearted and open-willed practices.[17] The extent of an individual's VoJ, VoC and VoF can be considered indicators of their resistance to change.[18] A sense of collectiveness, integration or Wholeness is often experienced by youth participating in such programmes and through the processes of generating knowledge and letting go of fragmented mental models, resulting in the integration of their views. In a scenario where real-life business situations are simulated by social technologies such as SHAPE, youths might not show initial fear of acting towards entrepreneurship because they perceive social technologies as assisting them in developing competencies within a safe learning space. Ecosystemic outlooks and values prevalent in the South African

---

[17] Gunnlaugson et al. (2013); Scharmer (2009); Scharmer and Käufer (2013); Senge (2012).
[18] Cox (2013).

culture also hamper the ability to clearly acknowledge and articulate the self and very individualistic worldviews, i.e., the individual as witnessed in Western society. For youths to deconstruct their mental models of perceived barriers, it is necessary to challenge the 'me' or 'self' to see an undifferentiated reality, not led by mental models, but rather 'learning a living' through living creatively.

The youths' feelings of not being separated from the system, coupled with feelings of co-inspiration and feelings of being-in-care through forming a relational framework, might contribute to youth entrepreneurs not demonstrating elements of VoJ, VoC and VoF in their early journey *en route* to entrepreneurial action. This is also a South African concept as it relates to the cultural notion of '*ubuntu*' which implies 'the potential for being human, to value the good of the community above self-interest'.[19] By applying the notion of *ubuntu,* youth entrepreneurs might develop competencies that enable them to counter the three enemies (barriers) but in relation to others. This poses a juxtaposition to traditional notions of individually driven entrepreneurial potentials and drives towards such activities.

However, some youth entrepreneurs will inevitably encounter the VoJ, VoC or VoF, perhaps from early stages *en route* to entrepreneurial action. Details of these possibilities are now considered.

7.3.1 Voice of Judgement

The Voice of Judgement (VoJ) shuts down the youth entrepreneur's Open Mind. An 'Open Mind' can be described as the capacity to suspend old ways of doing.[20] This 'open mind' process suggests that the youth entrepreneur has already decided to embark on the journey of entrepreneurial action and has now suspended their old ways of thinking about entrepreneurship, thereby deconstructing their traditional views on connecting to knowledge and on entrepreneurship (Fig. 7.2).

When they thought about entrepreneurship, they reflected upon this mode of thinking in the following ways:

---

[19] Chaplin (2006).
[20] Scharmer (2011).

Fig. 7.2 Reflections on the Voice of Judgement (*Source* Author)

The VoJ was the least referenced and coded of the three enemies in the project:

- *The big mean corporate world.*
- *Many think that being an entrepreneur is just having a business; I think it goes deeper than what other people think.*
- *An entrepreneur, you first must decide what the projects are. You must think about product development, marketing and accounting, among others. There is a great deal of uncertainty in this process, and you must rely greatly on your own judgements.*
- *There is a wide misconception that young people are laughed at in the business world.*

The internal domains of youth entrepreneurs are still growing in developmental maturity (initial transformation). This growth process is characterised by uncertainty around unlived experiences; therefore, they can only imagine what it feels like to be an entrepreneur. The internal domain is also a barrier to unlived experiences in relation to the external domain; therefore, perceived insecurities are experienced in relation to their own abilities and the manner youth entrepreneurs are perceived by role-players in the youth entrepreneurial ecosystem. Earlier in this chapter, youth entrepreneurs were described as connected to certain sources of inspiration: Self, the SHAPE programme, God or god and intermediaries. These sources of inspiration can enable youth entrepreneurs to let go of the old ego and self-centredness and construct views of *ubuntu*, caring collectiveness and systemic integration—thereby suspending old ways of doing and thus not encountering the VoC. This implies that the new knowledge and experience counteract the VoJ. One needs to consider that the personal changes that youth entrepreneurs are going through *en route* to entrepreneurial action are lifecycles that spiral forward.

It seems that early-phase youth entrepreneurs usually have an open mind in choosing entrepreneurship, therefore demonstrating a co-cooperativeness in suspending their old ways of doing (not taking entrepreneurial action) and letting new experiences and ways of doing come into their cognitive field.

7.3.2 Voice of Cynicism

The Voice of Cynicism shuts down the youth entrepreneur's Open Heart. 'Open Heart' can be seen as the ability to empathise with others and see the situation through the eyes of someone else.[21] Early-phase developing youth entrepreneurs do not show much evidence of the VoC.[22] If youth entrepreneurs do not demonstrate the ability to empathise with others and see situations through other people's eyes, this might be due to them being infatuated with their egos. A person's ego can be seen as his or her sense of self-esteem or self-importance.[23] However, a person with a high sense of ego might demonstrate a low sense of self-esteem and,

---

[21] Scharmer (2011).

[22] Van der Westhuizen (2016).

[23] Loevinger (2014).

therefore, low Entrepreneurial Self-Efficacy.[24] The VoC was the second-highest coded of the three enemies (Fig. 7.3).

Aspects of 'ego' as elements of constructing the VoC are evident from youth entrepreneurs' perceptions of barriers to youth entrepreneurship, details of which are given in later chapters. Should these perceptions relate to the youths' egos, their notions about how others see them or pose barriers for them might not be entirely true.[25] These might merely be fragments of mental models they constructed for themselves.

Participants stated the following as evidence of their VoC:

A part of me did not believe it but also expected it.

Fig. 7.3 Reflections on the Voice of Cynicism (*Source* Upton and van der Westhuizen, 2022)

---

[24] Ibid.

[25] Loevinger (2014).

I did not anticipate other people, particularly 'grown-ups', reaction to me wanting to become a businessperson. To be honest, I thought they would think of me as naive and would potentially patronise me or think it I was being 'cute'

Being an entrepreneur is not an easy career since you are faced with many uncertainties which need a lot of thinking, focus and confidence, not leaving out the most important skill of an entrepreneur: dedication.

Successful youth entrepreneurs require substantial resilience to add value to their ecosystem and sustain their businesses. Overcoming the VoC is crucial in building resilience, therefore, enabling the personality traits that might sustain the entrepreneurial endeavour. It is difficult to know 'what you do not know'. Cynicism is associated with limited-lived experiences and unexpanded mental models. Despite youth entrepreneurs' encounters with VoC, the ecosystemic approach of intermediaries interactively and interpersonally collaborating with one might create a continuum of entrepreneurial momentum and actions.

7.3.3 Voice of Fear

The Voice of Fear (VoF) shuts down the youth entrepreneur's Open Will. 'Open Will' describes the individual's ability to let go of old ways of doing things and accept new experiences and actions.[26] The VoF is evident in the quantitative chapters of this book (Chapters 5–8), where the youth entrepreneurs indicated that some of them did not feel comfortable moving into new situations (Fig. 7.4).

The voice of fear was found to be the most coded of the three enemies. There are multiple sources of concern expressed by some youth entrepreneurs. Among these was a lack of knowledge and industry know-how, and even a general lack of means to realise their ends— corresponding with views that other youths in South Africa have about entrepreneurial action.[27] This is evident in the following quote from a youth entrepreneur:

---

[26] Scharmer (2011).
[27] Herrington et al. (2015).

Fig. 7.4 Reflections on the Voice of Fear (*Source* Upton and van der West-huizen, 2022)

> I just did not know how to do it – to be successful that is. I always thought that I first had to finish my studies and obtain my degree, get a job, gain experience. Then think about starting up my own business

For this youth entrepreneur, it was daunting to start thinking about the emerging future and the possibilities of taking further entrepreneurial action. This individual was stuck in an old way of thinking about routine and felt that much more life experience was needed before even considering becoming an entrepreneur. They have been sold the usual purported trajectory of career development and advancement instead of challenging it and taking the risk earlier on and moving into entrepreneurial positioning vs employee, and gradual progression.

In addition, lack of self-confidence is a prominent factor in the early-phase development of youth entrepreneurs, as evidenced by these quotations:

I had a fear of being left behind by the world.
  I've hidden for a long time because I was scared to be a business-woman.

It also denotes gender relations and the positioning of women in society, especially in traditionally male-dominant positions and roles. Again, these Voices of Fear are indicators of certain fragments of mental models which the youth entrepreneurs created for themselves. Here, it seems as if some of them demonstrated a fear of exclusion, which might imply a fear of being excluded from the collective or *ubuntu* or being left behind in community advancement.[28]

7.3.4   Observation Regarding the Voices in the Study

The Voices of Fear the SHAPE youth entrepreneurs experienced were not strong enough to entirely block their open will as they continued to consider the emerging future *en route* to entrepreneurial action. Some fears are overcome as youth entrepreneurs develop their abilities over time, but in return, a new VoF can emerge as a barrier in the new situation in which youth entrepreneurs find themselves. Entrepreneurial action is still a nerve-wracking experience, even for youth entrepreneurs who have conquered initial barriers.

Despite these potential obstacles to developing the entrepreneurial heartset and mindset, certain positive inner enablers cause youth entrepreneurs to act and inform the method and content of programme delivery in order to overcome their disabling effect to activate potential, otherwise known as endorsing the Open Mind, Open Heart and Open Will. These are discussed in the following section.

---

[28] Wolff et al. (1996).

7.3.5 Enablers of Entrepreneurial Action Development: Open Mind, Open Heart and Open Will

During the reactive stages of applying the SHAPE social technology, participants are likely to need 'enablers' for evoking generative thoughts. This can occur through like-minded, like-hearted and like-willed individuals searching for certain key factors that could transform their inner aspirations to external realities: an open mind, open heart and open will, enabling them to act from the Whole Being.[29]

7.3.6 Open Mind

The Open Mind can be described as the capacity to suspend old habits of thought[30] and develop the ability to look at new (entrepreneurial) opportunities or challenges with fresh eyes.

Youth entrepreneurs who demonstrate an open mind are willing to deconstruct their mental models by carefully looking at concrete facts and suspending current reality and witness without judgement—thereby, in the same process, developing their entrepreneurial identity.[31] The consequence in the case of youth entrepreneurs is that they begin to operate from a generative rather than merely reactive response to external systemic stimuli (see Fig. 7.1)—thereby indicating once again a transformation or change in developmental maturity.

The initial step that youths take towards entrepreneurial action indicates that they want to suspend their old ways of doing things and make way for the future they want to see emerge. This change in attitude is important to note since it contradicts the literature findings, which show South African youths feeling negative—some even feeling helpless and hopeless—about becoming young entrepreneurs in South Africa (Fig. 7.5).[32]

---

[29] Southern (2013).
[30] Scharmer (2011).
[31] Fitch and O'Fallon (2013).
[32] Engelbrecht (2012); Herrington et al. (2015); Weinberg (2014).

Fig. 7.5 Reflections on an open mind (*Source* Upton and van der Westhuizen, 2022)

Through SHAPE, some students demonstrated an Open Mind, and this was roughly equal to the number who demonstrated an Open Heart:

Am I willing to sacrifice my whole life and dedicate it to my business[?]. Will I let go of late nights with friends, going out with my girlfriend for days and nights at the office desk?" I took some thinking and I realized that I would be driving myself down a path of misery.

It is rare as a student to engage in deep discussions about business orientated matters. We often bond over a chat of the weekend's game or other teen related matters.

I believe that it is a huge opportunity for someone as young, full of life and open minded as today's youth. Getting into shape will hopefully provide me with a large amount of information and experience about being a young entrepreneur and how to carry myself and face all the obstacles that come with being a young entrepreneur.

As a young entrepreneur I not only dream I dream, motivate myself to strive to achieve my dream and hope for success in all the risks that come with being a young wise, well minded, and motivated entrepreneur.

At first I didn't understand the shape program, but after I've attended the few classes it sank to my mind that wow now I'm really a young entrepreneur.

I personally consider SHAPE as a milestone in my future career. I see myself as a very successful global corporate leader in years to come.

I believe that my capabilities are beyond my perceptions, and with all hard work and effort needed I truly can out-perform at any situation given.

Entrepreneurial self-efficacy, individual entrepreneurial orientation and entrepreneurial intent are the concepts associated with psycho-neuro-endocrinological development. The reflections above are evidence of initial risk-taking, opportunity identification and personal innovation being taken by youth: A deliberate choice was made to change the future that they had made for themselves. Further, a choice was made to act and take charge of steering their future career path. Otto Scharmer refers to this process as 'leading from the future as it emerges'. During the application of social technology, the youth entrepreneurs also gave evidence of open minds and positive attitudes towards accessing collective capacities that are being accessed within an interpersonal space. This space, filled with open minds, hearts and wills, becomes the 'source' for the emergence of their best selves and highest future. Again, the African notion of *ubuntu* can be related to these attitudes.[33] The open heart of youth entrepreneurs will accordingly be discussed next. You can see from the above quotes that students are motivated to perform beyond the reality of their situations and see SHAPE as an important facilitator of this change.

[33] Chaplin (2006).

7.3.7 Open Heart

Open Heart refers to the ability to empathise with another and to see situations through the eyes of another.[34] The open heart can enable youth entrepreneurs to interact interpersonally with intermediaries and business friends and to offer the potential for a genuine collective sensibility to emerge, where they feel we are in this together.[35] However, potentially conflicting views, political interests and social complexities might provoke defensive routines and emotional distancing (Voice of Cynicism) that block the heart and create vulnerability, mutually essential for moving further down the U-Curve (Fig. 7.6).[36]

An open heart was evidenced in the social technology participants' reflections on socio-economic development:

As a young entrepreneur, I hope to make a valuable contribution or change to South Africa and the world. This is important to me as I see my ideas as a shift towards transformation and making people a whole lot happier.

I just want to make people smile and be happy or content; I want to make South Africa a better place to live in.

I want to transform how students view success; I want to introduce a different culture to its definition.

Yes indeed we all come from different backgrounds, we know different problems our community are faced with and I want to address those problems to the right people, who want to change our country.

So there is this one specific day that I will never forget and still think about to this very day. It's the day that I was introduced to "SHAPE". I was sitting in class waiting for it to commence and this lady called Thea van der Westhuizen showed us two videos – one of people who are demotivated easily, who have great ideas but don't go out there and implement them mainly because of the negative talk they have heard And. the second video it showed people that were completely the opposite of the first video- it showed go[-]getters, individuals who strived to do better,

---

[34] Scharmer (2011).
[35] Nicolaides and McCallum (2013).
[36] Ibid.

Fig. 7.6 Reflections on an open heart (*Source* Upton and van der Westhuizen, 2022)

be better, to make something of themselves and to develop their ideas into something huge because they believed and I knew that I was one of them.

One youth entrepreneur stated that he realised the importance and role of others, thus clearly indicating an open heart and ability to sense others:

I was ready to penetrate the business world with an iron fist. I was racing against myself with impossible deadlines. I had a fear of being left behind by the world. Being rich was the main objective no matter what the cost was. I never thought beyond other basic human needs like happiness, proper health. On our first day Thea made us do a kind of self-valuation exercise. One question that stood out for me was "Am I willing to sacrifice my whole life and dedicate it to my business. Will I let go of late nights with friends, going out with my girlfriend for days and nights at the office desk?" I took some thinking and I realized that I would be driving myself down a path of misery. Money won't necessarily give me the pleasures that I would have given up a few years ago.

The Open-Heart enabler mirrors the internal domain of entrepreneurial heartset directly. It is something that occurs neither in the brain nor in the mind. This is a very deep awareness and an experience often relating to Source. These quotes tie in with the previous discussions where the youths expressed their wishes to contribute to socio-economic development in South Africa. The experiences most of the respondents brought with them from their communities, together with the concentrated SHAPE social technology strategies to increase their awareness of local economic development and socio-economic development more broadly, may have contributed to these expressions of an open heart.

Further, the SHAPE programme allowed them to overcome the fear and the voices of judgement and cynicism that demotivated and promoted inaction on the part of youth entrepreneurs. It was a process of exploration where youths were encouraged to challenge their ideas and any barriers that withheld them from pursuing their potential. This is a co-constructed and interdependent process of facilitation that requires internal reflection and barrier dissolution in favour of moving forward and dissolving the invisible negative internalised ties holding youths back from dreaming beyond the circumstance.

7.3.8 Open Will

An Open Will refers to 'letting go of old ways of doing things and accepting new ones'.[37] The concept of open will can be interpreted as a 'causal state', which can be defined as a 'state that apprehends causal objectives such as awareness of awareness'. From a causal state or open will perspective, the viewpoint is that everything is 'empty-full' or that an individual's very own words and subtle boundaries are an illusion, a story that individuals themselves make up. When youth entrepreneurs let go

---

[37] Scharmer (2011).

of old ways of doing things and accept new ones through demonstrating an open will, they can develop the capacity to step into an interlacing of concrete/subtle/causal consciousnesses and look at self, other, contexts and the entire world from that position. However, reaching such views might take a prolonged period and further change in developmental maturity.[38] As evidenced throughout youths' reflections, this enabler constituted the highest saturation of coded transformations (Fig. 7.7):

As you can see from the Word Cloud above, the use of the word dreams has become evident, as has entrepreneur, idea and business. An Open Will relates to the internal domain of entrepreneurial intent as this is a process before engaging with entrepreneurial action—the entrepreneurial handset. An open will is a key associative factor with

Fig. 7.7 Reflections on an open will (*Source* Upton and van der Westhuizen, 2022)

---

[38] Fitch & O'Fallon (2013).

resilience and determination to sustain action. The participants at this stage have had to let go of simply being regular second-year students, having made an explicit choice in applying to participate in SHAPE and being prospective student entrepreneurs, followed in due course by the prospect of acceptance as a Young Entrepreneur.

Sometimes it will be necessary for youth entrepreneurs to make changes in their personal lives to achieve the Self and Work they wish to see in the emerging future:

> The meetings every Wednesday have also taught me commitment. Now I am planning to work hard, attend all meetings and have fun.
>
> I was ready to penetrate the business world with an iron fist. I was racing against myself with impossible deadlines. I had a fear of being left behind by the world. Being rich was the main objective, no matter what the cost was. I never thought beyond other basic human needs like happiness, proper health. On our first day, Thea made us do a kind of self-evaluation exercise. One question that stood out for me was 'Am I willing to sacrifice my whole life and dedicate it to my business? Will I let go of late nights with friends, going out with my girlfriend, for days and nights at the office desk?' I took some thinking and I realised that I would be driving myself down a path of misery. Money won't necessarily give me the pleasures that I would have given up a few years ago.
>
> Everyone dreams of owning their own companies and businesses and being recognised by almost everyone all around the world but what really is important is not having the dreams but what you do to achieve those dreams.
>
> As the shape program continues, I intend to give it my all, attend, interact and grow as much as possible to make sure this opportunity is not in vain.
>
> As a young entrepreneur, I will never forget where I am coming from, where I am at the moment and most importantly, where I want to be.

The reflections above indicate that the youth entrepreneurs involved in SHAPE realised that earning a big salary might not bring happiness, but rather living a life filled with creativity and 'learning a living' instead of 'earning a living'—an important indicator of change in developmental maturity.[39] Furthermore, they have realised the importance of persistence in realising their dreams, harnessing their past and their situational roots into something productive and aligned with growth.

> With this in mind I plan to stay focused, with my vision and dream in mind. Therefore I, as a young entrepreneur, am on a road that has neither directions nor a specific destination but I am willing [to] work endlessly and tirelessly to be a successful and noteworthy businesswoman.

Therefore, the journey to entrepreneurial action can be seen as one that is constantly changing and adapting, requiring perseverance. They are readying themselves and their will to do what is necessary to achieve their dreams that have now been stimulated.

7.4   Conclusion

As the youths engaged with their entrepreneurial ecosystem and started to develop their internal domains, they experienced a dichotomy of inspiration and fears at the same time. It was evident that both experiences contributed to the transformation—also referred to as growth in developmental maturity of internal domains. Enhances internal domains resulted in more entrepreneurial self-efficacy to co-initiate, co-sense, co-inspire, co-create and co-evolve with role-players in their external domains—the youth entrepreneurial ecosystem. The youth entrepreneurs received extensive initial support from their ecosystem. On the other side, role-players in their ecosystem's experiences came from interacting with the youth entrepreneurs and the educational institute. More interventions are needed in the youth entrepreneurial ecosystem to develop internal and external domains from the adult role-players in parallel to the youth entrepreneurs with the aim of breaking down systemic disconnect and co-create a continuum of co-inspiring (presencing). As the youth entrepreneurs participated in the SHAPE social technology, which aimed to facilitate inner-domain development, they

---

[39] Hannon et al. (2013).

came to a point where they needed to choose how they wanted to take forward entrepreneurial actions. Some move forward into starting up an enterprise; some continue to ideate entrepreneurial ideas. Others demonstrated that entrepreneurial transformation for some individuals could be a very long process to change the initial heartset, mindset and handset to become more entrepreneurial orientated.

The next chapters (8–10) reports on enablers and barriers the youth experienced as they continued their journey two years after co-initiation to SHAPE.

References

Adelakun, Y., & Van der Westhuizen, T. (2021). Delineating government policies and individual entrepreneurial orientation. *Journal of Sociology and Social Anthropology, 12*(3–4), 106–117. https://doi.org/10.31901/245 66764.2021/12.3-4.371

Awotunde, O. M., & Van der Westhuizen, T. (2021a). Entrepreneurial self-efficacy development: An effective intervention for sustainable student entrepreneurial intentions. *International Journal of Innovation and Sustainable Development, 15*(4), 475–495.

Awotunde, O.M. and Van der Westhuizen, T. (2021b, September). Entrepreneurial self-efficacy and the SHAPE ideation model for university students. In *ECIE 2021 16th European Conference on Innovation and Entrepreneurship Vol 1* (p. 37).

Chaplin, K. (2006). *The ubuntu spirit in African communities*. http://www.coe.int/t/dg4/cultureheritage/culture/Cities/Publication/BookCoE20-Chaplin.pdf [Retrieved 18 August 2015].

Cox LD. (2013). Presencing our absencing: A collective reflective practice using Scharmer's 'U' model. In: O Gunnlaugson, C Baron & M Cayer (eds). *Perspectives on Theory U: Insights from the field*. IGI Global.

Engelbrecht, K. (2012, October 2). 'SA youth entrepreneurship lags'. *Sunday Tribune*. http://www.news24.com/Archives/City-Press/SA-youth-entrepreneurship-lags-20150430

Fitch, G., & O'Fallon, T. (2013). Theory U applied in transformation development. In O Gunnlaugson, C Baron & M Cayer (eds.), *Perspectives on Theory U: Insights from the field*. IGI Global.

Gunnlaugson, O., Baron, C., & Cayer, M. (eds). 2013. *Perspectives on Theory U: Insights from the field*. IGI Global.

Guttenstein, S., Lindsay, J., & Baron, C. (2013). Aligning with the emergent future. In O Gunnlaugson, C Baron & M Cayer (eds.), *Perspectives on Theory U: Insights from the field*. Hershey, PA: IGI Global.

Hannon, V., Gillinson, S., & Shanks, L. (2013). *Learning a living: Radical innovation in education for work*. Bloomsbury.

Herrington, M., Kew, J., & Kew, P. (2015). *2014 GEM South African Report: South Africa: The crossroads – a goldmine or a time bomb?* www.gemconsortium.org/report/49154 [Retrieved 15 December 2017].

Kickul, J., & D'Intino, R. S. (2005). Measure for measure: Modeling entrepreneurial self-efficacy onto instrumental tasks within the new venture creation process. *New England Journal of Entrepreneurship, 8*(2), 6.

Korthaugen, F. A. J., Hoekstra, A., & Meijer, P. C. (2013). Promoting presence in professional practice: A core reflection approach for moving through the U. In O Gunnlaugson, C Baron & M Cayer (eds.), *Perspectives on Theory U: Insights from the field*. IGI Global.

Loevinger, J. (2014). *Measuring ego development*. Psychology Press.

Nhleko, Y., van der Westhuizen, T. (2022). The role of higher education institutions in introducing entrepreneurship education to meet the demands of industry 4. 0. *Academy of Entrepreneurship Journal, 28*(1), 1–23

Nicolaides, A., & McCallum, D. (2013). Accessing the blind spot: The U Process as seen through the lens of developmental action inquiry. In O Gunnlaugson, C Baron & M Cayer (eds.), *Perspectives on theory U: Insights from the field*. IGI Global.

Popper, K. (2014). *Conjectures and refutations: The growth of scientific knowledge*. Routledge.

Ruba, R. M., Van der Westhuizen, T., & Chiloane- Tsoka, G. E. (2021). Influence of entrepreneurial orientation on organisational performance: Evidence from congolese higher education institutions. *Journal of Contemporary Management, 18*(1), 243–269.

Scharmer, C. O., & Käufer, K. (2010). Theory U: Leading from the future as it emerges. *Developing Leaders*, 2010(2), 33. (Retrieved 4 September 2020). https://www.developingleadersquarterly.com/fb/Developing-Leaders-issue-2-2010/28/

Scharmer, C. O., & Käufer, K. (2013). *Leading from the emerging future: From ego-system to eco-system economies*. Berrett-Koehler Publishers.

Scharmer, C. O. (2009). *Theory U: Learning from the future as it emerges*. Berrett-Koehler Publishers.

Scharmer, C. O. (2011). *Leading the future as it emerges*. MA Thesis. Cambridge, Massachusetts: Society of Organizational Learning, University of Cambridge.

Schweikert, S., Meissen, J. O., & Wolf, P. (2013). Applying Theory U: The case of the creative living lab. In O Gunnlaugson, C Baron & M Cayer (eds.), *Perspectives on Theory U: Insights from the Field*. IGI Global.

Senge, P. M. (2012). Creating schools for the future, not the past for all students. *Leader to Leader, 2012*(65), 44–49.

Southern, N. 2013. Presencing as being in care: Extending Theory U in a relational framework. In O Gunnlaugson, C Baron & M Cayer (eds.), *Perspectives on Theory U: Insights from the field*. IGI Global.

Van der Westhuizen T. (2016). *Developing Individual entrepreneurial orientation: A systemic approach through the lens of Theory U*. PhD thesis. Durban: UKZN.

Van der Westhuizen, T. (2017a). The use of Theory U and Individual entrepreneurial orientation to increase low youth entrepreneurship in South Africa. *Journal of Contemporary Management, 14*, 531–553.

Van der Westhuizen, T. (2017b). A systemic approach towards responsible and sustainable economic development: entrepreneurship, systems theory and socio-economic momentum. In Z Fields (ed). *Collective creativity for responsible and sustainable business practice*. IGI Global. New York.

Van der Westhuizen, T. (2018a). The SHAPE project: Shifting hope, activating potential entrepreneurship. In D. Remenyi, D. A Grant (ed). *Incubators for young entrepreneurs – 20 case histories*. ACPIL

Van der Westhuizen, T. (2018b). Open Heart, open mind and open will in transformative individual entrepreneurial orientation pedagogies. *Academic Conferences and Publishing International Limited*. Redding, United Kingdom 443–448

Van der Westhuizen, T. (2019). Action! methods to develop entrepreneurship. In *18th European Conference on Research Methodology for Business and Management Studies*. (pp. 331–337)

Van der Westhuizen, T. (2021). Applying theory U through SHAPE to develop student's individual entrepreneurial orientation in a University Eco-System. In O. Gunnlaugson, W. Brendel (eds.), *Advances in pre-sensing volume III: Collective approaches, in theory U, trifoss Business Press*, pp. 395–435.

Van der Westhuizen, T. (2022). *Effective youth entrepreneurship*. Sunbonani. https://omp.sunbonani.co.za/index.php/sunbonani/catalog/book/6

Weinberg I. (2014). *The complete triangles model: Exploring the foundations of neuromodulation*. http://www.pninet.com/articles/Memory.pdf. (Retrieved 1 September 2017).

Wolff, G., Pathare, S., Craig, T., & Leff, J. (1996). Community knowledge of mental illness and reaction to mentally ill people. *British Journal of Psychiatry, 168*(2), 191–198.

Xavier, S., Kelley, D., Kew, J., Herrington, M., & Vorderwülbecke, A. (2013). . *Global Entrepreneurship Monitor (GEM) 2012 Global Report*. London: GERA (Global Entrepreneurship Research Association), London Business School. https://www.gemconsortium.org/file/open?fileId=48545

8

Key Barriers and Enablers to Youth Entrepreneurship

8.1 Introduction

The study described in this book was designed to explore barriers and enablers to youth entrepreneurship from a systemic perspective. The objective in investigating these was to find ways to overcome the obstacles that participants experienced and apply these solutions to entrepreneurship programmes and projects in general.

This chapter focuses on these key barriers and enablers identified in the study.

8.2 Key Barriers and Enablers to Youth Entrepreneurship

A potential solution to the unemployment problem in South Africa could come from addressing youth entrepreneurs' entrepreneurial traits. Table 8.1 shows the cumulative findings on personal barriers and enablers. The findings suggest that systemic intermediaries rank as the highest perceived barrier to entrepreneurship, while the lowest-ranking

© University of Kwazulu-Natal 2023
T. van der Westhuizen, *Youth Entrepreneurship*,
https://doi.org/10.1007/978-3-031-44339-8_8

barrier was educational institutions. An important finding was that the role-players in the SHAPE ecosystem for supporting youth entrepreneurs could be both barriers and enablers at the same time.

The finding that personal barriers in relation to systemic intermediaries rank highest reflects that the youth have limited self-leadership qualities and a complacent approach towards entrepreneurship. The lack of creativity towards solving business problems or coming up with new business ideas prevents them from starting a business, rather than lack of knowledge. The findings further show that the youth lack the skills, experience and resilience needed to secure funding and to have confidence in their idea creation, while funding itself presented another predominant barrier.

While personality traits and skills to view venture capital from a different perspective were lacking, equipping the youth with enabling aspects to bridge this barrier; for example (and as described in Part 3 of this book), using a variety of free online services and networks, enabled minimal-cost online start-ups. Not only did these alternatives

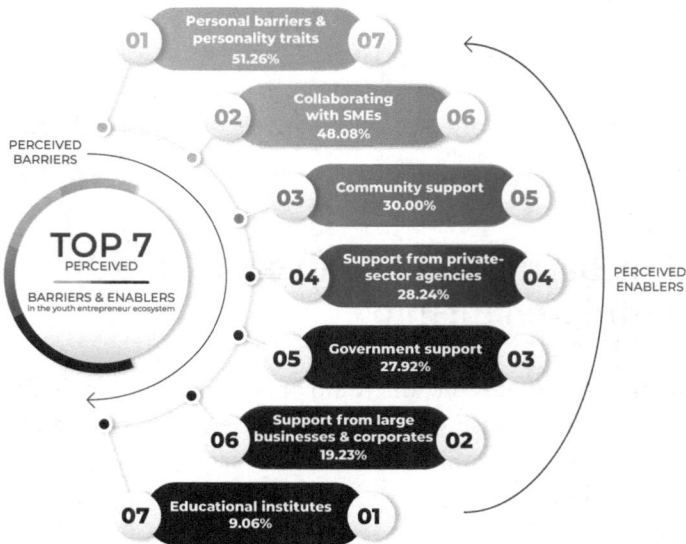

Fig. 8.1 Key barriers and enablers to youth entrepreneurship nexus (*Source* Van der Westhuizen, 2022)

minimise and resolve these barriers (as SHAPE had intended to do), but they allowed for online alternatives relevant to meeting the COVID-19 response while allowing the youth to recognise alternative methods to secure funding circumventing easy access to funding as an inhibitor of entrepreneurial activity.

The lowest-ranking barrier for youth entrepreneurs was found to be educational institutions. They saw University curricula inclusive of both academic and non-academic programmes at university supportive of youth entrepreneurship. There was a positive, moderate correlation between considering it important to have both academic and non-academic programmes at university to support youth entrepreneurship programmes, and SHAPE assisted me to have more self-confidence in becoming a young entrepreneur. Through SHAPE, youths found that educational institutions are increasingly becoming entrepreneurship-orientated through support, programmes, initiatives and activities. Through these types of initiatives, youths will benefit by participating and experiencing, leading to increased confidence as youth entrepreneurs. There is a positive correlation ($r = 0.342$) between UKZN becoming entrepreneurship-orientated and increased confidence in becoming a youth entrepreneur and heralding the increasing need to adopt an entrepreneurial approach towards its programmes. Confidence is an important precursor of entrepreneurial activity, and equipping students with the intrapsychic and intrapsychic tools (through networking with others in the industry and with fellow like-minded students) to facilitate entrepreneurial activities contributes positively to their confidence. As indicated in the previous chapter, youth entrepreneurs know that educational institutions are there to assist them in becoming more entrepreneurial. In addition, educational institutions are starting to offer entrepreneurship initiatives like SHAPE that benefit aspirant youth entrepreneurs who embrace the support. Although some results show educational institutions as a barrier, overall, youths recognise the importance of entrepreneurial programmes and embrace change from universities.

Successful entrepreneurs can be seen as being creative and proactive in the way they approach problem-solving. It, therefore, appears that entrepreneurial spirit determines success, not external barriers. This relates directly to the top-ranked barrier.

The importance of this study is that it provides useful knowledge about youth entrepreneurship and shows that future research needs to be conducted on internal barriers in relation to external barriers, rather than investigating external barriers alone.

8.2.1   Breakdown of Barriers to Youth Entrepreneurship's Constructs

The research investigated forty-four aspects of potential barriers and opportunities to youth entrepreneurs across seven different constructs, namely personal barriers, Educational Institutions, government agencies, private-sector agencies, communities and small—and medium-sized businesses. Table 8.2 shows the overall top ten ranked barriers to youth entrepreneurship identified. The table ranks these barriers from highest to lowest.

The barriers, ranked in descending order, were: difficulty accessing financial support to start their own business; personality traits in relation to systemic intermediaries hindering their progress in becoming an entrepreneur; government funding to pursue entrepreneurial activities; belief that small businesses are difficult to start due to high levels of competition; the difficulty of coming up with on-the-spot with ideas; crime hindering growth and development for the youth in South Africa; decision-making being challenging when planning a new business; limited awareness of private sector agencies, receiving limited training from large businesses; and lack of facilities within the community to assist youth entrepreneurs. The paragraphs that follow describe each of these barriers in more detail.

8.2.1.1   Financial Support

It is to be expected that financial difficulties would be the highest barrier to youth entrepreneurship since the youth lack the experience to create opportunities through being creative. Unrealised at this stage, this barrier

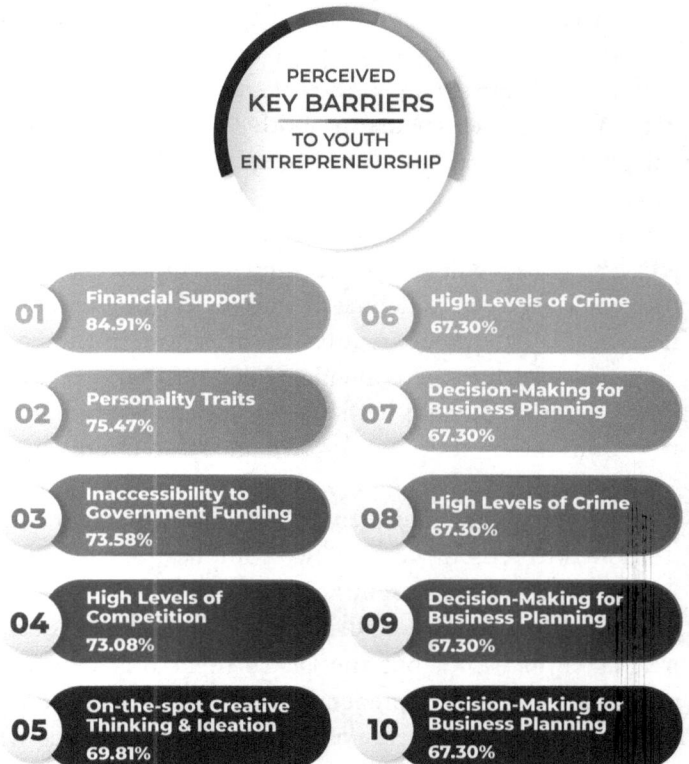

Fig. 8.2 Breakdown of key barriers to youth entrepreneurship

could be circumvented—for example, by creating a partnership with a friend through networks that could reduce the financial burden or by changing strategy to find a more affordable way to achieve outcomes. Further, the opportunities for online business and embracing the Fourth Industrial Revolution requires little or no capital layout to start up a business. However, this brings to the fore another question regarding the level of youths' technological skills as well as accessibility to data and stable internet reception.

It is common for youths to start businesses when they become unemployed or are in desperate need of money. In addition, youths do not capitalise on free opportunities, possibly due to inexperience and lack of skill. Youth entrepreneurs who own SMEs in South Africa require external debt financing from banks, but access to debt financing is a major barrier, which prevents youth entrepreneurs from achieving business growth. Youth entrepreneurs in South Africa are rejected by banks because of poor credit ratings, lack of security and inadequate business planning.[1]

Youth entrepreneurs need to understand the terms and conditions associated with an agreement, so governments and banks should offer support by providing clear guidelines to simplify the process of financing. In addition, youth entrepreneurs must be proactive and responsible in visiting financial institutions to obtain the documentation they need for financing.[2] This process could be further complicated by the economic recession within which the country and global economy have experienced as a result of COVID-19. Government and support agencies are working remotely, and universities and places of higher education have transitioned to remote working, with implications for networking, financing and entrepreneurial training initiatives.

Youth entrepreneurs in South Africa who own SMEs require external debt financing from banks, but the lack of debt financing is a major barrier preventing youth entrepreneurs from achieving business growth. They are rejected by banks because of poor credit ratings, lack of security and inadequate business planning. There are, however, some banks that offer a ten-year interest-free start up-loan to entrepreneurs.

These factors are to some extent associated with the second major barrier, which is personality traits.

8.2.1.2 Personality Traits

Personal barriers in youth entrepreneurs can be defined as personality traits exhibited by youths that inhibit their entrepreneurial intent to resolve an entrepreneurial action. Regarded as external influences, as previously explained, these personal barriers concerning systemic intermediaries may include personal barriers, entrepreneurship education

---

[1] Rector et al. (2016).
[2] Ibid.

and training, financial support, creative thinking, decision-making in planning a new business and working in teams.[3]

Many young people consider their personality traits themselves as a barrier hindering progress towards becoming an entrepreneur, which suggests that they believe they have limited control over outcomes and that they are a product of their environment rather than having control over their own lives. Their awareness that this is a barrier perhaps shows some degree of maturity in that they are aware of their weakness. The core personality traits of successful youth entrepreneurs are vision, resilience, teamwork, innovation, passion, leadership, integrity, quality customer focus and flexibility. Entrepreneurial personality traits are considered necessary to execute certain business tasks effectively.[4]

8.2.1.3 Inaccessibility to Government Funding

The third barrier is the perceived lack of funding from the government. This could be associated with the first barrier as youths appear to consider all finances a barrier. It is ill-informed to think that the government can provide funding for youths to start ventures. This barrier could be used as a convenient excuse; therefore, it is important to consider whether the barrier is more associated with personality than with finances. Financial social grants provided by the government can reduce incentives and motivation for entrepreneurs in the agricultural industry. There can consequently be a negative association with a dependency on such grants in the minds of rural entrepreneurs.[5].

8.2.1.4 High Levels of Competition and On-the-Spot Creative Thinking

The fourth-and fifth-rated barriers which appear to prevent youths from starting a business are the need for a high level of competition and

---

[3] Hormiga-Pérez et al.(2017); Kabukcu (2015); Luca and Robu (2016); Pruett (2012); Smolka et al. (2018).

[4] Ernst and Young (2017).

[5] Sinyolo et al. (2017).

limiting beliefs regarding their ability to creatively come up with ideas in planning the business. These two perceived barriers appear to be understandable because most business owners are constantly trying to outperform the competition by being creative. Entrepreneurship is a continuously changing discipline requiring innovation in a competitive market.

Being creative and innovative is a valuable skill for entrepreneurs seeking to leverage opportunities. Developing personal resilience and problem-solving ability could enable youths to add more value to their businesses and possibly find niches in the market. Creativity needs to be practised by the youth and should be included as a daily task. South African youth entrepreneurs starting SMEs should not resist competition but, instead, react by adding value within their own business. Embracing competition through ICT can provide networking capabilities that assist SMEs in improving staff interactions, supplier offerings and innovations. In this way, youth entrepreneurs can aim to react to opportunities and customer needs ahead of the competition.[6] However, converting creative ideas into reality is a challenge and requires being able to connect ideas and structure business plans for moving products to customers. Design, production and execution of projects in business are important—especially in the fashion industry, which requires seasonal changes every three months to attract demand from customers. Creativity and innovative products are consequently essential to remain in business.[7]

It benefits youth entrepreneurs by giving them real-world working experience and diverting their attention from possibly destructive behaviour, such as crime and drug addiction, towards artistic content which is engaging and interesting.[8]

8.2.1.5 High Levels of Crime

High levels of crime can prevent small businesses from achieving growth and development, and small businesses struggle more to recuperate from

---

[6] Adeniran and Johnston (2016).

[7] Kabukcu (2015).

[8] Montgomery (2017).

financial losses from crime than the larger businesses that can sustain these costs. Crime is a genuine barrier in South Africa and can deter businesses from reaching their potential, and high levels of crime reduce business entry in South Africa. In a longitudinal study from 2003 to 2015 calculating the variance in business registration in municipalities throughout South Africa, increased crime rates were shown to negatively impact business entry into the country.[9]

8.2.1.6   Decision-Making and Self-Accountability when Planning a New Business

The barrier to youth entrepreneurs represented by good decision-making when planning a new business could be associated with a lack of experience and an external locus of control. Entrepreneurs are reacting to the environment rather than becoming involved in planning. Correlations revealed a significant, moderate and positive correlation between the tendency to report difficulties in making decisions when planning a new business and showing a preference for working with others in a team environment when planning to start up a business. This shows how, when uncertain about their own abilities, they prefer to co-create and gain confidence through teamwork activities with others. Youth entrepreneurs are often exposed to uncertainty, ambiguity and emotionally charged scenarios, which can influence their decision-making.[10] Unpredictable environments make it difficult to plan a business, and it is recommended that entrepreneurs secure pre-commitments from third parties to ensure sustainability. Managing unpredictable circumstances requires entrepreneurs to be adaptable and proactive in seeking new opportunities. They also need to be empathetic and skilled in communications and negotiations with customers since this can greatly assist performance, including pre-commitment of goods and services, often creating sustainable partnerships.[11]

---

[9] Mahofa et al. (2016).
[10] Shepherd and Patzelt (2017).
[11] Smolka et al. (2018).

There can be problems; however, Nascent entrepreneurs sometimes stagnate in their decision-making for long periods and never move towards taking entrepreneurial action. They are often exposed to uncertainty, ambiguity and emotionally charged situations which can make decision-making difficult. To identify opportunities, entrepreneurs need to make assessments based on their experience, but this can result in negative emotions that reduce their motivation. In addition, opportunity-related decision-making from a static perspective, without assessing decisions, can change over time. Nascent entrepreneurs can nevertheless develop skills and gain more experience for making informed decisions. For example, decision-making is different for entrepreneurs motivated by non-economic goals that improve the environment and community rather than focusing on profits. These entrepreneurs are driven by positive change and base their decisions on uplifting the local community.[12]

8.2.1.7 Disconnect to Private Sector Agencies

Youth appear to be unaware of private sector agencies, which could act as a limit to business development, especially in regard to networking opportunities. This finding is expected as a few youths manage to establish business networks from an early age or be connected to business agencies. Youths' mental models are still expanding, and they might not have the necessary interpersonal abilities to initiate forming crucial business relationships. Youth entrepreneurs can greatly benefit from having associations with private sector agencies, and the lack thereof can even prevent youth entrepreneurs from starting businesses. Private sector agencies are sometimes prevented from achieving beneficial local community change because community members are not actively involved in the change process and lack control as a group.[13]

---

[12] Shepherd and Patzelt (2017).
[13] McEwan et al. (2017).

8.2.1.8 Skills Development

The next barrier is training and mentorship from large businesses or corporations to youth entrepreneurs for enabling business start-ups. This finding is surprisingly lower than expected, possibly reflecting a lack of awareness on the part of youth entrepreneurs. The benefits arising from structured training could provide youth entrepreneurs with an accurate understanding of industries and thus create employment opportunities. Educational programmes connected to the industry exist in South Africa but lack resources and expenditure from industry.[14] This explains, perhaps, why they hinge their hopes on initiatives from educational institutions in providing them with the necessary skills and confidence to start thinking creatively and engaging with networks with a little more confidence and thus constructive proactivity.

8.2.1.9 Lack of Facilities and Infrastructure

The final barrier is the lack of facilities and infrastructure in the community. This rating is also unsurprisingly low since youths throughout South Africa experience high levels of poverty, exacerbated by this lack. Youths are sometimes unaware of the benefits of properly functioning infrastructure and could achieve more when South Africa provides improved facilities to foster business. Inadequate long-term strategic planning has resulted in a lack of infrastructure, facilities and innovation for South Africans, stifling growth in the economy and creating a disconnect between geographical regions.[15]

8.2.2 Key Enablers for Youth Entrepreneurship

In identifying the top ten barriers to youth entrepreneurship (see Table 8.2), this research also identified the ten lowest barriers. These lowest barriers could be described as enablers for youth entrepreneurs

---

[14] Reinhard et al. (2016).
[15] Chitiga et al. (2016).

because they are perceived as areas that provide the least entrepreneurial resistance (see Table 8.3). They can accordingly benefit the youth and are discussed below.

Rated in descending order, the enabling factors for youth entrepreneurs were: university academic and non-academic programmes supporting youth entrepreneurs; municipality mentorship; educational institutions as an entrepreneurship-orientated institution through their support programmes and the initiatives on offer; benefit from SHAPE for youth entrepreneurs which is also an opportunity for them to become more entrepreneurial; greater self-confidence derived from

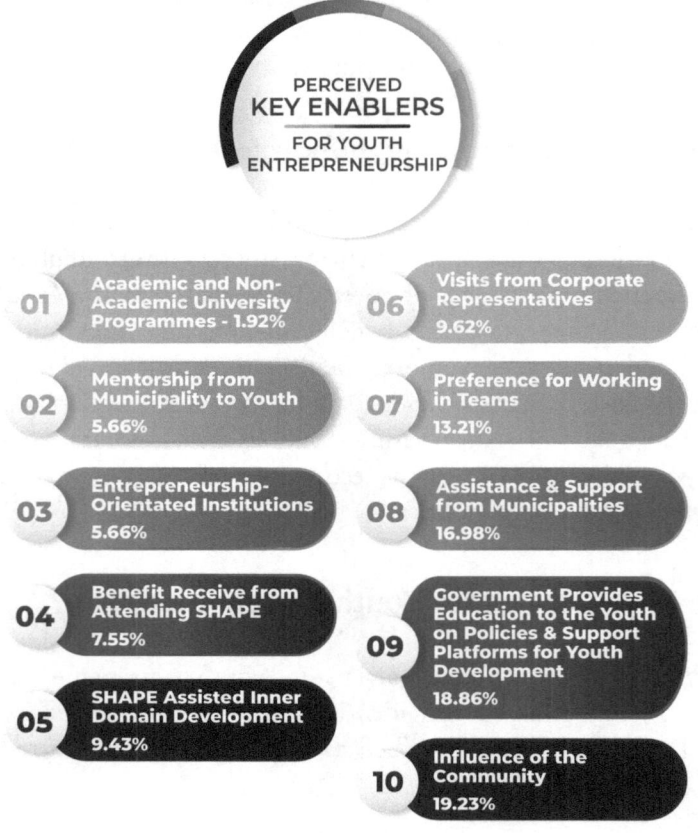

PERCEIVED
KEY ENABLERS
FOR YOUTH
ENTREPRENEURSHIP

01 **Academic and Non-Academic University Programmes - 1.92%**

02 **Mentorship from Municipality to Youth** 5.66%

03 **Entrepreneurship-Orientated Institutions** 5.66%

04 **Benefit Receive from Attending SHAPE** 7.55%

05 **SHAPE Assisted Inner Domain Development** 9.43%

06 **Visits from Corporate Representatives** 9.62%

07 **Preference for Working in Teams** 13.21%

08 **Assistance & Support from Municipalities** 16.98%

09 **Government Provides Education to the Youth on Policies & Support Platforms for Youth Development** 18.86%

10 **Influence of the Community** 19.23%

Fig. 8.3 Breakdown of key barriers to youth entrepreneurship

SHAPE, so that they were confident enough to take action; visits from representatives of large companies; working in teams, which can benefit entrepreneurial outcomes; municipal support for youth entrepreneurs; gaining information about government policies, and community influence in the type of businesses they would like to start. These ten key opportunities are now discussed in more detail.

8.2.2.1 Academic and Non-academic University Programmes

It is encouraging to see the enabling learning environment provided by academic and non-academic university programmes to support youth entrepreneurs. This was the youths' highest-rated enabler factor and suggests that systemic action-learning–action-research programmes are becoming more accepted. Youth entrepreneurs are starting to realise that universities require non-academic programmes that specifically focus on entrepreneurship from an innovation perspective.[16] There was a positive, moderate significant correlation between having received training from educational institutions to develop skills to start a business. SHAPE assisted them in having more self-confidence in becoming a young entrepreneur. It is thus evident that through SHAPE < and the training received. As a result, it has been vital in helping them develop the confidence needed to offset their perceived barriers in relation to their own entrepreneurial abilities. It attests to the need for educational institutions in assisting in developing the skills necessary for business and helping youth entrepreneurs gain the confidence they need to initiate entrepreneurial action. The key defining factor of youth entrepreneurs is exposure and relative lack of exposure to new ways of thinking and doing business. When exposed, it opens their mind to further possibilities and gives them the confidence needed to engage on the level necessary to facilitate action. Exposure occurs more within the older youth population, who are thus more inclined to positively rate the skills obtained from these educational programmes as more effective in starting a business.

---

[16] Rambe (2017).

Moving from immediate support or enablers: different systemic levels offer support and enabling aspects, but it might need time to tap into these systemic enablers. The youth's ever-expanding mental models that increase their worldview after being exposed to new realities and possibilities inform recognition of potential enablers within the system. It is therefore important to expose the youth to the nexus of systemic support around them and create the ecosystem which enables a bridging connection between youths and their nexus of systemic support. Without exposure to new mental model enablers, there might be no directional growth and awareness of the available business gaps within their environment.

Educational programmes can improve entrepreneurial intention, and indeed entrepreneurship education is often a motivator for the youth to consider entrepreneurship a possible career. However, the entrepreneurial intention is influenced more by community background than entrepreneurship education. To improve entrepreneurial education, working in real-life business scenarios, therefore, needs to be made part of the learning process.[17]

8.2.2.2 Municipality Mentorship

The second-highest-rated perceived enabler beneficial to youth entrepreneurs was municipality mentorship. This mentor's purpose was to strengthen the ecosystem by providing access to resources and networking opportunities. The tendency for the youth to rate the importance of not just academic but also non-academic initiatives as important was noted. Municipalities, considered informally as a non-academic source of skilling, could gain a better understanding of the needs of the youth through ongoing interactions from mentorship programmes. In addition, the youth could identify the strategic direction of the municipality and be more aligned. Municipal mentorship was enabled through SHAPE < showing a moderate, positive correlation between benefitting from sessions with their municipal mentor and ultimately leading to increased confidence through SHAPE on becoming a

---

[17] Herman and Stefanescu (2017); Pruett (2012).

young entrepreneur (r = 0.450). This attests to the need for collaborative peers in increasing confidence in one's own entrepreneurial ability and a more structured and focused approach towards securing mentoring from municipal mentors. These sessions are also shown to correlate with the perception of municipality support as a youth entrepreneur (r = 0.524). This also accounts for the high rating in perceptions regarding support but does not necessarily indicate a generalised view of support outside of the SHAPE programme.

The strategic objectives that local municipalities provide might offer a variety of platforms, including creating an environment that is safe and healthy. Many municipalities have developed a competitive environment by implementing support programmes through which small-and-medium-sized businesses can flourish, thereby empowering youth entrepreneurs and other entrepreneurs.

8.2.2.3 Entrepreneurship-Orientated Institutions

The third-rated enabler is that higher education institutions are becoming more entrepreneurially orientated institutions through support programmes and initiatives. The youth now perceive educational institutions as offering them support structures that can help them to achieve business goals. It appears that the youth welcome entrepreneurship programmes and embrace the new content and activities on offer.

8.2.2.4 The Benefit Received from Attending SHAPE

The fourth-ranked enablers were the benefit of attending the SHAPE social technology project (related to the third ranking). SHAPE contributed to entrepreneurial growth and exposure to new ways of thinking through collaborative efforts with key stakeholders in the industry. Among others, through attending SHAPE, youths felt the education and training prepared them sufficiently to become an entrepreneur ($r = 0.512$). Thus SHAPE and entrepreneurship education is key to preparing the youth and creating confidence in aspiring towards their hopes to become an entrepreneur. Attendance in SHAPE led to increased development of skills ($r = 0.400$), more self-confidence ($r = 0.502$). Thus, SHAPE was pivotal in creating the confidence needed in their skills and aptitude towards becoming successful entrepreneurs and suggests the need for further initiatives that are entrepreneurially oriented. SHAPE has provided youths with skills and experiences aimed at giving them opportunities to start their businesses, assisted them to create networks that they did not previously have and made them more entrepreneurial. Youth entrepreneurs who participated in the 2014–2015 SHAPE project received support and guidance from experienced entrepreneurs through business friends' or SMEs.

8.2.2.5 Visits from Corporate Representatives

The sixth enabler for youth entrepreneurs was receiving visits from representatives of large companies to inform them of business opportunities and provide access to up-to-date information on industry changes. Having access to the key players in the industry and engaging with them on a person-to-person basis is empowering within itself. These visits give young entrepreneurs a unique insight into large businesses and their operations and contribute to their confidence. In addition, these connections to large businesses could act as a bridge between unemployment and employment, thereby potentially reducing the unemployment rate. Youth entrepreneurs who complete these programmes are more employable than youths who have not been exposed to work because they provide practical experience.

8.2.2.6 Preference for Working in Teams

The seventh-rated enabler suggests that youth entrepreneurs are realistic about their capabilities and skills and therefore support working in teams rather than working alone, which tends to be associated with more experienced individuals. Moreover, young people do not consider working in teams as a barrier, which further suggests that they would embrace teamwork. Previous experiences significantly impact entrepreneurs' decisions to commence a business either alone or in a team.[18] This is a great inclination to be in possession of, as one of the key attributes of youth entrepreneurs is the ability to participate in teamwork and effectively execute entrepreneurial activities.

8.2.2.7 Assistance and Support from Municipalities

The eighth- and ninth-rated enablers suggest that youths would accept support from municipalities to assist them in becoming more entrepreneurial. They had already expressed openness to this opportunity, rating non-academic sources of inspiration and skilling as an important enabler of success. The many local municipalities provide essential support to SMMEs, all of which make a positive difference to the economy. This support aims to provide employment opportunities and assist in creating innovation and competition. Being informed about government policies is to some extent associated with receiving support from municipalities because youths have started to perceive external sources of information as useful, and this leads to perceptions of municipal support of youth entrepreneurs ($r = 0.422$).

8.2.2.8 Influence of the Community

The tenth enabler is youth entrepreneurs' perception of the influence of their community on the type of business they would like to start, suggesting that they are not limited by the community but rather are connected to the community through shared interests. Most business owners do not have a heritage and legacy enabling them to benefit from a family name—a benefit that takes years to achieve.[19] Those youths who do not have family businesses do not, however, see this as a limitation.

There was a positive correlation between the perception that people in their community influenced the type of business they would like to

---

[18] Hormiga-Pérez et al. (2017).
[19] Farrington et al. (2017).

start and their increasingly challenging decision-making when planning a new business (r 0.354). This indicates that perhaps this influence pulls youths in different directions, with the consequence of confusion and lack of personal belief further exacerbating the confidence in their own ideas and entrepreneurial ideation.

8.3   Conclusion

The majority of SHAPE first iteration participants graduated and progressed into employment or postgraduate studies, showing that SHAPE had a positive impact on its participants. The most significant barriers appeared to be the personal barriers formed in relation to systemic intermediaries: aspirant youth entrepreneurs have a limited self-leadership capacity and often display a complacent approach towards entrepreneurship. Their perceived lack of creativity and confidence prevents them from solving business problems or starting a business, rather than problems emanating from external intermediaries. They furthermore have not, at this stage, experienced and been exposed to many sources of inspiration that would not only expose them to new ideas but also bolster their confidence in engaging in any risk-associated entrepreneurial activities. Confidence and exposure are important requisites for opportunity identification and risk-taking. Attending academic and non-academic programmes towards this end help inspire confidence in their own skills, while networking and being exposed to key players in the industry put them on equal playing grounds, where they can actively engage in idea creation, without letting the voices overwhelm and immobilise activity.

Acknowledgement Chapter based on SHAPE research project work: Krieger, W., 2018. Barriers to youth entrepreneurship: a systemic approach (Masters dissertation). University of KwaZulu-Natal. Supervisor: Professor Thea van der Westhuizen.

References

Adelakun, Y., & Van der Westhuizen, T. (2021). Delineating Government Policies and Individual Entrepreneurial Orientation. *Journal of Sociology and Social Anthropology, 12*(3–4), 106–117. https://doi.org/10.31901/245 66764.2021/12.3-4.371

Adeniran, T. V., & Johnston, K. A. (2016). The impacts of ICT utilisation and dynamic capabilities on the competitive advantage of South African SMEs. *International Journal of Information Technology and Management, 15*(1), 59–89.

Awotunde, O. M., & Van der Westhuizen, T. (2021a). Entrepreneurial self-efficacy development: An effective intervention for sustainable student entrepreneurial intentions. *International Journal of Innovation and Sustainable Development, 15*(4), 475–495.

Awotunde, O. M. & Van der Westhuizen, T. (2021b September). Entrepreneurial self-efficacy and the SHAPE ideation model for university students. In *ECIE 2021 16th European Conference on Innovation and Entrepreneurship Vol 1* (p. 37).

Chitiga, M., Mabugu, R., & Maisonnave, H. (2016). Analysing job creation effects of scaling up infrastructure spending in South Africa. *Development Southern Africa, 33*(2), 186–202.

Ernst & Young. (2017). *Entrepreneurs share core traits: Decoding the DNA of the entrepreneur.* [Retrieved 15 September 2017], www.ey.com/gl/en/services/strategic-growth-markets/ey-nature-or-nurture-5-entrepreneurs-share-core-traits

Farrington, S., Venter, E., & Richardson, B. (2017). Stakeholders perceptions and the use of 'family' in selected marketing and branding practices of family

SMEs. In D. J. Nel (Ed.), *Proceedings of the 29ᵗʰ SAIMS Annual Conference*, Kopano Nokeng Country Lodge & Conference Centre, Bloemfontein, September 10–12.

Herman, E., & Stefanescu, D. (2017). Can higher education stimulate entrepreneurial intentions among engineering and business students? *Educational Studies, 43*(3), 312–327.

Hormiga-Pérez, E., Hancock, C., & Jaría-Chacón, N. (2017). Going it alone or working as part of a team: The impact of human capital on entrepreneurial decision-making. *Journal of Evolutionary Studies in Business, 2*(1), 210–231.

Kabukcu, E. (2015). Creativity process in innovation oriented entrepreneurship: The case of Vakko. *Procedia-Social and Behavioral Sciences, 195,* 1321–1329.

Luca, M., & Robu, A. (2016). Personality traits in entrepreneurs and self-employed. *Bulletin of the Transilvania University of Brasov. Special Issue Series VII: Social Sciences Law, 9(2):58.*

Mahofa, G., Sudaram, A., & Edwards, L. (2016). Impact of crime on firm entry: Evidence from southern Africa. *Economic Research Southern Africa,* ERSA Working Paper 652:1–19.

McEwan, C., Mawdsley, E., Banks, G., & Scheyvens, R. (2017). Enrolling the private sector in community development: Magic bullet or sleight of hand? *Development and Change, 48*(1), 28–53.

Montgomery, D. (2017). The rise of creative youth development. *Arts Education Policy Review, 118*(1), 1–18.

Nhleko, Y., & van der Westhuizen, T. (2022). The role of higher education institutions in introducing entrepreneurship education to meet the demands of industry 4. 0. *Academy of Entrepreneurship Journal,* 28(1), 1–23

Pruett, M. (2012). Entrepreneurship education: Workshops and entrepreneurial intentions. *Journal of Education for Business, 87*(2), 94–101.

Rambe, P. (2017). Developing context-relevant entrepreneurship: Experiences and lessons from advanced and emerging economies. In *Proceedings of the First International Conference on Entrepreneurship Development* (*ICED*), Faculty of Management Sciences, Central University of Technology, Free State, Bloemfontein, Hotel School, April 5–7.

Rector, M., Fatoki, O., & Oni, O. (2016). Access to debt finance by young entrepreneurs in Polokwane. *South Africa. Journal of Social Sciences, 49*(1–2), 67–95.

Reinhard, K., Pogrzeba, A., Townsend, R., & Pop, C. A. (2016). A comparative study of cooperative education and work-integrated learning in Germany, South Africa, and Namibia. *Asia-Pacific Journal of Cooperative Education, 17*(3), 249–263.

Ruba, R. M., Van der Westhuizen, T., & Chiloane- Tsoka, G. E. (2021). Influence of entrepreneurial orientation on organisational performance: Evidence from Congolese higher education institutions. *Journal of Contemporary Management, 18*(1), 243–269.

Shepherd, D. A., & Patzelt, H. (2017). *Trailblazing in entrepreneurship: Creating new paths for understanding the field*. Springer International.

Sinyolo, S., Mudhara, M., & Wale, E. (2017). The impact of social grant-dependency on agricultural entrepreneurship among rural households in Kwazulu-Natal, South Africa. *Journal of Developing Areas, 51*(3), 63–76.

Smolka, K. M., Verheul, I., Burmeister-Lamp, K., & Heugens. P. P. (2018). Get it together! Synergistic effects of causal and effectual decision-making logics on venture performance. *Entrepreneurship Theory and Practice, 42*(4), 571–604.

Van der Westhuizen, T. (2017a). The use of Theory U and individual entrepreneurial orientation to increase Low Youth Entrepreneurship in South Africa. *Journal of Contemporary Management, 14*, 531–553.

Van der Westhuizen, T. (2017b). A systemic approach towards responsible and sustainable economic development: entrepreneurship, systems theory and socio-economic momentum. In Z. Fields (Ed.), *Collective creativity for responsible and sustainable business practice*. IGI Global.

Van der Westhuizen, T. (2018a). The SHAPE Project: Shifting hope, activating potential entrepreneurship. In D. Remenyi & D. A. Grant (Eds.), *Incubators for young entrepreneurs—20 case histories*. ACPIL

Van der Westhuizen, T. (2018b). Open heart, open mind and open will in transformative individual entrepreneurial orientation pedagogies. *Academic Conferences and Publishing International Limited*. 443–448

Van der Westhuizen, T. (2019). Action! methods to develop entrepreneurship. In *18th European Conference on Research Methodology for Business and Management Studies*. (pp. 331–337).

Van der Westhuizen, T. (2021). Applying theory U through SHAPE to develop student's individual entrepreneurial orientation in a university eco-system. In O. Gunnlaugson & W. Brendel (Eds.), *Advances in pre-sensing volume III: Collective approaches, in theory U*, (pp. 395–435). Trifoss Business Press.

Van der Westhuizen, T. (2022). *Effective youth entrepreneurship*. Sunbonani. https://omp.sunbonani.co.za/index.php/sunbonani/catalog/book/6

9

Youth Entrepreneur Ecosystems: Barriers and Enablers Relating to Personal Systems, Educational Institutes and Communities

9.1   Introduction

This chapter expands on Chapter 8 by supporting the key barriers and enablers with empirical findings and discussions thereof. This chapter will be presenting data and findings related to:

- internal domains, personal aspects and traits;
- external domains as educational institutions; and
- communities.

The chapter concludes with a section focused on the COVID-19 epidemic. This section was developed during the initial outbreak of the pandemic and did not form part of the initial investigation. However, under the current socio-political and economic situation in the country, the impact of COVID-19 needs to be taken into consideration when discussing barriers and enablers to youth entrepreneurship. The COVID-19 epidemic has presented a serious barrier to youth entrepreneurship, which could, however, also act as an enabler if viewed from an entrepreneurial lens. The consequences of COVID-19 will be filtered into each aspect discussed in the chapter to follow.

© University of Kwazulu-Natal 2023
T. van der Westhuizen, *Youth Entrepreneurship*,
https://doi.org/10.1007/978-3-031-44339-8_9

9.2   Personal Barriers and Enablers Influencing Youth Entrepreneurs

To investigate how systemic personal barriers influence youth entrepreneurs' mindsets, certain aspects, as discussed in the paragraphs that follow, can be synthesised as the top barriers and opportunities to youth entrepreneurship.

The discussion that will follow will discuss the top barriers and their associated enabler. Within each dimension, a continuum existed along which youth entrepreneurs experienced barriers and associated enablers that helped leverage entrepreneurial potential. The discussion follows that with every perceived barrier within each dimension (personal and educational, etc.); there will be opportunities and enablers to entrepreneurial action that exist. Figure 9.1 shows the findings related to research Question 1 regarding personal traits/systems and their influence on developing youth entrepreneurs.

From Fig. 9.1, it appears that the top barrier that youth entrepreneurs experience (accessing financial support). Youth entrepreneurs experienced difficulties in accessing financial support to start their own businesses. Only 15.1% of respondents indicated that they had not had

Fig. 9.1 Research Question 1: Barriers and opportunities—Personal systems

trouble in accessing financial support to start their own business, whereas 84.9% of respondents agreed that they had had difficulty, with over half (52.8%, $N = 53$) of those agreeing 'entirely'. This question yielded a median score of 7 (entirely agree), with a left negative skew of −1.71, meaning the bulk of the distribution falls to the right, and the relative peaked-ness suggests that the majority are in clear alliance with the inability to access the necessary financial support.

Youth are not able to secure loans and get financial support, which is a major barrier and prevents them from achieving their business goals. At this point in their lives, they have relatively low access to networks or capital they can leverage efforts off. Youth entrepreneurs can stagnate because their poor credit ratings prevent them from obtaining small loans. These financial barriers are further worsened by banks not providing clear guidelines for youth, which makes the achievement of their business goals more problematic.[1] Youths with less financial support from their families are not able to apply the knowledge they learned from the entrepreneurial financial programmes. The effects of financial entrepreneurship programmes also vary according to age, background and gender.[2]

It is thus evident that the South African youth need to be incorporated into the financial system through banks and the government to overcome this major barrier. Without entrepreneurship education and training, youths are disadvantaged because they will not experience business scenarios reflecting real-life situations. Another problem is that unrealistic expectations are created when the youth believe that creating a successful business plan will lead to entrepreneurship. Youths who have negative experiences during entrepreneurship training do not perceive entrepreneurship as a viable career.

The establishment of financial support directly relates to their external environment, but it stems from within. There is complacency within which the youth expect to receive rather than generate from within. Essentially, the top barriers encountered by these youth entrepreneurs relate to the internal environment (intrinsic to the individual). It

---

[1] Rector et al. (2016).
[2] Bausch et al. (2016).

seems that youths struggle to adapt their personality traits to become more entrepreneurial. As discussed, youths find it difficult to think creatively and make effective decisions to propel them forward as youth entrepreneurs. This is a perceived internal mental block experienced by these youth. Creativity stems from within and relates to creating an innovative environment needed to leverage entrepreneurial activity, using resources innovatively and in constructive manners to build to an optimal point of breaking into the entrepreneurial space. These self-limiting beliefs held by the youth are such that they block creativity and disable creatively innovating towards utilising resources. The perception that they may be lacking in experience and resources is indicative of premature entrepreneurial self-belief through lack of exposure, and the inaccessibility to resources, including educational ones, needed to create and sustain entrepreneurial action. These findings are consistent with the findings in Fig. 9.2 on barriers to education, where the youth entrepreneurs indicated that the education they were currently receiving was not perceived as a barrier. The sought-after skilling presented to them reflects their internal positioning as relatively inexperienced and unexposed to opportunity but searching for instances and opportunities to equip themselves with the necessary resources to boost their confidence and creativity required to innovate and activate their entrepreneurial action. This might imply that youth entrepreneurs do not encounter personal barriers in relation to systemic intermediaries on a much deeper and more personal level than in relation to the education they receive, as they see them as enablers to equip them with the skills and exposure necessary to scaffold them more confidently into the entrepreneurial space.

9.2.1 Personality Traits

When understanding the perceived personality traits as the second-highest perceived barrier on the personality construct—the youth require pro-activity and an internal locus of control to exhibit those traits aligned with successful entrepreneurs. Without these traits, youths are less likely to influence outcomes and will thus be uncompetitive. Examination of

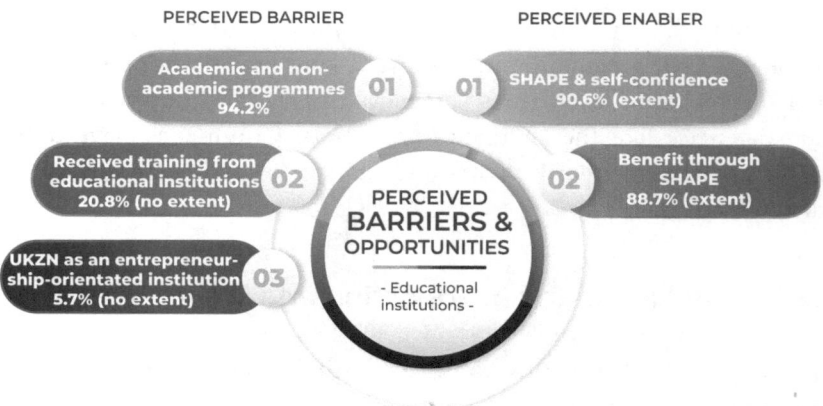

Fig. 9.2 Research Question 2: Barriers and opportunities—Educational institutions

the standardised regression weights for the personality trait dimension reveals it to be the second-highest regression weight attributable to a barrier to entrepreneurship. Although constituted as a barrier, it allows for the greatest opportunity requiring targeted intervention in taking the youth from a reactive to generating new ideas and seeking out the entrepreneurial activity.

The majority of respondents (75.5%, $N = 53$) agreed that they considered their personality traits a hindrance to their progress in becoming an entrepreneur, and 13.2% generally disagreed with this statement. The majority of the respondents were Africans, among whom business has been traditionally dominated by patriarchal authority. Gender differences are statistically significant across the data, showing that women are more likely to agree that their personality traits hinder their progress towards becoming entrepreneurs. This is somewhat unsurprising given that males within a patriarchally defined and dominated society are encouraged to take more risks and thus engage in more entrepreneurial activities. Further, women were more likely to feel empowered by initiatives offered by entrepreneurship education, indicative of a lack of personal confidence and empowerment to successfully pursue and consider oneself, as a woman, suitable to be an and embody an entrepreneur. This was evident in the self-section of the study, in which more than twice as many males as women participated voluntarily in the entrepreneurship initiative. Government organisations, such as the Small Enterprise Development Agency (SEDA) and business development agencies like the Durban Chamber of Commerce, have done a lot to uplift women in business and help to overcome gender-specific barriers.[3]

9.2.2 Entrepreneurship Education and Training

The second enabler in this construct is the effect of entrepreneurship education and training on preparing a student entrepreneur to become more entrepreneurial. Most respondents (81.2%, $N = 53$) agreed that their entrepreneurship education and training prepared them sufficiently for becoming an entrepreneur, and 69.8% of respondents agreed that it developed their skills to a moderate and very great extent. This shows that education and training is an important enabler providing an opportunity for the youth to overcome the negative entrepreneurial personality traits which prevent them from achieving entrepreneurial success. This is especially the case where there was a significant finding that the more mature youths, who have been increasingly exposed to educational skilling and training, find it more impactful in assisting in developing those skills and readying them for entrepreneurial action.

When contextualising these findings with existing research, we come to understand how personality traits act as barriers to youth entrepreneurship. Youths who have an internal locus of control are more entrepreneurial than those who believe the world controls outcomes.[4] The difference between youths and older adults might be related to personal and biological growth and maturity and explains why older youths participate more meaningfully in systems geared towards initiating entrepreneurial activation. Entrepreneurship education and training improve entrepreneurial intention and shift the perception of

[3] Van der Westhuizen and Upton (2017).
[4] Ernst & Young (2017).

the youth to understand their personality traits, which provides awareness of their barriers.[5] Moreover, real-world education and training provide a beneficial platform for building entrepreneurial skills in South Africa.[6] Education and training are considered to be crucial for youth entrepreneurs. It is also important to deconstruct systemic barriers and break down the systemic disconnect through bringing the ecosystem in interpersonal contact with one another. As a consequence, the SHAPE respondents were provided with a unique opportunity to grow and develop throughout the programme, shifting their attitudes to prepare them for the world of work.[7]

There was a significant gender-based difference in opinion as to whether entrepreneurship education and training prepared the respondents sufficiently to become entrepreneurs ($U = 182.50$, $p = 0.02$), with males being more likely to opt for a 'disagree' or 'neutral' stance, and women being more inclined to agree that it does sufficiently prepare them. Entrepreneurship education, including the Chamber of Commerce, had been perceived to have contributed significantly more to the growth and feelings of support received by women compared to males, indicating their importance in empowering women and youths in general and initiating entrepreneurial activity. Because of inherited and subversive ecosystemic, political and socio-economic reasons, educated and uneducated South African women experience difficulty entering the workforce because they lack opportunities. In addition, only 6% of South African women engage in entrepreneurial activities, which is concerning because this figure has shown a significant decline— of 9%—since 2014.[8] These statistics show that in South Africa; men engage in higher levels of entrepreneurial activity than women. Understanding the nature and origins that manifest women as marginalised in economic activities is complex and multifaceted and can be traced to the origination of Capitalism, Marxist ideologies and Hegel's conceptions around master–slave theory, and understanding gender ascribed roles and

---

[5] Herman and Stefanescu (2017).
[6] Van der Westhuizen (2017a, 2017b, 2017c); Venter (2017).
[7] Van der Westhuizen (2017a, 2017b, 2017c).
[8] Herrington and Kew (2016).

responsibilities embodied by men and women, socialised and inculcated into the culture, reproducing systems of submission and disempowerment. The large absence of women participating in the economy also means that there is little exposure to persons modelling and normalising economic activity for women entrepreneurs, thus further creating a barrier of entry for women. This lack of role models, the decreased networking opportunities and low capital are all major contributors to this gender disparity between men and women. In addition, female businesses tend to be smaller and generate less profit than men's businesses. Female business owners each employ around 23 employees, whereas male business owners employ around 29 employees.[9]

9.2.3 Creative Thinking

The third expressed barrier within this construct relates to creative thinking and ideas when youth entrepreneurs plan a business and is a derivative of the personality traits and held self-beliefs discussed above. Of the respondents, 18.9% indicated that they did not find it challenging to come up with ideas, especially on-the-spot creative thinking when planning a business, whereas a majority (69.8%, $N = 53$) of respondents agreed that it was challenging. A majority of the respondents found it difficult to produce or generate new ideas. This corresponds with earlier research that the author did with this cohort, in which they demonstrated an inability to product-innovate, showing that self-innovation is a long process of deep intrinsic reflections, realisations and personal growth to develop the entrepreneurial mindset and heartset. Even with financial training, youths with less financial support from families struggle to implement what they learn from the entrepreneurial programmes. The literature on creative thinking being a barrier to youth entrepreneurs does not provide a clear cause and effect. This, however, is seen as a complex topic and was not considered in the survey.

---

[9] Van der Westhuizen and Upton (2017).

9.2.4 Decision-Making

The fourth expressed barrier within this construct provided information on decision-making when planning a new business. Just over half (54.6%) of the respondents agreed that decision-making was a challenge when planning a new business. This makes sense if the youth are operating from a place of poor confidence in their skill and ability and lack the necessary exposure to empower them into a creative and confident space. There was a significant difference in respondents' highest level of education and decision-making being challenging when planning a new business ($F(4, 48) = 3.94$, $p= 0.01$), where post hoc tests revealed that the difference lay between third-year and honours students ($c^2(1) = 7.71$, $p= 0.01$). Honours students were more likely to agree that decision-making was a challenge when planning a new business. Second-year students were the least likely to agree. This could be taken to mean that second-year students are less entrepreneurially skilled than honours students and that they lack understanding of the efforts required to start a business and have a false sense of reality needed to realistically challenge their inner domains. In addition, second-year students could have more unrealistic expectations of the decisions required to be successful because of their lack of experience compared to honours students and are thus underwhelmed in terms of the complexity of decision-making and possession of the skill needed to bridge into that gap. Moreover, honours students are closer to exiting university. They could already have attempted ventures, and hence, understanding that decision-making is challenging when planning a new business. As previously indicated, they could have higher levels of exposure and skill in addressing potential challenges but are, inter alia, more cognisant of them.

This finding that decision-making when planning a new business is a barrier to youth entrepreneurs is supported by research showing that the youth are exposed to uncertainty and ambiguity and often lack the work experience to accurately assess situations.[10] In addition, business activities are unpredictable, and entrepreneurs consistently need to seek new opportunities to be sustainable, making decision-making

---

[10] Shepherd and Patzelt (2017).

more difficult.[11] As with creative thinking, the literature on decision-making does not provide clear cause and effect regarding barriers to youth entrepreneurs.

9.2.5 Working in Teams

Teamwork is considered an enabler of success, and this component analysed whether youths prefer working in teams when planning a start-up. A small percentage of respondents (13.2%) generally indicated that they preferred not to work with others in a team environment when planning to start up a business, whereas an overwhelming majority (81.1%) of the respondents generally agreed that they did. This finding could support the view that those sampled found decision-making difficult and that the youth struggle to work alone and preferred collaboration and input from other team members. Teamwork ascribes a level of confidence individuals' battle to harness by making decisions alone and allows the verification of constructs and ideas when mutuality is sought and achieved with others. It also helps mitigate perceived risks and blind spots associated with individualistic paradigms of understanding. Given that youths are relatively unconfident in their level of skill, and they expressed concern over the validity of their decision-making and confidence in idea creation; they actively seek out initiatives to help boost their confidence in their ability. Teamwork is part of these opportunities for learning and vetting ideas. Examination of the standardised regression weights reveals that the highest regression weight and therefore greatest barrier among the personal attributes construct was attributable to 'Decision-making is challenging for myself when planning a new business' (0.86, with a factor weighting of 0.63),

This finding is consistent with past research explaining that youth entrepreneurs are more inclined to work in teams because they lack previous work experience. Moreover, youth entrepreneurs will benefit from the support and guidance associated with teams providing diverse

---

[11] Smolka and Verheul et al. (2018).

skills. Working alone is more likely for individuals with industry-specific experience and the confidence to achieve successful business outcomes.[12]

Considering that youths prefer to work in teams, it is worth mentioning that working in teams could be as difficult as working alone. Working in teams is likely to require a high level of social skill, negotiation and management, which could make decision-making difficult. They indicated that individual decision-making is difficult when planning a business, so decision-making among team members could perhaps be equally difficult. The literature shows that working in teams does not appear to be a barrier for youth entrepreneurs but working alone is considered a barrier as it requires more skills and experience.

Whether a business is commenced individually or as a team will be influenced by several factors, including social awareness, previous experience and external motivation. Entrepreneurs exhibiting higher social awareness can form strong bonds, even from only one or two interactions. These entrepreneurs will consequently network more with people because this adds value to a business and encourages people to start a business in a team. Previous experience also significantly influences an entrepreneur's decision to commence a business alone or in a team. Individuals who have gained previous experience in a specific industry may, however, have in-depth knowledge and be able to work alone. External motivation can influence an entrepreneur to work individually or in a team, depending on their reaction to events. For example, failure of a venture could lead to reduced self-confidence and influence an entrepreneur to search for support and guidance from a team environment. Conversely, motivation can have the reverse effect in cases where continued success working as an individual is likely to reinforce belief in continuing alone. The entrepreneur and his or her personality traits and experiences can therefore either bring opportunities to entrepreneurship or provide barriers to entrepreneurship.

---

[12] Hormiga-Pérez et al. (2017).

9.2.6 Summary

In summary, the problems most frequently experienced as personal barriers in relation to systemic intermediaries were accessing financial support, coming up with ideas and respondent's personality traits. Women are more likely to be affected by their personality traits, which creates a unique gender barrier. Entrepreneurship education and training sufficiently prepared the respondents for becoming entrepreneurs and is thus a vital component in preparing the youth to pursue entrepreneurial activities.

Youth entrepreneurs are aware of their financial limitations; however, they need to be willing to create cost-effective solutions through networking, building teams and upskilling. In addition, the youth need to adopt proactive behaviours to attract business opportunities rather than waiting for the business to come to them. They also need to create an internal locus of control so that they can influence the environment around them.

9.3   External Enablers and Barriers Encountered in Relation to Educational Institutions

Figure 9.2 shows the findings related to research Question 2 regarding educational institutions and their influence on developing youth entrepreneurs.

The negative view of receiving additional training could also be associated with a non-proactive attitude in which students may want to complete only those courses that they are required to complete.

9.3.1 Previous Training in Business Skills

The first question of this construct assessed whether participating youth entrepreneurs had received previous training from an education institute to develop business skills. Of the overall response, 20.8% indicated that training from educational institutions to develop skills to start a business was met to a 'small' extent, whereas 69.8% of respondents agreed that their skills were developed. The third aspect in this construct gives the data on university support to youth entrepreneurs through academic and non-academic programmes. A very small proportion of the respondents said that it is not important to have both academic and non-academic programmes at university to support youth entrepreneurship programmes, whereas a large proportion (94.3%) agreed that it is important to a 'moderate' or 'very great' extent. It is important to note that of those responses, 63.5% indicated the importance of 'very great extent' to have both academic and non-academic programme support. These results suggest that students require further support from universities to develop their businesses.

There is limited research on the impact of entrepreneurial programmes. This response raises more questions about the current curriculum in South Africa and whether the monitoring system should be changed to include external entrepreneurship programmes.

Research conducted at the University of Massachusetts shows that it is beneficial to have youth entrepreneurship programmes that link. However, it is important not to assume cause and effect from entrepreneurship programmes because entrepreneurial activities are sometimes more influenced by regional factors relating to geographical development.[13]

9.3.2 Entrepreneurial Orientation of Institutions of Higher Learning

Of the respondents, 5.7% indicated 'no' to a 'small extent' in answering whether higher education institutes were becoming entrepreneurship-orientated through support, programmes, initiatives and activities on offer; 15.1% opted for a neutral answer, and 79.3% said they were improving to a 'moderate' or 'very great' extent.

---

[13] Bergmann et al. (2016).

9.3.3 Benefits of SHAPE

A small percentage (7.5%) of respondents said they had benefited through SHAPE to a 'small' or 'no' extent, whereas 88.6% said they had benefited to a 'moderate' or 'very great' extent.

9.3.4 Summary

In summary, the greatest educational institutional barrier was seen to be the lack of a combination of both academic and non-academic programmes of support, especially as there has been very little thrust towards this end within youth training experiences and histories. Entrepreneurial success has received very little focus within areas of commerce and higher education institutions and has thus actualised very little potential towards this end. Where initiatives have been implemented and involved youth, youths perceive the benefits as great in assisting them to have more self-confidence in becoming youth entrepreneurs. It, therefore, appears that SHAPE is vital in the development of entrepreneurs.

There was a difference in both the highest level of education and employment status in the perceived benefit of training programmes, mainly between third-year and honours students, and full-time postgraduate students respectively. Honours students were more likely than third-year students to indicate 'a greater extent' to which educational institutions could develop the skills required to start a business, whereas full-time postgraduate students and entrepreneurs were more likely to rate their skill-development efficacy at a 'lesser' or 'no' extent.

It is encouraging to see that youths are embracing new entrepreneurially orientated programmes that can benefit them. It is accordingly recommended that youths attend these programmes and communicate their feedback to staff. There is a further requirement to improve the entrepreneurship orientation of training initiatives both within the industry and institutions of higher learning, and increased emphasis needs to be placed on the training and involvement of marginalised persons within society, such as women.

9.4   External Barriers and Enablers Encountered in Relation to Communities

The finding that communities do not have an entrepreneurial attitude or orientation as expressed by the youths and as shown in Fig. 9.3 highlights the importance of a more granular level of exploration and understanding. Context is undoubtedly a major precursor of entrepreneurial attitude, as participants are socialised into self-limiting ways of thinking, as they adopt the material and non-material values and beliefs of the culture within which they are socialised.

To investigate communities' influence on the development of youth entrepreneurs: the criteria in Fig. 9.3 can be synthesised as the top barriers and opportunities to youth entrepreneurship.

9.4.1 Barriers and Opportunities to Youth Entrepreneurship—Communities

The following paragraphs discuss barriers and opportunities to youth entrepreneurship related to communities.

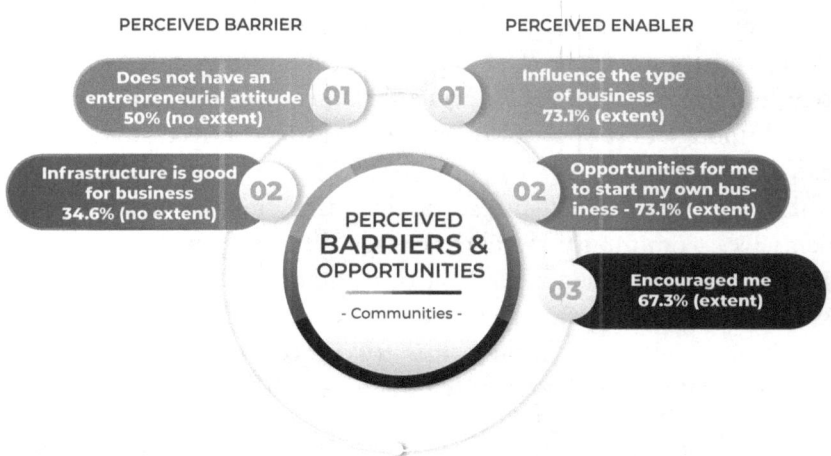

Fig. 9.3 Research Question 3: Barriers and opportunities—Communities

9.4.1.1 Community Encouragement

The first aspect in this construct gives the data on community encouragement to youth entrepreneurs. More than two-thirds (67.3%) of the respondents rated the extent to which people in their community encouraged them to become a youth entrepreneur as 'moderate' to 'very great', whereas 23.1% of respondents rated it as 'none' to 'small' ($N = 53$). The median was 5 (moderate extent), with a slight negative left skewness, suggesting that communities are perceivably assisting the SHAPE youths to become entrepreneurs. However, these respondents could be limited by being encouraged only to be entrepreneurs in fields that have limited growth. There were some differences in their perceptions of whether people in their community encouraged them to become youth entrepreneurs between Kruskal–Wallis respondents' level of education, regarding, again, between third-year and honours students ($c^2(1) = 10.08$, $p= 0.00$). There was more perceived encouragement from community members of those persons completing their honours compared to third-year students. As previously mentioned, honours students not only report to have engaged more confidently and to a greater extent of upskilling than their third-year counterparts, but they also have experienced more exposure and experience to the management and entrepreneurial activity. This could possibly contribute to their confidence, and thus their level of engagement with other members within communities, with the consequence that they may more favourably be looked-upon, and supported, or encouraged in a youth-led dynamic and interaction with the other, stemming from their own beliefs. The inverse of this argument is that instead of stemming from within the youths themselves; community members engage differently with older youths held in higher esteem as a result of being a postgraduate student. These assumptions around competencies as a result of their graduate status cannot be denied, nor can they be assertively concluded upon.

Interestingly enough, there was a significant difference in respondents' opinions on whether people in their community encouraged them to become youth entrepreneurs between men and women (U = 178.50, p = 0.03). Crosstabs revealed that men rated the extent to which they received community encouragement lower than that reported by women.

9.4.1.2   Community Influence on the Type of Business

The second aspect in this construct explored the influence of the community on the type of business for youth entrepreneurs. Of the respondents, 19.2% believed that people in their community influenced the type of business they wanted to start to a 'very little' extent, whereas 73% said their community members influenced their type of business in a 'moderate' to 'great' extent. This suggests that although communities were influencing SHAPE youths to become entrepreneurs; the respondents could be limited by their communities in the type of businesses they intended to start. It implies an inherent culturally derived orientation and delimits the possibilities of entrepreneurial activity. In this way, it acts as a barrier towards innovation when the lines of practice are demarcated by cultural values and normative social systems. With COVID-19, youth entrepreneurs can now adopt further lean resource bases and venture into buying and selling face masks as an extension of existing goods. They can further capitalise on local and community needs as SMEs are community businesses and can concentrate on servicing the needs of the community. The business owner, being part of the community, can gain the upper hand when venturing into the new needs of the community.

There is limited information on community influence on the type of business the youth could potentially start, which makes the results from this aspect somewhat difficult to interpret. This finding could mean that youths are influenced by the community—either to develop or to stagnate. The community influence could mean the youth are being motivated to commence businesses that are beneficial only to the local community without having a global perspective. This response creates more questions for the researcher around how the youth are being influenced, which could generate solutions for the youth to be more entrepreneurial.

This results in this aspect somewhat contradict past research, which explains why a majority of entrepreneurs do not advertise their businesses as family-owned businesses—suggesting that the community does not influence the type of business.[14] This discrepancy could exist because these studies examined different constructs, as the respondents might not have been considering family business influence but rather influences from friends and business associates.

9.4.1.3 Community Entrepreneurial Attitudes

The third community aspect gives data on community entrepreneurial attitudes. There was a roughly even split, where 50% of respondents rated a 'moderate' or 'very great' extent of agreement with the statement that their community did not have an entrepreneurial attitude, whereas 38.5% agreed to a lesser extent ($N = 53$), with a median measure was 4.5 (neutral to a moderate extent). The highest barrier, with a negative loading, was 'I feel my community does not have an entrepreneurial attitude' (–0.21), with a negative factor weighting of –0.03. This is in parallel and supplementary to the notion that programmes that bring radical transformation (growth in developmental maturity) are necessary as they help expose individuals' mental models and plant the seed towards entrepreneurial action. Whether the poor entrepreneurial orientation of communities is an objective fact, or a subjective projection placed into the outside world from a person with a lack of entrepreneurial agency remains to be seen.

9.4.1.4 Opportunities Provided by Communities

The fourth aspect in this construct gives the data on whether the community provides opportunities to start a business. Of the respondents, 65.4% indicated that their community offered opportunities for them to start their own business to a 'moderate' or 'very great' extent, and 23.1% said to a lesser or no extent ($N = 53$). The median measure was 5 (moderate extent), indicating that community support can therefore be seen as an important enabler within the ecosystem to support youth entrepreneurs in understanding and fostering an entrepreneurial

---

[14] Farrington et al. (2017).

spirit. It is unique that those who volunteered themselves onto the study also believe that opportunities and support exist within their community. Even if cultural nuances are directing their entrepreneurial activity—the spirit of opportunity identification is present and presents potential in harnessing it into the proper domain. Perhaps this community spirit can be understood to have enabled an open will that oriented the youth towards participation in the programme and is what separates them from peers who did not. This situation will need to be reconsidered under the current global pandemic, as the economic recession has not only crushed the economy but also closed numerous businesses (especially with the more recent political unrest). More than 45,000 small and micro enterprises shut their doors, as the economy suffered in excess of R16 billion in stock and damage to infrastructure. This means that where there has been a decline in financial resources; there has been an associated incline in opportunities available in response to both COVID-19 and the recent political unrest. This would need some entrepreneurial creativity in harnessing business activity effectively into those spaces, but first starts with opportunity identification.

9.4.1.5 Facilities and Infrastructure in Communities

The fifth aspect in this construct indicates responses on facilities and infrastructure in communities. Of the respondents, 34.6% indicated a 'lesser' or 'no' extent when alluding to that the facilities and infrastructure in their community as good for business development, and 61.6% agreed to a 'moderate' or 'very great' extent ($N = 53$). Opportunities were purported to exist within communities for entrepreneurial engagement and development. Examination of the standardised regression weights reveals that the highest regression weight, and therefore, the greatest opportunity in the community composite was attributable to 'Facilities and infrastructure in my community are good for business development' (0.86) with a factor weighting of 0.42. Again, answer varied according to Kruskal–Wallis to respondents' highest level of education with regard to their perceptions of community facilities and infrastructure for business development, and again the difference existed between third-year and honours students. Honours students indicated a higher extent to which the facilities and infrastructure were good for business development, consistent with other findings regarding exposure, maturity and opportunity identification. At this level, their academic development is steering them towards being ready for the world of work, ideally becoming job creators and not job seekers.

These results are not supported by past research, which indicates that there is a lack of infrastructure and facilities in South Africa due to poor long-term planning.[15] Moreover, there are issues with funding for key water resources, and the current models are outdated and need to be redesigned.[16] A possible reason for this contradiction is that respondents in this study may not have experienced the high levels of infrastructure and facilities associated with developed countries such as the United States. This could mean that respondents are not aware of developed infrastructure—similar to their lack of awareness of private sector agencies in South Africa.

A major inhibiting factor for entrepreneurship development is the inaccessibility of youth entrepreneurship support and the youths' lack of awareness of such structures and initiatives in local communities. In addition, poor planning has resulted in the absence of infrastructure, facilities and innovation for South Africans, a major barrier for youth entrepreneurs. This has stifled economic growth and created a disconnect between geographical regions. It seems that there is a prevailing expectation among some youths that the government 'owes them'. They feel that government should create entrepreneurial opportunities and that they should be able to 'get' from governance instead of leading self-directed change and becoming the change agent.

9.4.2 Summary

In summary, people in the community are influential and are pivotal in encouraging those hoping to become youth entrepreneurs, especially women. The influence of community members on the type of business

---

15 Chitiga et al. (2016).
16 Ruiters and Matji (2016).

being considered is very important. There seems to be a generally negative attitude towards entrepreneurship in communities, which suggests that future studies should be aimed at communities, investigating the influence they may have over the motivations of youth entrepreneurs. In addition to community attitudes acting as a barrier, opportunities within communities also seem to pose problems. The overall consensus is that community members are highly influential in youths' selection of the type of business they want to start. The statement the respondents agreed with least was that their community had an entrepreneurial attitude.

Acknowledgement Chapter based on SHAPE research project work: Krieger, W., 2018. Barriers to youth entrepreneurship: a systemic approach (Masters dissertation). University of KwaZulu-Natal. Supervisor: Professor Thea van der Westhuizen.

References

Adelakun, Y., & Van der Westhuizen, T. (2021). Delineating government policies and individual entrepreneurial orientation. *Journal of Sociology and Social Anthropology, 12*(3–4), 106–117. https://doi.org/10.31901/245 66764.2021/12.3-4.371

Awotunde, O. M., & Van der Westhuizen, T. (2021a). Entrepreneurial self-efficacy development: An effective intervention for sustainable student entrepreneurial intentions. *International Journal of Innovation and Sustainable Development, 15*(4), 475–495.

Awotunde, O. M., & Van der Westhuizen, T. (2021b). *Entrepreneurial self-efficacy and the SHAPE ideation model for university students.* In ECIE 2021

16th European Conference on Innovation and Entrepreneurship (Vol. 1, p. 37).

Bausch, J., Dyer, P., Gardiner, D., Kluve, J., & Kovacevic, S. (2016). *The impact of skills training on financial behaviour, employability, and educational choice of youth.* https://www.ilo.org/wcmsp5/groups/public/---ed_emp/documents/presentation/wcms_506175.pdf (Retrieved November 15, 2017).

Bergmann, H., Hundt, C., & Sternberg, R. (2016). What makes student entrepreneurs? On the relevance (and irrelevance) of the university and the regional context for student start-ups. *Small Business Economics, 47*(1), 53–76.

Chitiga, M., Mabugu, R., & Maisonnave, H. (2016). Analysing job creation effects of scaling up infrastructure spending in South Africa. *Development Southern Africa, 33*(2), 186–202.

Ernst, & Young. (2017). *Entrepreneurs share core traits: Decoding the DNA of the entrepreneur.* www.ey.com/gl/en/services/strategic-growth-markets/ey-nat ure-or-nurture-5-entrepreneurs-share-core-traits (Retrieved September 15, 2017).

Farrington, S., Venter, E., & Richardson, B. (2017). Stakeholders perceptions and the use of 'family' in selected marketing and branding practices of family SMEs. In DJ Nel (Ed.), *Proceedings of the 29th SAIMS Annual Conference, Kopano Nokeng Country Lodge & Conference Centre*, Bloemfontein, September 10–12.

Herman, E., & Stefanescu, D. (2017). Can higher education stimulate entrepreneurial intentions among engineering and business students? *Educational Studies, 43*(3), 312–327.

Herrington, M., & Kew, P. (2016). Is SA heading for an economic meltdown? *Global entrepreneur monitor: South African Report 2015/16.* www.gemconsor tium.org/report/49537 (Retrieved January 15, 2018).

Hormiga-Pérez, E., Hancock, C., & Jaría-Chacón, N. (2017). Going it alone or working as part of a team: The impact of human capital on entrepreneurial decision-making. *Journal of Evolutionary Studies in Business, 2*(1), 210–231.

Nhleko, Y. & van der Westhuizen, T. (2022). The role of higher education institutions in introducing entrepreneurship education to meet the demands of industry 4.0. *Academy of Entrepreneurship Journal, 28*(1), 1–23.

Rector, M., Fatoki, O., & Oni, O. (2016). Access to debt finance by young entrepreneurs in Polokwane, South Africa. *Journal of Social Sciences, 49*(1–2), 67–95.

Ruba, R. M., Van der Westhuizen, T., & Chiloane- Tsoka, G. E. (2021). Influence of entrepreneurial orientation on organisational performance: Evidence from Congolese higher education institutions. *Journal of Contemporary Management, 18*(1), 243–269.

Ruiters, C., & Matji, M. P. (2016). Public-private partnership conceptual framework and models for the funding and financing of water services infrastructure in municipalities from selected provinces in South Africa. *Water SA, 42*(2), 291–305.

Shepherd, D. A., & Patzelt, H. (2017). *Trailblazing in entrepreneurship: Creating new paths for understanding the field*. Springer International.

Smolka, K. M., Verheul, I., Burmeister-Lamp, K., & Heugens, P. P. (2018). Get it together! Synergistic effects of causal and effectual decision-making logics on venture performance. *Entrepreneurship Theory and Practice, 42*(4), 571–604.

Van der Westhuizen, T. (2017a). The use of theory U and individual entrepreneurial orientation to increase low youth entrepreneurship in South Africa. *Journal of Contemporary Management, 14*, 531–553.

Van der Westhuizen, T. (2017b). A systemic approach towards responsible and sustainable economic development: Entrepreneurship, systems theory and socio-economic momentum. In Z. Fields (Ed.), *Collective creativity for responsible and sustainable business practice*. IGI Global.

Van der Westhuizen, T. (2017c). Theory U and individual entrepreneurial orientation in developing youth entrepreneurship in South Africa. *Journal of Contemporary Management, 14*, 531–553.

Van der Westhuizen, T. (2018a). The SHAPE Project: Shifting hope, activating potential entrepreneurship In: D. Remenyi & D. A. Grant (Eds.), *Incubators for young entrepreneurs—20 case histories*. ACPIL

Van der Westhuizen, T. (2018b). *Open Heart, Open Mind and Open Will in transformative individual entrepreneurial orientation pedagogies* (pp. 443–448). Academic Conferences and Publishing International Limited.

Van der Westhuizen, T. (2019). Action! Methods to develop entrepreneurship. In *18th European conference on research methodology for business and management studies* (pp. 331–337).

Van der Westhuizen, T. (2021). Applying Theory U through SHAPE to develop student's individual entrepreneurial orientation in a university ecosystem. In O. Gunnlaugson & W. Brendel (Eds.), *Advances in Pre-sensing Volume III: Collective approaches, in theory U* (pp. 395–435).Trifoss Business Press

Van der Westhuizen, T. (2022). *Effective youth entrepreneurship*. Sunbonani. https://omp.sunbonani.co.za/index.php/sunbonani/catalog/book/6

Van der Westhuizen, T., & Upton, J. (2017). *Ethekwini Municipal Women Entrepreneurship Program: An assessment*. Paper presented at the 29th Southern African Institute of Management Scientists: Management Research: Science Servicing Practice Conference, Bloemfontein, January.

Venter, M. (2017). *How serious are we about entrepreneurship?* EDHE Lekgotla (conference), Johannesburg, 16 March 2017.

10

Youth Entrepreneur Ecosystems: Barriers and Enablers in Relation to Government Agencies, Private sector Agencies, SMEs, Large Businesses and Corporates

10.1 Introduction

This chapter reports on the findings of the research regarding barriers and enablers influencing youth entrepreneurs, namely those related to:

- government agencies;
- private sector agencies;
- small- and medium-sized enterprises (SMEs); and
- large businesses and corporates.

These types of agencies and corporate influences are important as they inspire and co-create with the youth. Networking with like-minded individuals who can inspire is imperative in helping the youth towards an entrepreneurial orientation. To date, the youth had very little exposure to business friends and thus had not been able to connect and co-inspire. They had, as previously detailed, received very little support from government and private agencies as a whole but once this connection was forged, so too was the co-initiate, co-create and co-inspire process enabled, and the necessary mechanisms of entrepreneurial action triggered. There were numerous reports of the absence of support, financial,

© University of Kwazulu-Natal 2023
T. van der Westhuizen, *Youth Entrepreneurship*,
https://doi.org/10.1007/978-3-031-44339-8_10

network or other, from government and municipal agencies, which were offset by increased access and collaboration by municipal or government mentors. Access is a large barrier but is overcome through collaborative efforts from varied parties in inspiration.

10.2 Barriers and Enablers Encountered in Relation to Government Agencies

Figure 10.1 shows the findings related to barriers and enablers that youths perceived to experience in relation to government agencies and their influence in developing youth entrepreneurs.

When looking at the above table, funding again was the largest barrier and the lack of municipal business support. While these operated as barriers to entrepreneurial action and success, they were removed when assigned a municipality mentor, when the government was informed and when they received municipal support. Thus, indicating that barriers are essentially those items where support structures are removed from the process and absent, whereas having contact and information when providing support, the entrepreneurial achievement is better sustained

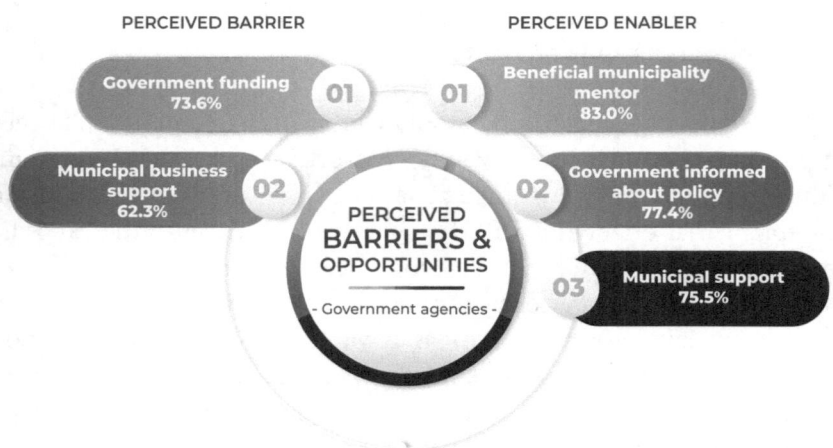

Fig. 10.1 Barriers and enablers—Government agencies

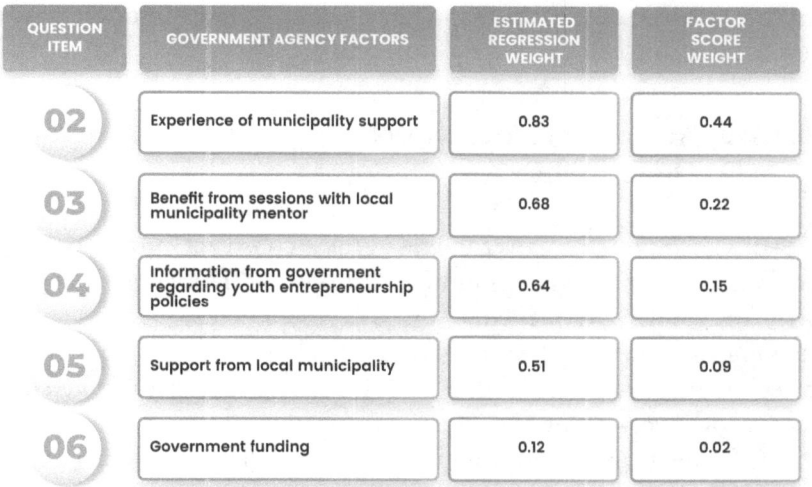

QUESTION ITEM	GOVERNMENT AGENCY FACTORS	ESTIMATED REGRESSION WEIGHT	FACTOR SCORE WEIGHT
02	Experience of municipality support	0.83	0.44
03	Benefit from sessions with local municipality mentor	0.68	0.22
04	Information from government regarding youth entrepreneurship policies	0.64	0.15
05	Support from local municipality	0.51	0.09
06	Government funding	0.12	0.02

Fig. 10.2 Standardised regression and factor score weights—Government agencies

and secured. It is not surprising that financial difficulties (access to government funding) are the highest barrier because the youth could be entrepreneurially inexperienced. A deeper underlying issue could be the lack of resilience associated with youth, perhaps meaning that blaming financial barriers is a convenient excuse.

A common theme is expressed by the youth that governments and municipalities prevent them from achieving their business goals. Perhaps governments and municipalities are not to blame, but rather the problem is the lack of focus and determination of the youth to solve complex problems, which is time-consuming and difficult.

10.2.1 Barriers and Enablers to Youth Entrepreneurship—Government Agencies

To investigate the impact of government agencies on youth entrepreneurs: the aspects discussed in the paragraphs that follow can be synthesised as the top barriers and opportunities to youth entrepreneurship.

10.2.1.1 Awareness of Municipal Support Offerings/ Opportunities

The first item on the government agency construct provided insight into youths' awareness of municipal support offerings and opportunities to youth entrepreneurs. Of the respondents, 75.5% reported knowing what support the municipality would provide for them as youth entrepreneurs, and 24.5% did not. This was unsurprising given the amount of involvement and exposure provided to youth entrepreneurs by government agencies throughout the SHAPE programme. As part of SHAPE, they had weekly mentoring sessions with an officer from a local municipality, and several municipality communications regarding business development opportunities and support from the municipality were communicated to the youth. The group that indicated they did not know about existing opportunities and support from the municipality business development unit might relate to a personal barrier of not being proactive in seeking opportunities. It is important to establish these connections and networks with members within agencies and infrastructures that could offer insight and support of initiatives and develop ideas that the youth may have, and in so doing, give confidence to their inner voice.

10.2.1.2 Interpretation of Municipal Support Received

This construct interpreted how youths experienced the municipal support offered to them during and after the SHAPE social technology. An examination of the standardised regression weights reveals that the highest regression weight, and therefore the greatest opportunity in the government composite was attributable to 'The municipality provides mentorship support for me as a youth entrepreneur' (0.83) with a factor weighting of 0.44. This support accounts for the highest variability in outcomes with regard to government agencies and thus possesses the highest potential to offset the barriers experienced on this dimension. Of the respondents, 17% said the municipality did not provide support for them as youth entrepreneurs, whereas 75.4% agreed that support had been provided. These findings appear rather contradictory, as only 25% of respondents were aware of the support provided by the municipality. A possible explanation is that the municipality provided support during SHAPE, but not once the respondents had left the programme. They were reporting from a place where the most recent exposure was that of a municipal mentor, and they were operating from the present. This attests to the power mentors and support have in mitigating the perception of the lack thereof. Here is limited information on municipal entrepreneurship support to youth entrepreneurs. This could be because entrepreneurship programmes are difficult to implement and require support from a wide variety of stakeholders, including government, universities and business professionals.

In addition (based on the limited information sourced from the official websites of major cities in South Africa), there was no established or in-depth information on youth entrepreneurship programmes available from local municipalities.[1] This is further exacerbated with the dispensation of COVID-19, as municipal workers are largely working remotely, and increased inaccessibility to officials is a reality.

10.2.1.3 Benefit from Municipality Mentor Sessions

The above attests to the perception that participants felt they had benefited from their sessions with a mentor from the local municipality, with most respondents agreeing (83.1%, $N = 53$) that the sessions were beneficial to them, with only 5.7% disagreeing.

There is a prevailing lack of past research on the extent to which the youth receive support for youth entrepreneurs from municipalities. Despite the results from this study suggesting otherwise, it could be because, in SHAPE, municipality representatives were encouraged to provide support to the participants, which could have led the participants to respond favourably towards municipal mentors. The municipality

---

[1] City of Johannesburg (2017); Walford (2017)

mentor was introduced to the SHAPE youth entrepreneur ecosystem as part of the intervention under assessment. This institutionalised and systematic programme that built-in municipal support from mentors is otherwise known to be lacking, reactive, rather than proactive and engaging.

10.2.1.4 Perceptions of Government Policies for Youth Entrepreneurial Development

The fourth dimension is related to governmental and municipal support, youth entrepreneurial orientation and participants' perceptions of government policies for youth entrepreneurial development. Of the respondents, 18.9% disagreed with the statement that the government informed them about their policy of youth entrepreneurial development, and 77.4% agreed that they were informed. This response supports the positive relationship which youth entrepreneurs experienced with the municipality mentor in the SHAPE project, shown by the 83% who said they had benefited. Again, students are operating from a position of the present and will gradually move towards a future orientation. There was a statistically significant Kruskal–Wallis difference in response, based on respondents' employment status, regarding their perceptions as to how well the government had informed them about their policy of youth entrepreneurial development ($H(8) = 15.64$, $p = 0.05$), and post hoc tests and cross-tabulations revealed that full-time employed, part-time employed and full-time undergraduate students were likely to agree that the government had given them information, whereas full-time undergraduate students with entrepreneurial activity, entrepreneurs working for themselves and part-time undergraduate students were more likely to disagree. Perhaps those already engaged in the entrepreneurial action had previously tried to engage with existing policy but failed to do so outside of a structured programme. When they engaged in entrepreneurial activity outside of SHAPE, those youths had been faced with situations wherein they either had little familiarity with existing policy to guide their behaviour, realising the extant focus and regulatory guidance aimed towards youth entrepreneurial development by government and municipal agendas. It is thus useful to interrogate the data, looking at those who do not agree, as only those who had previously initiated entrepreneurial activity were aware of the scarcity in policy. Others, only now starting to engage with the help of SHAPE, were most likely to be missing in this exposure and thus fail to realise the true state of affairs as they exist systemically and outside of SHAPE.

10.2.1.5   Support from the Municipality to Assist Youth Entrepreneurship Activities

Congruent with the findings above, perceptions regarding support from the municipality to assist youth entrepreneurship activities were largely supported, with almost two-thirds (62.3%, $N = 53$) of respondents agreeing that they had received business support from the municipality to assist in their entrepreneurship activities. 24.5% generally disagreed, with a median of 5 (somewhat agree). It was through SHAPE that such a positive rating of municipal assistance was achieved, and when one breaks this down further, the Kruskal–Wallis test showed a significant difference in this response from respondents with different employment statuses. The difference was largely accounted for between part-time and full-time employed: Full-time undergraduate student respondents were more likely to agree that they had received business support from the municipality, whereas part-time undergraduate students and full-time postgraduate students were more likely to disagree with the statement. Again, this could be understood in terms of previous exposure to and experience with the entrepreneurial process and the level of support and assistance they received within this activity while being employed. The extant assistance would not have otherwise been noted if the youths had not been engaged in entrepreneurial action or some type of activity oriented towards revenue generation.

Generally, the overall perception of support from municipal bodies was bolstered when engaging in sessions with mentors ($r = 0.322$) and being informed about government policy of youth entrepreneurial development ($r = 0.359$).

10.2.1.6 Government Funding

The sixth aspect of this dimension gives data on whether the government provided youth entrepreneurs who participated in SHAPE with funding. Just over half the respondents stated that the government had not provided them with funding to pursue their entrepreneurial activities (entirely disagree), with 73.6% of the overall response indicating a general disagreement with the statement. This is consistent with previous findings regarding the lack of funding necessary to initiate and support entrepreneurial opportunities and activities. Funding is a huge feature of actively engaging in entrepreneurial activities, and unless it is secured, the youth are not yet able and skilled to seek alternative revenue-generating activities or ideas. Only 22.7% of the sample indicated a level of agreement with the statement. The median measure for this statement was 1 (entirely disagree) and suggested that government should aim to provide financial support, possibly as small loans, to provide momentum for the youth to start and sustain entrepreneurial activity. The literature supports the opinion that the government in South Africa is still not providing sufficient financial assistance to youth entrepreneurs.

This result is consistent with research, which suggests that youth entrepreneurs lack funding from the government to develop their businesses and that funding from the government can sometimes create dependency and lead to entrepreneurs being demotivated when they do not receive support.[2] Youths based in townships are only one-third as likely as their demographic counterparts to receive loans from banks, which is considered a barrier to youth entrepreneurship.[3]

This result, which shows that youth entrepreneurs are not being funded by the government to support their entrepreneurial activities, could, however, mean that youths are using the government as an excuse for their business failures or the lack of initiating entrepreneurial activity in the first place, remaining in a state of helplessness, poor opportunity identification, risk-taking and remaining dependent on contingent handouts from outside of themselves. It almost appears as if youth

---

[2] Sinyolo et al. (2017)
[3] GEP (2014)

entrepreneurs rely on the expectation of support to establish a business, and without support, they feel failure is justified. This could be a barrier that prevents the youth from achieving business success, not because of lack of funding, but perhaps from the attitude that they are unable to run a business without funding.

The lowest regression weights on the government agency composite were 'The government has provided me with funding to pursue my entrepreneurial activities' (0.12), and 'I have received business support from the municipality to assist in my entrepreneurship activities' (0.51) with a factor weighting of 0.09. This has previously been discussed in relation to SHAPE and the variability in outcomes because all respondents were operating from within the systematic and structured SHAPE programme, which forced interaction, mentorship and support with government agencies and municipal mentors. This is somewhat artificial as it occurs within the context of SHAPE and not outside in naturalistic business environments. As such, the item 'experience of municipality support' had the highest regression weight and factor loading as it was well felt within the context of SHAPE, which structured the co-imitation and co-creation between the youth and municipal officials. There is a correlation between the perception that the municipality provided them with support as a youth entrepreneur and SHAPE assisting youths in having more self-confidence in becoming a young entrepreneur ($r = 0.477$) and ultimately benefitting from SHAPE ($r = 0.330$). This indicates that this type of co-creation and co-initiation was made possible through SHAPE. It can be argued that similar experiences do not as readily exist outside a structured entrepreneurship programme. Despite this, however, support from the municipality and funding contributed to the lowest factor weights, thus falling outside the construct of support, contributing to a different factor, loading outside of support to more of a barrier, or lack of support when it came to municipalities themselves and funding. These two elements, going forward, need to be fostered into fortified and inculcated into a culture focused on youth entrepreneurial development and awareness. Integral to offsetting these barriers is mentorship and support from persons already in business in initiating and triggering entrepreneurial mindset, heartsets and handsets, especially enshrined within governmental structures, with abundant resourcing and knowledge of programmes and infrastructure aimed at economic growth and development.

10.2.2 Summary

In summary, respondents are aware of the support that the municipality ostensibly provides them but believe that it fails to do so. However, where support does happen, it is perceived as highly beneficial. In addition, there is a perception of a major failure on the part of the municipality to keep youth entrepreneurs informed. It seems that the more entrepreneurial and the closer potential entrepreneurs get to actualise their entrepreneurial activities, the more aware they become of the failure on the part of the government to support their entrepreneurial activities and aspirations. Students who had reached points where they needed to seek assistance from the municipality were more inclined to rate the support they received positively. Another significant barrier was the lack of funding from the government to pursue entrepreneurial activities. If we look summatively at Fig. 10.1, we see that most respondents considered that the government had not provided them with funding to initiate entrepreneurial activities (i.e., it was the greatest barrier), but where there were sessions with their municipal mentor, it was seen as highly beneficial, and in that way, students felt supported by the municipality. The youth need to accept that government cannot solve all their entrepreneurial problems. Rather than being deterred when a government cannot support them, they need to act resiliently to overcome difficulties. It is possibly best to support students and provide them with mentorship and guidance to move them from a place of complacent dependency on external funding to initiate entrepreneurial activity to a place where they identify opportunities to trigger entrepreneurial action and innovate towards action in proactive and self-initiating ways. Support and guidance, more than unlimited funding, is necessary, and programmes of support and mentorship are vital in initiating youth entrepreneurial activity.

10.3 Barriers and Enablers Encountered in Relation to Private Sector Agencies

In contrast to the previous section detailing government agencies, this component of the SHAPE programme investigated the youths' perceptions of the barriers and enablers regarding the private sector in the pursuit and experience of entrepreneurial mindsets. Figure 10.3 shows the findings related to research Question 5 regarding private sector agencies and their influence on developing youth entrepreneurs. This construct was reliably measured, indicating internal consistency on balancing with this construct ($a = 0.726$, $N = 5$).

Youth entrepreneurs are of the opinion that, despite being aware of the role and purpose of private sector agencies, and their potential in contributing to their growth as entrepreneurs, they had limited exposure and experience with networked key individuals within the private sector. As such, they received very little support and information from this sector. The greatest barrier with regard to private sector agencies is the awareness, communication and support received from this sector, while the importance and contribution that can stem from this sector will help to offset these barriers. It could conceivably be

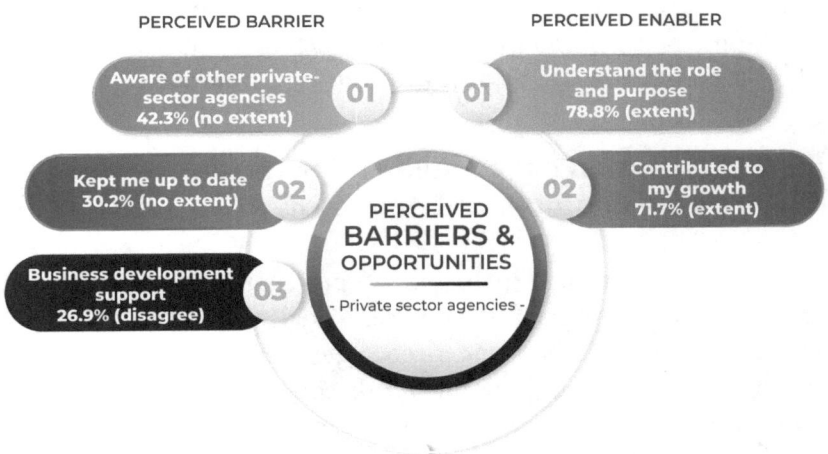

Fig. 10.3 Barriers and enablers—Private sector agencies

difficult to source private sector agencies which specifically support youth entrepreneurs through structured programmes. Outside of these structured and fortified programmes, it is necessary for private sector agencies to combine their resources to form a central support system for youth, to keep them informed regarding business development support opportunities, in order to offset the barriers and perceived blockers of initiated and sustained entrepreneurial activity. Perhaps a deeper underlying concern is that private sector agencies are not prepared for the complex problems that the youth encounter, calling for deeper reflection on current processes. Youths, if not acting from a place of confidence and in the absence of exposure to this sector, and individuals within it will invariably fail to seek out private sector partners in business with whom they can connect and engage on an entrepreneurial journey. Outside of SHAPE, these types of business partners are not possible and explains why the responses to this question are somewhat confusing as youths commented that the private sector did contribute towards their growth, but perhaps the reported and experienced support was mediated through SHAPE, so these comments do not reflect private sector agencies, external to programmes. Student acknowledgement of the role and importance in private sectors attests to the importance of creating feelings of support and connection within this sector. It is almost as if government agencies were perceived to be the source of financial aspects in start-ups, whereas the knowledge and experience in entrepreneurial and business activities are best provided for by the private sector.

10.3.1 Perception of the Role and Purpose of the Chamber of Commerce

This section investigated participants' perceptions of the role and purpose of the Chamber of Commerce. A majority (78.8%) of respondents indicated that they understood the role and purpose of the Chamber of Commerce regarding youth entrepreneurs from 'some' to a 'very great' extent, whereas 13.5% indicated that they did not understand it. The median understanding was 5 (to some extent), which may explain how students perceive their role, and thus, the extent to which they feel empowered by receiving their support. This means that they are aware and business-minded to the extent of appreciating the role of such a business developer and agent. This understanding was correlated with participation in SHAPE ($r = 0.405$) and contributed to the self-confidence in becoming a young entrepreneur.

10.3.2   Awareness Relating to Private Sector Agencies

When it came to awareness of private sector agencies within themselves, 42.3% indicated that they had 'no' to 'small' awareness of private sector agencies other than the Chamber of Commerce, whereas 53.9% indicated 'some' to a 'great' extent of awareness. This suggests that the youth are not provided with the knowledge to access essential support to start their businesses, nor are they operating with the confidence needed to seek out, engage and network with key players in the private sector.

It was difficult in this study to locate information on private sector agencies other than the eThekwini Chamber of Commerce. Further, the youth have not as yet proactively sought out assistance from this group. This could have led to the youth being unaware of such agencies. In addition, most of the respondents were based in KwaZulu-Natal and possibly not exposed to other private sector agencies around South Africa. Another possibility is that private sector agencies do not provide support for nascent entrepreneurs but rather support entrepreneurs who are already established and operational.

These results are supported by past research and show that private sector agencies are not prepared for the complex needs of youth. Moreover, private sector agencies are somewhat disconnected from community development programmes and are not actively involved. In addition, it appears that private sector agencies are not focused on assisting youths to build entrepreneurial skills.[4]

Among private sector agencies, the Technology Information Agency promotes technology information by offering support to the public. This

---

[4] McEwan et al. (2017)

agency focuses on stimulating growth in the economy by focusing on entrepreneurial innovation. Besides the local Chamber of Commerce, most respondents indicated an awareness of the Small Enterprise Development Agency (SEDA) (11.5%). This was followed by Shanduka Black Umbrellas (5.8%), The Biz Farm (3.8%) and Ithala Development Bank (3.8%, $N = 53$). The median was 1, indicating unknown organisations with positive right skewness, with the bulk of the distribution falling to the left and a peak of 2.51.

10.3.3 Contributions of the local Chamber of Commerce

The first aspect in the private sector construct measures the extent to which the local Chamber of Commerce contributed towards the growth of youth entrepreneurs. The majority of respondents said that the Chamber of Commerce contributed to their growth to 'some extent' or 'a very great extent', with only 28.3% indicating little to no extent. The median measure was 5 (some extent), with a slight left, negative skew, indicating some variability in the construct. Mann–Whitney indicated a significant gender difference in the opinion that the Chamber of Commerce contributed to their growth ($U = 178.00$, $p = 0.02$), where women indicated a greater extent of contribution to their growth by the Chamber of Commerce. Males were more likely to express a 'small' or 'some' extent of the contribution made by the Chamber. This is an interesting finding and perhaps attests to the previously perceived lack of support in ideas and confidence afforded to their ideas and activities, especially women, operating within gender stereotypical roles where they often are perceived not to possess or part-take in entrepreneurial action. Thus, it came as more surprising when engaging with the Chamber of Commerce and receiving their support at a level of mutual engagement in helping them be more entrepreneurial. This boosts their confidence and could arguably help to significantly contribute to innovative risk-taking, opportunity identification and other entrepreneurial activities as it indicates a degree of interest in their ideas and acknowledges their potential as entrepreneurs.

10.3.4 The Ability of the Chamber of Commerce to Keep the Youth up to Date

The second aspect in this construct provided insight into the Chamber's ability to keep the youth up to date. Nearly two-thirds (64.2%) of the respondents indicated that the Chamber of Commerce kept them up to date with information and news on Chamber activities, which helped them be more entrepreneurial to 'some' or 'very great' extent, whereas 30.2% indicated 'no' or to a 'small extent' in whether the Chamber had updated them. The median measure for this item was 5 (to some extent), a simple act of asserting confidence in youth entrepreneurial potential and ideas. The findings that more than a third of the sample was 'not updated' suggest that more direct assistance is required to develop youth entrepreneurship, especially if associated with increased confidence within which to engage in entrepreneurial activities. There were Kruskal–Wallis significant differences in the extent to which they felt the Chamber kept them up to date, based on respondents' highest level of education, with third-year and honours students ($\chi^2(1) = 5.52$, $p = 0.02$) differing in their opinion. Third-year students rated a lesser extent of receiving up-to-date information than their honours counterparts, who were more likely to rate the degree of updated information as 'to a great' extent. Honours students are arguably more confident as a simple fact of feeling more educated and skilled, with the result that they more confidently engage with members of the Chamber of Commerce, thus creating a more open channel by which they could seek support. The importance of the eThekwini Chamber of Commerce in keeping the youth up to date with information and news on Chamber activities in an effort to be more entrepreneurial led to positive-correlated outcomes in the perception that they had received training from educational institutions to develop skills to start a business ($r = 0.470$). The government has provided me with funding to pursue my entrepreneurial activities ($r = 0.370$), and particularly, the perception that the eThekwini Chamber of Commerce contributed to their growth ($r = 0.634$).

10.3.5 Business Development Support from the Chamber of Commerce

The third aspect of this construct gives the data on receiving business development support from the Chamber of Commerce. Only 26.9% of respondents indicated that they had, from 'small' to 'no' extent, received business development support from the Chamber of Commerce, whereas 65.3% experienced support from 'some' to a 'very great' extent. The median was 5 (to some extent). This response is supported by the respondents' opinions on being kept up to date. This support was mediated through participation in the SHAPE project and suggests a continued need for similar initiatives in sustaining this level of support of youth entrepreneurs ($r = 0.300$).

This result is consistent with past research, showing that the Chamber of Commerce provides support to youth entrepreneurs through a variety of platforms. These platforms include lobbying and representation from the business community. Moreover, the Chamber of Commerce provides members with networking opportunities to grow their businesses and promotes growth through training opportunities.[5] Despite these platforms, it is up to youth entrepreneurs to engage and ensure their uptake when trying to initiate and support their entrepreneurial action, but they have to first get to that point where they experience self-belief enough to seek them out. The greatest barrier experienced and expressed on this construct was 'I am aware of other private sector agencies besides the local Chamber of Commerce' (−0.04), with a factor score of −0.00. This means that very little support was perceived to have been received by students from the private sector and accounted for very little variability in support of youth entrepreneurs.

Past research indicates no negative literature associated with the Chamber of Commerce, which could suggest that the Chamber does indeed act as a contributor towards youth entrepreneurship. Considering that the purpose of the Chamber of Commerce is to represent businesses, it is reasonable to assume that their intentions as an organisation are aligned with the results.

---

[5] Durban Chamber of Commerce (2017)

A Mann–Whitney test revealed a significant difference in response, based on gender, regarding the respondents' perception of having received business development support from the Chamber of Commerce ($U = 190.50$, $p = 0.05$), with women indicating more development support than their male counterparts. This is consistent with women's increased perceptions and experience of support from other agencies on other constructs. Again, perhaps the extent to which it is experienced is more so for women as their entrepreneurial self-belief is lower and thus more impactful when bridging that gap into support action. Women are traditionally home-makers and thus experience elevated perceptions of support when acknowledged for their potential as entrepreneurs, and this external validation manifests in higher perceptions of support.

Kruskal–Wallis revealed significant differences in perceptions about receiving business development support from the Chamber of Commerce between varying levels of education. Again, the difference existed between third-year and honours students ($c^2(1) = 4.08$, $p = 0.04$), with honours students reporting that they received more development support from the Chamber of Commerce than their third-year counterparts did. A possible explanation for this is that youths in their fourth year of study are more aware of the immediate future and reality that after completing this qualification; there will be options of either continuing for a master's degree or other postgraduate qualifications, looking for a job or becoming self-employed. They also engage more confidently, and thus more actively seek out support, and foster networks support of their entrepreneurial ideation. An examination of the standardised regression weights reveals that the highest regression weight, and therefore, opportunity in the private sector composite was attributable to 'I have received business development support from the local Chamber of Commerce' (0.98). This means that receiving development support has the greatest impact on mitigating the effects of the lack of support from industry and consequentially halted and unsupported entrepreneurial action. It is the biggest enabler of perceptions of support needed from the private sector and the actualisation of the importance of the roles expected of this sector in contributing to their growth and support as entrepreneurs.

10.3.6 Summary

In summary, the youth participants, especially women, reported that the Chamber of Commerce had contributed to their growth and business development. The lack of information provided by the Chamber of Commerce in this regard was considered a barrier. Honours students rated the updates more favourably than third-year students did. The majority of respondents indicated support from the Chamber of Commerce, contrary to previous findings. Women indicated higher levels of perceived support than males. Honours students reported more development support from the Chamber of Commerce than third-year students. Students understood the role and purpose of the Chamber of Commerce, and as such, this is not a barrier. Almost half of the respondents have little awareness of other private sector agencies and were also unable to name any. This is a barrier.

The greatest private barriers were the unawareness of private sector agencies other than the Chamber of Commerce, followed by the lack of contribution to the growth and business development support received from the Chamber of Commerce. The youth appear to embrace support from private sector agencies, but they need to reach out to businesses and mentors, potentially creating further opportunities. Moreover, the youth need to recognise that businesses are under pressure to generate profits and that their involvement can sometimes be at a cost to the company. The youth should accordingly value time spent in businesses and attempt to add real value rather than being a hindrance. According to the literature, private sector agencies are ineffective in delivering information and support. Two major reasons for this are that these agencies deal with complex communities and that their primary focus has been healthcare and education rather than entrepreneurial education. This is considered a barrier to youth entrepreneurs.

10.4   Barriers and Enablers Encountered in Relation to Small- and Medium-sized Enterprises

The last component, explored through youth entrepreneur experiences, was in relation to small- and medium-sized enterprises (SMEs). Figure 10.4 shows the findings related to research Question 6 regarding SMEs and their influence in developing youth entrepreneurs. SMEs are operating in what is considered one of the most competitive landscapes, made more challenging through socio-economic and political landscapes characterised by high levels of unemployment, poor access to education, a struggling economy due to corruption, fraud and more recently, COVID-19. As a result, businesses have to fend off the daily intrusion of potential fraudsters and criminality.

To investigate the impact of SMEs on youth entrepreneurs: The aspects discussed in the paragraphs that follow can be synthesised as the top barriers and opportunities to youth entrepreneurship.

The two highest reported perceptions relating to barriers experienced by SMEs was the high level of competition and crime in South Africa.

Fig. 10.4   Barriers and enablers—SMEs

Findings showed that the participants considered a high level of competition a barrier. However, high levels of competition are common for most businesses and should be embraced, but can be intimidating when, as previously discussed, one's self-confidence and confidence expressed in their ideas and creativity serve more as a barrier than a challenge that needs to be overcome in order to secure and sustain entrepreneurial success. As such, one's personal traits, values and beliefs will act in conjunction with confronted challenges in ways that are disabling. Youths should practice innovation and collaboration with skilled persons to increase their value, rather than negatively reacting to competition or being immobilised by fear or internal doubt. Youths need to upskill themselves and build their confidence through sustained activity, rather than perceiving competition as a barrier, and find solutions to add more value to their businesses. Crime, however, is a real barrier, and youths require support from the government and municipalities to solve the resulting problems. Crime, unfortunately, is something that the youth can do very little about but indicates the relative lack of entrepreneurial activities that are geared towards creative success rather than creative criminality. It serves as a barrier, and one which will disable even the most creative start-ups, and trying to fend or protect against it, requires capital investment or innovative ways around the prevention thereof.

Participation in SHAPE mediated the perception of having received business development support from small to medium-sized businesses to assist in their entrepreneurship activities ($r = 0.308$).

To offset these two major barriers: It is held that increased support and rallying of numerous stakeholders across the various groups, including government agencies and private sectors, together with training and empowerment, will help to overcome these perceived barriers. It is through collaborative support that a front can be built and implemented to sustain activity through adversity. Thus, collaborative partnerships, support and skill development from experts in the field cannot be understated.

10.4.1 High Levels of Crime

This section measured perceptions relating to the environment within which SMEs operate and that could potentially act as a barrier to entrepreneurial success. It measured the effect that crime might have on respondents' growth and development. Of the respondents, 19.2% agreed to a 'small' to 'no' extent with the statement that high levels of crime had affected their growth and development, whereas 67.3% agreed to a 'moderate' and 'very great' extent ($N = 53$). The greatest barrier was 'High levels of crime have affected my growth and development' (0.24), and a factor loading of 0.02. There is very little the youth can do, from their current positioning, about crime, and thus, there is a lack of variability in response in the outcome variable and lowest in their locus of control.

Undoubtedly, crime is something that acts as a real threat to entrepreneurial success, especially in a context rife with socio-political and economic unrest. KwaZulu Natal has more recently fallen victim to looting and the destruction of property through arson amounting to over R20-billion and the loss of over 150 000 jobs. This is critically disabling in an environment already battling to sustain and recover from the negative effect of COVID-19. Responding to these threats in the economic climate is paramount and requires entrepreneurs to be agile and sufficiently skilled to think creatively and innovatively in their response. Unfortunately, however, skills and creative thinking is not enough, and over 45 000 businesses have shut their doors as a result of the looting and unrest alone.

Kruskal–Wallis revealed significant differences in response, based on respondents' gender, regarding their perceptions of whether high levels of crime affected their growth and development ($U = 179.00$, $p = 0.03$). Women indicated a 'moderate' to 'very great' extent in their level of agreement with the statement that high levels of crime affected their growth and development.

These results are supported by past research, which suggests a significant decrease in business entries for SMEs associated with high crime prevention costs compared to larger businesses that make more profit.[6]

There is, however, contradictory research that suggests that crime does not entirely affect growth and development but rather that the youth are negatively affected by large geographical boundaries between formal and informal areas.[7] This could mean that 67% of the respondents are affected by geographical boundaries between formal and informal areas, rather than crime being the primary contributor to their perceived lack of growth and development.

10.4.2 High Levels of Competition

Another feature investigated in this section was the effect of high levels of competition exacerbating the difficulty with which to start a small business. Only 15.4% of respondents expressed 'small' to 'no' extent in agreement with the statement that small businesses are extremely difficult to start due to high levels of competition. By contrast, 73.1% of respondents indicated a greater agreement ($N = 52$). There was a significant difference in their perceptions of whether small businesses are difficult to start due to high levels of competition between varying employment statuses. Cross-tabulations showed that part-time and full-time employed people and those who were already entrepreneurs were more likely to rate this item higher than undergraduate students, who rated the extent as 'small' to 'none'. There is a significant positive correlation between believing small businesses are extremely difficult to start due to high levels of competition and having received training from educational institutions to develop skills to start a business ($r = 0.333$). This indicates that as youths become increasingly aware of the details around starting their own business; they become more aware of the conditions within which they are operating. They are more realistic about the demands on them as entrepreneurs in attempting to establish a successful business and thus note the role of competition in doing so.

---

[6] Mahofa et al. (2016)

[7] Grabrucker and Grimm (2016)

Past research supports these results and explains the importance of being able to change and adapt to different business environments. It is, however, difficult and expensive to maintain information technology systems, so entrepreneurs need to be creative and innovative.[8]

The responses to this survey could be related to youths not having access to finance, which could make competition in business more challenging.

Past research also suggests that small businesses experience high levels of competition and are at a disadvantage compared to large businesses, which have greater resources and can employ specialists to outperform the competition. Further research explains that there is a skills shortage in the townships of South Africa, which could make these respondents more vulnerable to high levels of competition.[9] This makes training vital in disabling the total effect of crime and competition on entrepreneurial action.

10.4.3 Training Received from SMEs

The first aspect of this construct was the training being received by youths from SMEs. Of the respondents, 26.9% indicated 'lesser' to 'no' agreement that they had received training from SMEs to develop business start-up skills, whereas 67.4% expressed a greater extent to which they had received training from SMEs ($N = 53$). As indicated, training from experts in the field who are in possession of the know-how of operating within the economy is vital. The extent to which training was reported indicates participating in SHAPE, which harnesses these training interactions and efforts. Given this, it is imperative, given their disablement of features in the economy, such as competition and crime, to sustain entrepreneurial action.

Kruskal–Wallis revealed significant differences in response, based on respondents' employment status, regarding their perceptions of receiving training from SMEs to develop business start-up skills ($H(8) = 18.02$, $p = 0.02$). Seven pairs of differences were found.

---

[8] Adeniran and Johnston (2016)
[9] Mbinda and Spencer (2016)

A further examination of the crosstabs revealed that both full-time undergraduate students and full-time undergraduate students with entrepreneurial activity were likely to state that they had received training from SMEs to develop business start-up skills to only a 'small' or 'no' extent, whereas part-time and full-time employed were likely to indicate a greater extent of agreement with the statement. This is understandable if employment activity implies increased exposure to enterprises operating within the economic environment, with limited exposure to those youths who are primarily focused on studying.

10.4.4 Business Development Support

The second aspect in this construct gives the data on business development support from SMEs to youth entrepreneurship activities. Of the respondents, 71.1% expressed the extent of their agreement with the statement that they had received such support as 'moderate' to 'very great', whereas 25% reported 'small' to 'no' agreement with this statement ($N = 53$).

SHAPE participants engaged with entrepreneur practitioners and small- and medium-sized enterprise (SME) owner-managers during an interactive business engagement intervention known as 'Meet your Business Friend Day'. Student entrepreneurs were paired with practitioners and had a full day opportunity of engagement. Those attending the occasion were encouraged to exchange contact details and continue exchanging 'business friendship' to develop entrepreneurial endeavours. The responses from this sample could therefore be expected to be different from those of youths not given an explicit opportunity to engage with a business friend. Examination of the standardised regression weights on the SME composite reveals that the highest regression weight and, therefore, the greatest opportunity to entrepreneurial action was attributable to 'I have been receiving training from SMEs to develop skills to start a business' (0.95). Changes on this plane indicated a good response in the outcome variable and thus acted as an effective enabler of entrepreneurial activity and success.

10.4.5 Summary

In summary, just over half of the respondents indicated that they had received training from SMEs; this is not a lot and thus creates a barrier. Those still studying reported less training than their employed counterparts, probably more exposed to business. Many students reported favourably about receiving business development support from SMEs to assist in their entrepreneurship activities, and this is, therefore, not a barrier. Crime seems to have a slight degree of influence. Competition is a significant barrier, especially for people already engaging in some form of entrepreneurial activity. The belief that small businesses are difficult to start due to high levels of competition was rated as the highest barrier; however, the median measure for all items was 5 (moderate extent), and therefore, crime and start-up costs are the biggest barriers experienced by SMEs.

The study suggests that youths should attempt to conduct business in different communities around South Africa, which would increase potential opportunities. The benefit of extending oneself to different communities is that this creates larger networks and more diverse experiences. It is further recommended that youths engage more with communities to provide feedback on their business ideas and prototypes.

We suggest that youth entrepreneurs embrace competition from SMEs and perceive it as an opportunity to learn rather than a barrier. Youth entrepreneurs must develop their skills by learning from SMEs and challenge themselves to be more creative.

10.5 Barriers and Enablers Encountered in Relation to Large Businesses and Corporates

The last section detailing perceived barriers and enablers of success examined the effect of large businesses and corporates. Figure 10.5 shows the findings related to research Question 7 regarding large businesses and corporates and their influence in developing youth entrepreneurs. It reveals that while not having received training from large corporates and not being recognised and recruited as potential talent and investment, increased encounters and networking with large companies and awareness of entrepreneurial support offered by these large corporates are vital in offsetting barriers to entrepreneurial success. This is in line with what has previously been discussed. Whereas youth entrepreneurs are still relatively unconfident in their skill and ability, they are not networking or engaging with large corporates in due recognition of their own talent and perceive any training with these invaluable sources of success will better equip and empower them towards recognition as entrepreneurs. To investigate the impact of large businesses and corporates: The aspects discussed in the paragraphs that follow can be synthesised as the top barriers and opportunities to youth entrepreneurship.

Unlike SMEs, some large businesses and corporates can initiate corporate social investment (CSI) programmes. However, these programmes are not reaching their full potential due to poor monitoring and evaluation from third parties. Large businesses and corporates need their CSI processes to be evaluated and scrutinised to improve their service offering for youth.

Findings in this regard are somewhat misleading. Respondents stated that they had received several visits from large companies; however,

Fig. 10.5 Barriers and opportunities—Large businesses and Corporates

these visits were within SHAPE and not external, suggesting that youths require further support from large businesses. Training has repeatedly recurred throughout findings as vital in creating, initiating and sustaining youths' confidence in their abilities and skilling them with the requisites of entrepreneurial success. Training needs to occur from across all sectors and operations within the economy and provide for versatility in response.

10.5.1 Skills-Development Training

Skills-development training received from large businesses and corporates to develop business start-up skills was rated as 'moderate' to 'very great' by just over half (55.7%) of the respondents rated the extent to which they received training as, compared to 38.5% who rated the training received as 'small' to 'none' ($N = 52$). Of these, eleven respondents rated no extent. This variability means that students have had varied exposure and success in initiating these engagements and could be an artefact of the life-positioning and period within which youth entrepreneurs are in. These perceptions of support are important in developing the skills to start a business ($r = 0.466$).

Kruskal–Wallis revealed significant differences in response, based on respondents' highest level of education, regarding their perceptions of receiving training from SMEs to develop business start-up skills ($H(3) = 10.75$, $p = 0.01$). The difference lay between third-year and honours students ($c^2(1) = 8.21$, $p = 0.00$), with the former rating the development of skills through training as having taken place to a 'lesser', 'small' or 'no' extent, and the latter rating it as a 'moderate' or 'great' extent. The training received was rated as of 'small' or 'no' extent by 42.3% of the third-year students ($N = 26$).

Research supports the results from this study and suggests that businesses show only weak support to youth entrepreneurs through training. Youths are not provided with business support through work-integrated learning. However, partial support is evident when companies are financially invested in these programmes.[10] This corresponds with the lack of CSI programmes in South Africa and could mean that businesses lack incentives from the government to create programmes that could impact youth entrepreneurs.

10.5.2 Awareness of Entrepreneurial Support

Another aspect measured as part of the large corporate construct indicates youths' awareness of entrepreneurial support for youth entrepreneurs from large companies. A mere 17.3% of respondents rated the extent to which they are aware of entrepreneurial support from large companies as 'small' to 'none', whereas 74.9% of respondents rated the extent as 'moderate' to 'great' ($N = 52$). These findings indicate a large awareness of entrepreneurial support from large companies, perhaps an artefact of participation in SHAPE moderating this relationship. Examination of the standardised regression weights reveals that the highest regression weight and therefore the greatest opportunity, and the highest factor loading on the construct in enabling entrepreneurship within in the large businesses composite was attributable to 'I am aware of entrepreneurial support that large companies offer to support youth entrepreneurs' (0.91). Thus, the greater the support, the more likely it accounts for positive changes in entrepreneurial action. The support emerges again as a large indicator of entrepreneurial success and cannot be underplayed. Where youths are uncertain of their own internal competencies and their possession of the skills required to engage in entrepreneurial activities and respond to potential threats in the system such as crime, competition and other barriers, support is imperative in offsetting these doubts.

Awareness of entrepreneurial support that large companies offer to support young entrepreneurs is vital in preparing them sufficiently for

---

[10] Reinhard et al. (2016)

becoming an entrepreneur ($r = 0.348$), developing skills to start a business (0.375), and having more self-confidence in becoming a young entrepreneur ($r = 0.301$).

Kruskal–Wallis revealed significant differences in response, based on respondents' employment status, regarding their perceptions of entrepreneurial support that large companies offer to youth entrepreneurs ($H(8) = 16.30$, $p = 0.04$). It was found that full-time undergraduate students were more likely to rate the support as being to a 'lesser' or 'no' extent, whereas full-time postgraduate students; full-time postgraduate students with entrepreneurial activity, unemployed and part-time employed students were more likely to rate the entrepreneurial support to a 'moderate' or 'very great' extent. This makes sense as seeking out support for entrepreneurial activity while studying full-time is less important as moves towards entrepreneurial activity are not yet generated, as students are in the process of upskilling towards this targeted action in the future.

10.5.3 Talent Recruitment Programmes

The fourth aspect measured in this construct, relating to large companies, is the talent recruitment programmes for youth entrepreneurs. Just over a fifth (21.2%) of respondents indicated a 'small' to 'no' extent rating in agreeing with the statement that large companies offer talent recruitment programmes that will help them progress to become successful entrepreneurs, whereas 74.9% indicated a rating of 'moderate' to 'very great' extent ($N = 52$).

Kruskal–Wallis revealed significant differences in response, based on respondents' highest level of education, regarding their perceptions of how large companies offer talent recruitment programmes that would help them progress to become successful entrepreneurs. Third-year students were less likely to feel that the talent recruitment programmes had helped their progress than honours students, who rated this as 'moderate' to 'very great' extent. Again, the lack of entrepreneurial intent and subsequent move towards engaging in entrepreneurial or economic action is minimal. It is likely that those students who are to be identified and who qualify as eligible for talent programmes are not, as yet, suitable candidates at this stage.

Talent recruitment programmes help to prepare youths sufficiently for becoming an entrepreneur ($r = 0.358$), and through SHAPE have assisted youths to have more self-confidence in becoming young entrepreneurs ($r = 0.486$).

10.5.4 Informational Visits by Large Companies

The measure of students receiving visits from large companies to inform them about business opportunities was rated as 'small' to 'no' extent rating for the statement 'While being a student entrepreneur we received several visits from large companies' representatives to inform us about business opportunities' by a very small percentage (9.6%) of respondents. Comparatively, 84.6% indicated a 'moderate' to 'very great' extent rating ($N = 52$) and showed the lowest regression weight and factor loading onto the construct. Again, this finding is expected as networking and facilitating collaborations within large companies, forging relationships between youth entrepreneurs and business partners within the various sectors of the economy was a principal focus in harnessing an entrepreneurial spirit through co-sensing, co-creating, co-initiating and co-evolving through collaboration.

These visits correlate with more self-confidence in becoming a young entrepreneur ($r = 0.418$) and thus are important in contributing towards initiating entrepreneurial activity.

10.5.5 Corporate Social Investment Programmes

With due knowledge of the impoverished CSI initiatives throughout SA, it was empirically investigated in this section of the questionnaire. Only 19.2% of respondents gave a 'small' or 'no' rating as the extent to which they agreed with the statement that corporate social investment programmes had invested in them as student entrepreneurs, compared to 69.2% of respondents who indicated a 'moderate' to 'very great' extent ($N = 52$). These findings are somewhat unsurprising given the time and resources invested in them as part of SHAPE, which provided a unique opportunity and platform to harness the benefits from large corporates in their investment in youth entrepreneurial potential. The simple act of investing one's time is empowering and gives value, moving students across the inner domain towards proactive risk-taking and confidence needed to initiate and sustain entrepreneurial action. These findings further suggest that CSI programmes in South Africa need to provide more support for youths to become entrepreneurial. It also demonstrates that applying social technologies such as SHAPE enables the youth and gives them an advantage over other young people without access to such an enabling ecosystem. This demonstrates the success of co-initiating, co-sensing, co-inspiring and co-evolving within an ecosystem.

Kruskal–Wallis revealed significant differences in response, based on respondents' employment status, regarding their perceptions of whether corporate social investment programmes were investing in them as student entrepreneurs ($H(8) = 16.29$, $p = 0.04$). Investigation of the cross-tabulations revealed that full-time undergraduate students, full-time undergraduate students with entrepreneurial activity and entrepreneurs were more likely to rate the programme investment to 'lesser' or 'no' extent. Full-time postgraduate students, full-time postgraduate students with entrepreneurial activity, part-time employed and full-time employed respondents were more likely to rate the investment as 'moderate' to 'great' extent, perhaps in recognition of the potential source of skillsets necessary to sustain success.

There has been limited research on corporate social investment programmes in South Africa and the extent of their impact, which leads us to believe that more resources need to be committed to encouraging businesses to assist youth entrepreneurs.

These results are supported by past research, which shows that CSI programmes are not generally supported by businesses. These programmes are often implemented as a marketing strategy to gain loyalty and credibility with clients, rather than focusing on creating actual change for youth entrepreneurs. In addition, companies that offer support for employees to implement these programmes can compromise their effectiveness.[11]

It appears that further research needs to be conducted to motivate businesses to implement CSI programmes for youth. Despite this, some evidence shows that businesses that provide work-integrated learning for youths and are financially invested have a greater commitment to social-economic development.[12]

An examination of the means plot revealed significant differences in response, based on respondents' highest level of education and current employment status, regarding their perceptions of whether CSI programmes were investing in them as student entrepreneurs ($F(8, 43) = 2.78$, $p = 0.02$). Results reveal higher extents of agreement that corporate social investment programmes were not investing in them as youth entrepreneurs.

In South Africa, industries and businesses show a weak contribution to work-integrated learning, which is a major problem because youths are not provided with valuable experience. In addition, businesses not financially invested in work-integrated learning show less engagement than those so invested. This is consequently a barrier to youth entrepreneurs.

10.5.6 Summary

In summary, these responses suggest that CSI programmes in South Africa need to provide more support to youths to become entrepreneurial. This was found to be especially true for the employed. Those with higher levels of employment were more likely to rate the degree of CSI lower, suggesting that investment is lacking for this group and is acts as a barrier. A majority rated the skills-development training from large businesses favourably, suggesting that this is a barrier, especially among third-year students, of whom eleven (42.3%) reported 'small' or 'no' extent of training from large businesses. There seems to be an awareness of the entrepreneurial support that large companies offer to support youth entrepreneurs, and as such, this is not a barrier, especially

[11] Penn and Thomas (2017)
[12] Reinhard et al. (2016)

for those involved in more entrepreneurial activities. In addition, neither the degree to which large companies offer talent recruitment programmes that would aid respondents' progress, nor the number of visits received from large companies seems to be barriers.

The extent to which respondents were visited by large companies offering talent recruitment programmes to help with their progress was rated highest, making this the least obtrusive barrier for large businesses and corporates. The most significant barrier was the lack of training received from large businesses and corporates to develop start-up skills. The second most significant barrier was the lack of investment from CSI programmes. Youth entrepreneurs require support from large businesses and corporates; however, it appears that they are not receiving support through structured representation but instead only from short-term interventions aimed at marketing the businesses. It is difficult for youths to engage with these large businesses, and educational institutions should, therefore, create pathways for youths to participate in the entrepreneurial programmes offered by large businesses.

10.6 Conclusion

The two-year post hoc analysis provides insights on the youths' journey further the initial co-initiation, co-sensing, co-inspiring and co-creating with their youth entrepreneur ecosystem. A novel finding is that these youths mostly were able to further their studies with an education institution while taking steps in entrepreneurial action—some being business owners. It is evident that in youth SHAPE and SALAR interventions; there was a transformation (growth in developmental maturity) in the youths entrepreneurial heartset, mindset and handset. It is evident that more all-round support for the youth entrepreneur ecosystem should be provided to facilitate the continued growth of the youth's personality traits to build self-confidence and resilience. The post hoc analysis showed that nearly all of the youths under assessment were strongly committed to continuing their education and gaining academic qualifications. 49% were now in their honour's year at university, and 36% were doing postgraduate courses such as a master's degree. Furthermore, of those still at university, 36% were in part-time employment, well above the national employment rate for this age group, and an incredible 59% were engaged part-time in entrepreneurial activities. At the time of assessing SHAPE's initial iteration, the second iteration was coming to an end. From this group, 73 new business concepts were prototyped and were ready for the next incubation phase.

The author is not interested in making claims that this study can be generalisable. However, this effective youth entrepreneurship case can perhaps provide a blueprint for other organisations or teams to create a similar youth entrepreneur ecosystem within a different unique socio-location.

10.7 Chapter Conclusion

This chapter provides a quantitative lens and presents data with discussions thereof to support the findings from Chapter 6. The data was gathered through a post hoc analysis of the SHAPE social technology participants two years after their participation in the intervention stopped. Further discussions were added to this chapter around barriers and enablers that the pandemic situation is bringing to your entrepreneurs and their ecosystem. It can be concluded that personality traits and internal domains of people are the key facilitators of crucial relationships with the external domains. This re-emphasises the importance of developing a microsystem's inner propensities as a starting point when creating the youth entrepreneur ecosystem. These crucial relationships will need to be fostered, nurtured and further developed over time for youth entrepreneurs to upkeep entrepreneurial action and, most importantly, to sustain value creation and socio-economic development.

Acknowledgement Chapter based on SHAPE research project work: Krieger, W., 2018. Barriers to youth entrepreneurship: a systemic approach (Masters dissertation). University of KwaZulu-Natal. Supervisor: Professor Thea van der Westhuizen.

References

Adelakun, Y., & Van der Westhuizen, T. (2021). Delineating government policies and individual entrepreneurial orientation. *Journal of Sociology and Social Anthropology, 12*(3–4), 106–117. https://doi.org/10.31901/245 66764.2021/12.3-4.371

Adeniran, T. V., & Johnston, K. A. (2016). The impacts of ICT utilisation and dynamic capabilities on the competitive advantage of South African SMEs. *International Journal of Information Technology and Management, 15*(1), 59–89.

Awotunde, O. M., & Van der Westhuizen, T. (2021a). Entrepreneurial self-efficacy development: An effective intervention for sustainable student entrepreneurial intentions. *International Journal of Innovation and Sustainable Development, 15*(4), 475–495.

Awotunde, O. M., & Van der Westhuizen, T. (2021b, September). Entrepreneurial self-efficacy and the SHAPE ideation model for University Students. In *ECIE 2021 16th European Conference on Innovation and Entrepreneurship Vol 1* (p. 37).

Bloomberg. (2020). This is not a pause, it's a reset—Johann Rupert. https://businesstech.co.za/news/business/398335/this-is-not-a-pause-its-a-reset-joh ann-rupert/ (Retrieved May 15, 2020).

City of Johannesburg. (2017). *Joburg in new move to enhance SMMEs* https://support.joburg.org.za/index.php?option=com_content&view=article&id=11601&catid=88&Itemid=266 (Retrieved December 15, 2017).

Durban Chamber of Commerce. (2017). *Welcome to the Durban Chamber of Commerce and Industry NPC*. Official website of the Durban Chamber of Commerce. www.durbanchamber.co.za/ (Retrieved December 6, 2017).

GEP (Gauteng Enterprise propeller). (2014). *Gauteng township economy revitalisation strategy 2014–2019.* (Retrieved September 1, 2017) https://www.gep.co.za/wp-content/uploads/2018/12/Gauteng-Township-Economy-Revitalisation-Strategy-2014-2019.pdf (Retrieved September 1).

Grabrucker, K., & Grimm, M. (2016). Does crime deter South Africans from self-employment? *Journal of Comparative Economics, 46*(2), 413–435.

Harrell, W. (1995). *For entrepreneurs only.* Career Press.

Mahofa, G., Sudaram, A., & Edwards, L. (2016). Impact of crime on firm entry: Evidence from southern Africa. *Economic research Southern Africa,* ERSA Working Paper 652, 1–19.

Mbinda, B., & Spencer, J. P. (2016). Risks connected to the workforce at the small, medium and micro enterprises. *Risk Governance & Control: Financial Markets and Institutions, 6*(4), 161–238.

McEwan, C., Mawdsley, E., Banks, G., & Scheyvens, R. (2017). Enrolling the private sector in community development: Magic bullet or sleight of hand? *Development and Change, 48*(1), 28–53.

Meyer, K., Pedersen, C. L., & Ritter, T. (2020, April 12). The coronavirus crisis: A catalyst for entrepreneurship. *The Conversation.* https://theconversation.com/the-coronavirus-crisis-a-catalyst-for-entrepreneurship-135005

Nhleko, Y., & van der Westhuizen, T. (2022). The role of higher education institutions in introducing entrepreneurship education to meet the demands of industry 4. 0. *Academy of Entrepreneurship Journal, 28*(1), 1–23.

Penn, C., & Thomas, P. H. (2017). Bank employees' engagement in corporate social responsibility initiatives at a South African retail bank. *Acta Commercii, 17*(1), 1–10.

Reinhard, K., Pogrzeba, A., Townsend, R., & Pop, C. A. (2016). A comparative study of cooperative education and work-integrated learning in Germany, South Africa, and Namibia. *Asia-Pacific Journal of Cooperative Education, 17*(3), 249–263.

Ruba, R. M., Van der Westhuizen, T., & Chiloane- Tsoka, G. E. (2021). Influence of entrepreneurial orientation on organisational performance: Evidence from congolese higher education institutions. *Journal of Contemporary Management, 18*(1), 243–269.

Sinyolo, S., Mudhara, M., & Wale, E. (2017). The impact of social grant-dependency on agricultural entrepreneurship among rural households in Kwazulu-Natal, South Africa. *Journal of Developing Areas, 51*(3), 63–76.

Van der Westhuizen, T. (2017a). The use of theory U and individual entrepreneurial orientation to increase low youth entrepreneurship in South Africa. *Journal of Contemporary Management, 14*, 531–553.

Van der Westhuizen, T. (2017b). A systemic approach towards responsible and sustainable economic development: entrepreneurship, systems theory and socio-economic momentum. In Fields, Z. (Ed.), *Collective creativity for responsible and sustainable business practice*. IGI Global.

Van der Westhuizen, T. (2018a). The SHAPE project: Shifting hope, activating potential entrepreneurship In Remenyi, D. Grant, D.A. (Ed.), *Incubators for young entrepreneurs—20 case histories*. ACPIL.

Van der Westhuizen, T. (2018b). Open heart, open mind and open will in transformative individual entrepreneurial orientation pedagogies. *Academic Conferences and Publishing International Limited*. (pp. 443–448).

Van der Westhuizen, T. (2019). Action! Methods to develop entrepreneurship. In *18th European Conference on Research Methodology for Business and Management Studies*. (pp. 331–337).

Van der Westhuizen, T. (2021). Applying theory U through shape to develop student's individual entrepreneurial orientation in a University Eco-System. In Gunnlaugson, O. & Brendel, W. (Eds.), *Advances in pre-sensing Volume III: Collective approaches, in theory U*, (pp. 395–435). Trifoss Business Press.

Van der Westhuizen, T. (2022). *Effective youth entrepreneurship*. Sunbonani. https://omp.sunbonani.co.za/index.php/sunbonani/catalog/book/6

Walford, L. (2017, April 16). eThekwini municipality hosts youth innovation challenge: The eThekwini Municipality is attempting to drive economic growth through the youth innovation challenge. *Berea Mail*. https://bereamail.co.za/108047/municipality-hosts-youth-innovation-challenge/

WHO (World Health Organization). (2020). Coronavirus. *WHO: Health topics*. https://www.who.int/health-topics/coronavirus#tab=tab_1 (Retrieved May 13, 2020).

Index

© University of Kwazulu-Natal 2023
T. van der Westhuizen, *Youth Entrepreneurship*,
https://doi.org/10.1007/978-3-031-44339-8